Dynix

MAN THE MEASURE

By the same author

VON HÜGEL AND THE SUPERNATURAL

Man the Measure

AN ESSAY ON
HUMANISM AS RELIGION

By

ARTHUR HAZARD DAKIN

PRINCETON
Princeton University Press
LONDON : HUMPHREY MILFORD
OXFORD UNIVERSITY PRESS
1939

SET UP AND PRINTED
BY PRINCETON UNIVERSITY PRESS
AT PRINCETON, NEW JERSEY, U. S. A.

To

CLEMENT C. J. WEBB

CONTENTS

		PAGE
INTRODUCTION		xi
CHAPTER I.	The Background of Humanism	3
CHAPTER II.	American Humanism	51
CHAPTER III.	Humanism and Scientific Method	91
CHAPTER IV.	Humanism and Psychology	129
CHAPTER V.	Humanism and Practical Ethics	153
CHAPTER VI.	Humanism and Speculative Ethics	195
CHAPTER VII.	Humanism and Religion	223
CONCLUSION		267
INDEX		273

INTRODUCTION

INTRODUCTION

R ELIGIOUS HUMANISM," or simply "humanism," indicates, if not a theoretical denial, at least a neglect or a practical denial, of theism, for the sake of substituting as a religion a would-be scientific and ethical absorption in human affairs without reference to God. So well established has this use of the word now become that it appears in the unabridged second edition of *Webster's New International Dictionary,* where it is defined as "A contemporary cult or belief calling itself religious but substituting faith in man for faith in God." The dictionary then cites a sentence of Dr. C. F. Potter's: "Humanism is faith in the supreme value and self-perfectibility of human personality."

Traditional theism, specifically Christianity, strikes most humanists as intellectually, socially, morally, and spiritually bankrupt. They would drop sentimental alliances with the past and present connections with hypocrisy and reaction. Free and fresh would they pursue truth. Supplementing their logic with charms like a clear eye, a sure hand, and a head unbowed by fear, pretence, or cloudy devotion, they seek the renewal of man's soul and civilization.

Though more spectacular kinds of atheism appear in certain totalitarian countries, and the worship of mammon we have with us always, nevertheless humanism offers a fairly promising field in which to observe some current, popular, and honest objections to belief in God. Whether humanism as an organized movement is alive, dying, or dead, matters little compared with the influence and the prevalence in English-speaking countries of the ideas it celebrates. The insistent ubiquity of those ideas has already evoked a large literature for their analysis, of which this essay is a tardy fragment.

xi

Because it is interested primarily in humanistic ideas in relation to God rather than in humanism for its own sake, this study presents a somewhat arbitrary account of only that side of humanism and of humanists. A brief outline of a group as a whole, especially an outline inspired by such a definite and narrow interest, can hardly treat each member of the group and the subtleties of his thought with the nuances they merit. As humanism is largely a popular mood, it expresses itself quite as much in publications that the discriminating shun as in those that they enjoy. To have concentrated on only the ablest humanists, to have banned citation from "cheap and vulgar" documents, would have meant ignoring an important part of humanistic propaganda.

Frequent reference to individuals, far from indicating a desire to indulge in personalities, has been reluctantly admitted as a way of pinning down ideas, in order to facilitate the work of any who may want to investigate further their sources and affinities.

The conceptions here loosely called theism and Christianity, though not without substance, are purposely left amorphous, so that whoever will may be his own Pygmalion. They are introduced not for logical or theological appraisal, proselytizing persuasion, or religious edification, but simply for rough comparison with humanism.

For kind assistance in the preparation of this book I thank him to whom it is dedicated. Its title was one of many welcome suggestions from Miss Helen G. Sahler. The generosity of several leading humanists in furnishing the material attributable to them in Chapter I is gratefully acknowledged. In correcting the proofs, I have enjoyed the able help of Mr. William W. Stifler, Jr.

The many quotations, inserted for "local color," prove the courtesy of their original publishers and authors. Although every one receives at least the Quaker headstone of a footnote acknowledgment, George Allen and Unwin, Ltd., on account of the unusual number of passages that they have allowed to be reproduced, merit special mention.

As for the pages to come, Chapter I introduces humanists themselves and briefly sketches their intellectual ancestry. After quoting

in full the Humanist Manifesto, Chapter II discusses some of its
tenets. Because humanists call science the touchstone of their
thought and action, Chapter III examines the meaning and the use
of that standard of their faith. And because on psychology they
rely most for their own defense and for their dismissal of theism,
Chapter IV glances at humanistic psychology. Chapter V proceeds
to the first, or this-worldly, stage of humanistic ethics. Chapter VI
ascends to the metaphysical justification of that ethics. As such
speculations invariably soar into theology, the seventh and last
chapter reviews humanistic religion.

CHAPTER I

SYNOPSIS OF CHAPTER I

The point of view from which this study approaches humanism. The meaning of humanism. The places where it is strongest. The kind of people humanists are. The humanism of human thought. The schools of humanism, optimistic, pessimistic, and mediating. "Literary humanism." The atheism of humanism. Humanism and Lâo-tse, Confucius, and Buddha. Humanism and sophism. Humanism and the Renaissance and the Reformation. Some post-medieval tendencies in science, philosophy, and theology, affecting current humanism.

THE BACKGROUND OF HUMANISM

THE major interests of humanity express themselves, or seek to do so, in established institutions and traditions. Although different civilizations surpass one another in certain respects, ordinarily one seeks satisfaction by the usual methods of the culture into which one was born. As a rule one renounces these only if through ignorance, exceptional circumstances, or "exhaustive" knowledge, one believes something better is to be found elsewhere. These great products and defenders of human interests require, like other living things, a combination of conservatism and hospitality in order to grow in age and stature. Christianity, for example, which in one form or another is the dominant expression of religion in the occident, in spite of the revolutionary character of its early days, has been extraordinarily assimilative. Beginning as a small, heretical offshoot of an ancient Hebrew cult, it grew not by its novel elements alone but often by absorbing and adapting itself to religions and philosophies with which it came in contact—by showing that it destroys by fulfilling.

It could probably be maintained that at most times the average working ideals of these institutions are slightly above the equivalent average ideals of the majority of the community that they serve and slightly below the best current thought, which may or may not be represented in the institutions themselves. But when Christianity, for example, falls noticeably below the usual standard of truth and goodness environing it (and instances of this are not confined to the Reformation), no amount of vested interest and human lethargy can long save it. Yet its ever growing abundance

3

and its need, for both itself and humanity, to take the greatest variety of things into consideration and to avoid hasty commitments handicap it against forms of research devoid of such responsibilities and adapted to pursue truth in a swift, thin, straight line rather than in a more complex, comprehensive, and expanding sphere. Thus certain movements (like humanism) on special points not infrequently outstrip a slower, more cautious mass of traditions and institutions (like Christianity), while on the whole remaining inferior to it in balance, depth, solidity, and completeness. By showing that what is true in discoveries made by others is either already present in it (perhaps even an unrecognized by-product of it) or is not incompatible with it, and by taking steps to adopt what has been well proved, so far Christianity has utilized criticism for purification and advance.

> "Leur venin, qui sur moi brûle de s'épancher,
> Tous les jours en marchant m'empêche de broncher.
> Je songe, à chaque trait que ma plume hasarde,
> Que d'un oeil dangereux leur troupe me regarde.
> Je sais sur leurs avis corriger mes erreurs,
> Et je mets à profit leurs malignes fureurs.
> Sitôt que sur un vice ils pensent me confondre,
> C'est en me guérissant que je sais leur répondre;
> Et plus en criminel ils pensent m'ériger,
> Plus, croissant en vertu, je songe à me venger."[1]

In a common love of humanity and desire to improve its earthly lot, Christianity (the mother of most philanthropy in the West and of much in the East) and humanism are closely allied. They differ, though, in their attitude towards God. If the new naturalists did not deny God's reality and insist that some sort of sugar-coated positivism was the only legitimate form of religion, there would be little or no friction. As God, for Christians, is real and adorable and enhances life, they cannot avoid the conviction that the humanist denial of His existence, or description of Him, if existing, as a mere shadow of what He is for them or as a menace

---

[1] "Epître à M. Racine," Nicolas Boileau-Despréaux.

4

rather than a deity, must rest on misinterpreted, inadequate evidence, which gains its plausibility more from theoretical and practical failings of Christians than from true sources opposed to their faith. A study like this, therefore, must investigate some of the principal reasons for the rejection of God by humanism, in enough detail to arrive at an opinion about the truth or the falsity of its own initial bias.

The popular meaning of "humanism," already noted in the Introduction, may be better conveyed by descriptions of it given by several humanist leaders in response to inquiries.[2] Humanism, they said, is an inevitable result of the progress of secular knowledge and of the growing indifference to the claims of the Christian Church. By organizing that knowledge into a consistent philosophy of life, humanism seeks to augment human values through man's efforts apart from God. Because it believes theistic religion to be "the most active and pervasive menace to civilization which confronts us today," and because it is not "too dignified to take notice of ignorance and bigotry and inefficiency,"[3] humanism not merely disregards but actively attacks any relation with what it calls the "supernatural." It would fuse a "reasonable," this-worldly residue of Christian ethics with science. Guaranteeing free discussion, humanist centers serve as "super-clubs"[4] for those who cannot honestly describe themselves as other than "intelligent, liberally [sic] minded, and emancipated." "Scientific method" is the kernel of humanism; its shell, "a naturalism that includes man." If not in practice, at least in theory, humanists hold naturalism less as a dogma than as the best working hypothesis available. Because

[2] With few exceptions, which do not materially alter the results of the investigation, most leaders of important humanist groups answered the inquiries addressed to them. Figures on membership, etc., appearing in the following pages, though not purporting to be more than the guesses of these leaders in 1936 and 1937, are probably the most reliable statistics obtainable.

[3] cf. pp. 145-7 of "Humanism—the Hope of the World," an address (March 22, 1931) by J. H. Dietrich, no. 10, series XIV, of *The Humanist Pulpit,* published by the First Unitarian Society, 1526 Harmon Pl., Minneapolis, Minn.

[4] cf. *Fellowship,* September 1935, a leaflet published by the Unitarian Church of Evanston, 1405 Chicago Ave., Evanston, Ill., R. Lester Mondale, minister.

5

"people who are sufficiently enlightened and of that temperament leading to Humanism are not apt to associate in organizations,"[5] humanism as an institution is insignificant. But the spirit of humanism, implicit, so we are told, in "the whole trend of modern thought," is "destined increasingly to shape the minds of men."[6] It is best for humanism, according to these leaders, to be not a discrete body but a leaven working in religious and social groups. Believing that nurture is humanism's chief present need, most of them hesitate (as a humanist adept in mixed metaphor puts it) "to separate sheep from goats within the Unitarian Church, for fear of killing the goose that lays the golden eggs."

From late 1930 until early in 1937 *The New Humanist* (published bimonthly in Chicago by the Humanist Press Association,

[5] Quoted from a letter from a humanist minister.

[6] From another letter. cf. "There is a real danger that, with the spread of the culture, which is based on the satisfaction of economic needs and inspired by physical science, civilization will lose its soul; for it is a people's religion that is the soul of its civilization, and this kind of culture may easily seem to leave no room for religion." C. C. J. Webb, *The Contribution of Christianity to Ethics* (Calcutta: Calcutta University Press, 1932), p. 59.

For many—simply to indicate a point of view different from that in the text above—humanism as an intellectual and social force of much novelty and merit died before it was born. Professor J. B. Pratt writes of it as a belated echo of the reaction of the last century to the supernatural and the other-worldly. When that reaction wore away (largely because theism had adapted its concepts to meet new circumstances), humanism, apparently ignorant of the changes of decades, resurrected long interred issues without noticing anything outmoded about them. The limitations of the "new" humanistic religion preached from 1915 on—in gist Joseph Monneron's, "Il faut croire à l'homme, mon fils. C'est la véritable religion et le véritable Évangile"—had been previously remarked, as, for example, in Paul Bourget's *L'Étape* (1902). An instance of "cultural lag," humanism, like many political and social "advances" and "reforms," grew by flattering and exploiting the finer feelings of the partially educated "reading public." The peak of interest in it was probably reached, as Mr. C. S. Braden has calculated, between 1929 and 1931. Whether again it can ever attract as much attention to itself as a specific movement is less important than its steady, imperceptible absorption by the secularism of today. If humanism "is no longer expounded formally in the serious journals it is found often enough in the popular journals and its spirit permeates many an article in the Sunday newspapers and even the pulp magazines. There it is by no means dead. It takes some time for an idea to get down into this class of journals, but when it does and when it is not argued but assumed as true and the normal way to think, it is likely to have very far-reaching effects on the people at large. Nor is it dead on the college campuses. As a teacher of religions the writer finds constant evidence of the prevalence of the humanistic point of view among students. And sometimes among workingmen or the man on the street one

Inc.[7]) was (apart from books by individual humanists) the principal written means of spreading humanism. For several years, Dr. John H. Dietrich's Sunday morning humanist addresses in Minneapolis were broadcast by wireless and later printed in *The Humanist Pulpit* series. When *The New Humanist* expired,[8] its readers and contributors were advised to turn to periodicals like *The*

discovers it. They do not know it as humanism, they may not even know that such a well defined school ever existed, but the ideas are there and the attitudes, and it seems likely [that they] will continue to manifest themselves for a long time to come." (C. S. Braden, "Is Humanism Dead?"—one of the articles in a symposium on humanism by A. E. Haydon, Charles Hartshorne, John Dietrich, J. B. Pratt, and C. S. Braden—*The University Review* (University of Kansas City, Kansas City, Mo.), summer 1937, p. 249. Clarence Decker, editor of *The University Review,* and Harold Buschman, associate editor, were formerly on the staff of *The New Humanist.*)

The slump in humanist activity, at least prior to Dr. Eliot's election to the presidency of the American Unitarian Association in 1937, has been explained as a matter of political strategy. Humanists then thought it would be "a loyal thing to subordinate discussion of a divisively doctrinal nature and especially in local parish work to avoid the use of labels in any manner possibly confusing to Unitarian laymen." Dr. Eliot elected, humanists are now "mindful of their opportunity to carry on." What they call "wise tactics" at present amounts to retirement from the intellectual front and concentration on popular propaganda and practical organization. Although atheistic ministers can apparently excuse themselves for remaining in sects that, like the Unitarian Church (which holds "in unity of spirit a diversity of conviction"), do not put belief in God before the sanctity of debate, such a course must be more questionable to members of officially theistic bodies. (cf. "Religion Today," by A. C. Dieffenbach, *Boston Evening Transcript,* October 23, 1937.)

Professor D. L. Evans in his article called "The Persistent Claims of Humanism" (*The Journal of Religion,* University of Chicago Press, July 1937), finds in democracy, modernity, and reason, enduring elements of humanism.

[7] In 1939 the officers of the Humanist Press Association were: president, Curtis W. Reese, 700 Oakwood Blvd., Chicago, Ill.; vice-presidents (U.S.A.), L. M. Birkhead, Ernest Caldecott, John H. Dietrich, A. Eustace Haydon, Corliss Lamont; vice-president (England), F. S. Marvin, Welwyn, Garden City; secretary-treasurer, Edwin H. Wilson, 301 North Mayfield Ave., Chicago, Ill.; secretary, Dale DeWitt, 8925 190th St., New York, N.Y.; executive committee, E. Burdette Backus (in 1939 minister of the Unitarian church, Indianapolis, Ind.), Raymond B. Bragg, R. Lester Mondale, Edward W. Ohrenstein, Curtis W. Reese, and Edwin H. Wilson. On the editorial staff of *The New Humanist* in 1937 were: editor, Raymond B. Bragg, Minneapolis, Minn.; managing editor, Edwin H. Wilson, Chicago, Ill.; associate editors, Oliver L. Reiser, University of Pittsburgh, Pittsburgh, Pa., Clarence R. Decker, University of Kansas City, Kansas City, Mo.; literary editor, Alexander P. Cappon, Bozeman, Mont.

[8] On account of a deficit and the claims of other duties upon those who gave their editorial services free. On March 30, 1938, the secretary-treasurer of the Humanist Press Association announced the reduction of the deficit from $700 to $50.

American Freeman,[9] *Unity,*[10] and *The Christian Register.*[11] The Humanist Press Association remains the nearest approach to a national organization of humanists. After occasionally mailing to its members a mimeographed *News Letter* about six pages long, it published in February 1938 the first issue of *The Humanist Bulletin,* on about the same scale, to appear quarterly or at any rate "as often as possible."

The north central states of America probably contain more humanists than any other part of the world. California and New York[12] have their quota. Individuals holding the principal tenets of "religious humanism" may be found wherever "modern, scientific" naturalism has spread.[13] But nowhere are they more numerous and

[9] Haldeman-Julius Publications, 229 East Forest Ave., Girard, Kan.—a monthly "for the enlightenment of the masses" (No. 1980, September 1937, p. 4), claiming to have 25,000 subscribers (*ibid.,* p. 1).

[10] Unity Publishing Co., Abraham Lincoln Centre, 700 Oakwood Blvd., Chicago; John Haynes Holmes, editor; Curtis W. Reese, managing editor; Raymond B. Bragg, Albert C. Dieffenbach, A. Eustace Haydon, and M. C. Otto, among the editorial contributors.

[11] Unitarian; 25 Beacon St., Boston, Mass.; Llewellyn Jones, editor.

[12] The First Humanist Society of New York, N.Y. (in 1939 with an office at 1775 Broadway and with Sunday morning meetings at 113 West 57th St.) was founded in 1929 by its present leader, Dr. Charles Francis Potter. In the same year the Rev. Theodore Curtis Abel started the Hollywood (Calif.) Humanist Society. Before these there were no "humanist centers" not connected with a church. About 1915 Dr. John H. Dietrich began preaching "humanism" under that name in the Unitarian Church. "A few years later, Mr. Curtis W. Reese, then the Unitarian minister in Des Moines," Iowa, changed the name of his "Religion of Democracy" to "Humanism." ("The Advance of Humanism," address—October 2, 1927—by J. H. Dietrich, p. 38 of no. 3, series XI of *The Humanist Pulpit.* cf. also "The Humanist Controversy in History," by Edwin H. Wilson, *The Christian Register,* January 5 and January 12, 1939.)

[13] Outside the United States there seems to be no body exactly like the "religious humanists." The Humanist Club of Bangalore, India, is said to potter with the occult. In England and Canada, except for a few individuals, the movement is embryonic. The Positivist Society, founded by Auguste Comte, encourages, in France, South America, and England (where it flickers faintly), an attitude towards life and religion with which humanists as a rule sympathize. Rationalist, freethinking organizations critical of the religions around them and dedicated to "the scientific spirit" are usually allies of humanism. The Rationalist Press Association (4-6 Johnson's Court, Fleet St., London, E.C. 4), of which humanists like Dr. John Dewey, Professor Julian S. Huxley, and Bertrand Russell are honorary associates, fulfils, among other and broader functions, some similar to those of the Humanist Press Association. But as groups interested in science, ethics, and sociology, assembling regularly for inspiration, discussion, and social purposes

8

better known to one another than in the Middle West. Their "centers" are usually Unitarian churches; for most of the leaders of American humanism are or were Unitarian ministers.[14] Though probably no more than twelve predominantly humanistic churches exist in the Western Unitarian Conference, with about six more churches in which a large part of the congregation is humanistic,[15] nevertheless humanism claims to be the prevailing point of view "among Unitarians of the mid-west."[16] Throughout the United States about fifty Unitarian ministers and about fifteen thousand people (most of whom belong to the one hundred and twenty-six thousand laity in the three hundred and fifty-five Unitarian churches) are said to be humanists.[17] At times this minority has

probably the Ethical Societies in the United States and the British Empire most closely resemble humanist centers. Regardless of theism or atheism or any other theories, members of the Ethical Societies seek the true, the beautiful, and the good, without leaning on theology (indeed leaving to each individual the definition of his ideals) and, unlike humanists, without elaborating a "scientific," metaphysical system like "new naturalism." "To help one another to know, love, and do the right; to promote a Religion of Human Fellowship and Service": this "general aim" of the Ethical Societies appeals not merely to humanists and Christians but to all well intentioned people. Catholicism, Protestantism, traditional Unitarianism, modernism, Ethical Culture, humanism—in this rough order humanism would be more "advanced," "radical," "naturalistic," and "materialistic" than Ethical Culture. However, except as the "new naturalism" has colored the thought of a group of people officially open-minded and reluctant as a body to subscribe to anything (or even to exist as a closely knit organization), the similarities between humanism and Ethical Culture greatly outweigh their differences. Ethical Culture has been called "the humanism of the Jews," because the ratio of Jews to Gentiles is greater in Ethical Culture than in humanism. This seems to be more true of the United States, especially of New York, N.Y., than of England. Brief expositions of Ethical Culture appear in the pamphlet, *The Ethical Movement Explained,* by Lord Snell, published (1935) by The Ethical Union, 12 Palmer St., London, S.W. 1, and in "Ethical Culture," by H. J. Bridges, being Chap. XI of *Varieties of American Religion,* edited by C. S. Braden (Chicago: Willett, Clark, 1936).

[14] *News Letter,* February 15, 1937, p. 4, published by the Humanist Press Association.

[15] Based on the personal estimate, in 1936, of the secretary of the Western Unitarian Conference.

[16] *News Letter,* February 15, 1937, p. 6.

[17] According to estimates in Dr. C. F. Potter's article entitled "Humanism" in *The New International Yearbook* for 1937. Also cf. *ibid.,* article on Unitarianism. Because in England Unitarianism has never been so "advanced" or so strong in numbers and standing, humanism has had less chance to grow there than in the United States.

been powerful enough to threaten a rift between theists and non-theists in American Unitarianism.[18]

Humanist centers vary in size from less than a hundred people to the larger groups in Hollywood,[19] Minneapolis,[20] Kansas City,[21] and New York.[22] With nothing asked of them except general agreement with humanist principles, the congregations are largely the personal following of their preachers. Barring unusual local conditions,[23] the membership of a humanist center represents (with a few regular and striking exceptions) an average cross section of its community. The occasional presence of Unitarian churches in small cities and towns somewhat mitigates Mr. Raymond Bragg's declaration that "any attempt to start a Unitarian Society in a city

[18] In 1937 a humanist, Dr. Frederick M. Eliot, was elected president of the American Unitarian Association.

[19] The Humanist Society, Box 605, Hollywood; Theodore Curtis Abel, director; slightly over 3,000 "contributors," 308 active members, average Sunday morning attendance 250. On account of "the depression," this society met usually not more than once a month during 1935-1937, but a resumption of weekly meetings was expected soon after that.

[20] First Unitarian Society, 1526 Harmon Pl., Minneapolis; John H. Dietrich, minister 1916-1936, senior minister 1936-1938, now minister emeritus; Raymond B. Bragg, minister 1936-; 1,500 nominal members, 750 average attendance at Sunday morning meetings held in a theater.

[21] The Liberal Centre (legal name, All Souls Unitarian Church), 3425 Baltimore Ave., Kansas City, Mo.; L. M. Birkhead, minister; 1,185 nominal members, 340 active members. Early in 1939 Dr. Birkhead "resigned from his church work to take up the leadership of the organization known as Friends of Democracy, combating anti-semitism and American fascist trends." (*The Humanist Bulletin,* March 1939, p. 2.)

[22] See footnote 12, above. Nominal members 500, active members 250, average Sunday morning attendance 100. The Advisory Board of this society, according to its official stationery, includes M. J. Aronson, Harry Elmer Barnes, L. M. Birkhead, Albert Boni, Edwin Arthur Burtt, John Dewey, John H. Dietrich, Will Durant, William Floyd, Daniel Frohman, Edwin Franko Goldman, Lawrence Gould, Irwin D. Hoffman, Helen Keller, Julius Kessler, Gilbert D. Lamb, Henry Goddard Leach, James H. Leuba, Robert Morss Lovett, Clarence H. Low, George E. O'Dell, Fulton Oursler, John Herman Randall, William Jourdan Rapp, George W. Rappleyea, Oliver L. Reiser, B. Sachs, Roy Wood Sellars, Herbert Bayard Swope, Frederick Tilney, Oswald Garrison Villard, Albert Edward Wiggam, and Ira S. Wile.

[23] As at Ann Arbor, Mich., the seat of the University of Michigan, where almost all the regular attendants at the Unitarian church (The Fellowship of Liberal Religion, State St. and Huron St., Harold P. Marley, minister) are engaged in educational work.

under sixty thousand is doomed to failure."[24] Nevertheless the fact
that (in answer to inquiries) only one minister reported farmers
in his congregation, and then to the extent of ½ per cent, suggests
that humanism is not appreciated in rural areas. Representatives
of the army, the navy, and the air forces, as well as persons engaged in politics, diplomacy, and government service, are also
conspicuously rare on humanist rolls. In only two humanist centers did more than 5 per cent of the faithful belong to the laboring
class, and those two centers reported 14 and 20 per cent[25]—probably an average below that of most Christian churches in the
United States. Clearly humanism is not a representative cross section of the country as a whole (or of most communities in it) so
long as "the masses" play the smallest part. But what would disturb the conscience of a Christian church apparently flatters humanists. Possibly confusing a certain level of instruction with
native intelligence and emotional insight, they sometimes intimate
that, because they speak a language "above the heads" of the
"uneducated," they skim the mental and the spiritual cream of the
nation. As a rule, about half their members have attended some
sort of college or professional school, and one in ten has drunk
deeper of the Pierian spring. In the occupations of humanists,
business, commerce, and trade about evenly balance engineering,
transport, communication, and technical or quasi-scientific work.
The professions and teaching claim, ordinarily, from a tenth to a
fifth of a center's membership,[26] leaving a small remainder to be
divided among literature, art, dramatics, music, banking, insurance, and brokerage. With unbroken uniformity and apparently
regardless of the size or the location of the center, between 50 and
75 per cent of its members have an annual family income from
$1,500 to $3,000. From 5 to 30 per cent more, depending upon the
kind of city the center is in, earn between $3,000 and $6,000.

[24] Quoted in *Fellowship*, September 1935.
[25] Kansas City and Hollywood, respectively.
[26] In Ann Arbor about 95 per cent are engaged in education and 5 per cent in
business. In Hollywood 30 per cent are "technical."

11

Those with incomes exceeding that are few[27] compared with those managing to live on less than $1,500 a year. In political and social views, no humanist center admits a "liberal" majority of less than 70 per cent. Coinciding with the number of unusually large or unusually small incomes reported, the remaining 30 per cent or so is prevailingly either "conservative" or "radical." The only exception is the New York center, which having but 10 per cent with an income below $1,500 and as much as 10 per cent with an income over $12,000 can afford the luxury of being 30 per cent radical and totally untainted by conservatism. Although manners, tastes, and spirit cannot always be correlated with income, and although other classes are also represented in humanism, the figures indicate that, as far as material circumstances are concerned, most humanists belong in the lower rather than the upper half of the provincial urban middle class. And this seems to be true not merely of external circumstances but also of the general tone of popular humanism. Besides the "educational" value of the Sunday addresses, humanists attend centers for the sake of "dinners, parties, and entertainments of the better sort."[28] One of the largest centers has a "poets' corner"; yet the intelligentsia, and still more the bohemians, do not run away with the movement. Birth control, crime prevention, consumers' cooperatives, and various forms of charitable work find support in some centers. For the most part this is carried on by voluntary contributions of money and service. Though the minister will, like the janitorial and the clerical staff, ordinarily accept compensation, often he works at considerable personal sacrifice and turns over to the cause anything earned by his books or lectures.

A psychologist might assert that from the prosaic, restricted sphere to which circumstances confine most of its devotees, humanism promises escape. In humanism they seek an oasis of reason,

[27] Kansas City reports 3 per cent, $6,000 to $12,000; 1.5 per cent, $12,000 to $25,000; and 1 per cent over $25,000. New York estimates 5 per cent for each of those three categories.

[28] From a circular distributed by the First Humanist Society of New York.

hope, and disinterestedness. Those happily ignorant of the life to which many are condemned should be the last to accuse Mr. Sinclair Lewis of describing it with unjustifiable exaggeration. Mr. Lewis has, to quote the vivid words of Mr. Robert Cantwell, "a sense of the physical variety and the cultural monotony of the country [U.S.A.], an easy familiarity with the small towns and square cities, the real estate developments and restricted residential areas, the small business men, the country doctors, the religious fakers, the clubwomen, the county officeholders, the village atheists and single-taxers, the schoolteachers, librarians, the windbags of the lower income groups, the crazy professors and the maddened, hyperthyroid, high-pressure salesmen—the main types of middle-class and lower-middle class provincial society, conspicuous now because he has identified them so thoroughly. . . . The message of *Babbitt, Arrowsmith, Elmer Gantry,* however Lewis might deny that it was his intention to preach it,[29] was simply that American society was death to any disinterested effort, to any human tolerance, almost to any human sympathy; that it was regimented within an inch of its intellectual life; that any deviation from its norm of self-seeking, money-grubbing, career-making, throat-cutting, treachery, slander, blackmailing, was instantly punished with exile and disgrace; that spontaneity or generous emotions or a freedom from calculation, among the calculating wolves of business, amounted to suicide of a long drawn out and painful kind. . . . In his best books he has caught, better than anybody else, the desultory, inhibited, half-sad and half-contented middle-class life of the Middle West, a life of spiritless conflicts and drives in the country, of social gatherings as nerve-wracking and exhausting as final examinations, of interminable business plots and fears of ruin, of frightened infidelities, limitless ambitions, of forced enthusiasms and false simplicities—a life hedged in behind social barriers set by the least enlightened members of the community

[29] Is this a signal that from here on Mr. Cantwell will "interpret" Mr. Lewis with more "freedom" than Mr. Lewis might have expected or desired?

and existing under a dictatorship that is no less powerful for being masked and unadmitted by those who bow to it."[30]

Even if this is a bitter, indiscriminate, and, in parts, almost hysterical, description of "American society," and even if similar and worse conditions prevail elsewhere, reason enough exists why serious, sensitive people living in an environment tending to approximate the one described should turn to prophets of a better order. What is the intellectual and the spiritual value of the prophets' message? Does it surpass, as it claims to, the potentialities of theistic religion, to which for centuries the western world has gone for a renewal of spiritual power?

A consideration of some of the meanings and affinities of humanism may place it in better perspective. To the extent that all our thought is inevitably anthropomorphic, a basic humanism colors every point of view. In this sense theism, which admits the existence of a spiritual reality greater than man and the material universe, a reality that man can apprehend, love, and worship, only according to his limited capacities, and likewise science, the very impersonality of which reflects human nature as much as the objects of its study, may both be called humanistic. A vague, partial humanism like this, which through religion in one form or another relates man intimately to what he believes to be ultimate forces and values of existence, and through some sort of knowledge and control of nature makes him feel at home in the physical world, is probably the implicit working philosophy of most people. An experimental outlook, expanding and contracting with the vicissitudes of life, neither fully realistic nor completely subjective, in referring everything to man it distinguishes him only to blend him better into that environment apart from which he would be nothing.

From concentration upon certain aspects of this general feeling of union with what is above and with what is below mankind, a union strengthened and warmed rather than hindered by our pecu-

[30] "Sinclair Lewis," by Robert Cantwell, *The New Republic,* October 21, 1936, pp. 298-301. cf. also Mr. Cantwell's article, in the same magazine, called "America and the Writers' Project," April 26, 1939, pp. 323-5.

liarities, arise the more sharply defined types of humanism. As philosophy tries to clarify fundamental interests and pursuits, the validity of these secondary humanisms depends upon the fidelity and the competence with which they describe and develop the experience from which they sprang.

Impressed by the fact that our knowledge is a product of our minds, current humanists, with few exceptions, stand for man first and last. God and values they draw from the heights above us and transform into fictions of primitive desires, useful perhaps but to be supplanted by scientific concepts. They do this not merely on psychological grounds but because some of them feel that God necessarily impairs instead of improves man's initiative, responsibility, and dignity. Although most of them, except the "literary humanists," eulogize science and pride themselves on diffusing its glory, and although some of them speak well of its disinterestedness, the characteristic note, especially of the religious humanists, is the demand (like Comte's) for the "humanization" of science, by which they mean its exercise only so far as that is compatible with its subordination to their idea of human welfare. The external world is also ordinarily regarded from this angle of efficient control. Humanists seldom suggest that inanimate nature has an intrinsic value which we can enjoy or that there is any possibility of our communing with it. In sermons, in hortatory moments, in sentimental lapses, they sometimes refer to its ability to refresh and stimulate our spiritual life, but in the less "inspirational" moods common to most of their writing, they hint at air-conditioned houses, well planned cities, more satisfactory transport, and other desirable examples of better arranging the furniture of our earthly stage. The furniture may dwarf us, but we are doing the moving and the acting. The spotlights focus on our self-expression. When that is thwarted, when optimism fails, and when all other bonds with nature (like the intangible ones of morality and religion), except that of material continuity with it, have been broken, humanists fall back on hopeless endurance or anger in the face of an indifferent or hostile world.

15

Starting from the postulate that since nothing is better known than man he must be the norm of thought and action, humanists portray him each according to his own likeness. They can be classified in three groups, depending upon their estimate of our place in the universe. The optimistic school (if "school" may here be used without involving, in all cases, an awareness of affinity on the part of those assigned to it) finds the ultimate nature of things eminently suited to the flowering of our moral and religious powers. Professor Nicolai Hartmann approaches without reaching this goal. To have gone farther, as Dr. Paul Elmer More did in his theism, would have been to go beyond virtually all contemporary humanism, which, owing to its suspicion of anything superior to man, feels obliged to reject religion in its ordinary sense.

The pessimistic school, represented by Bertrand Russell and Mr. J. W. Krutch, with defiance or resignation faces a complicated brief career in a material and social environment like that described principally by recent popularizations of physics and psychology. Believing that science is the only way to truth and that, aside from ourselves, reality is indifferent to values, the pessimistic school stresses the subjectivity, the relativity, and the frustration, of human desires. Granted that the appreciation of value is as much part of man's constitution as his senses are, his senses, drilled by science, reveal, according to these thinkers, the true nature of things around him, whereas his acts of valuation, bathing all in subjective radiance, create (notably in science itself when made an instrument of the emotions) a purely human world within, and often incongruous with, the encompassing universe.

Only by limiting attention to the best features of our precarious and ephemeral civilization can other humanists accepting the premises of Mr. Krutch and Bertrand Russell keep up their spirits. If they look beyond that, they must become either theists, which their science forbids, or apathetic or indignant naturalists, at which their moral temperament rebels. Efforts resembling those of "right-wing pragmatists," like Professor William James and Dr. F. C. S. Schiller, to reconcile rich, broadly cultural, personal points of view with clear, abstract, scientific points of view, are still, whether they recognize it or not, the dominant motives of a mediating school of humanists, including Dr. John Dewey and his disciples—Dr. E. S. Ames, Professor A. E. Haydon, Professor M. C. Otto, and Mr. Walter Lippmann (in his *Preface to Morals*)—together with Professor J. H. Leuba, Professor R. W. Sellars, Dr. C. F. Potter, and, in England, Professor J. S. Huxley. This group, which (through its attempts to devise a new naturalism less closely bound than the optimistic school to tradition and more in harmony than the pessimistic school with common feelings and beliefs) has become a characteristic expression of a widespread mood, will be analyzed in the next chapter.

Professor Hartmann's right to be called a humanist lies chiefly in his rejection of theism as incompatible with man's moral dignity and freedom. While starting with virtually a Kantian faith in conscience and in ethical personality as an end in itself, he does not conclude with Kant that the existence of God is an implicate of that faith.[31] The reason for this divergence seems to lie in Professor Hartmann's idea that the transcendence of God must necessarily be of such an external nature as to preclude His immanence in our thought and will. Were that so, disinterested devotion to truth and goodness, instead of suffering by falling short of its divine impulsion and norm, might conceivably suffer by running counter to a being greater than ourselves and indifferent to our broadest and profoundest aspirations. To forestall such a contingency, Professor Hartmann rules out God and places the justification and the ultimate springs of morality in eternal values or self-subsisting Forms. Since by due recognition of these values man can find stable satisfaction, the general tone of Professor Hartmann's work admits him to the optimistic school. Aside from the Platonic aspects of his metaphysics, which to some degree are shared by neo-realists, his general view of ethics so much resembles the type of sensitive, secular morality recommended by the mediating school that the

[31] cf. Chap. III of Dr. C. C. J. Webb's *Religion and Theism* (London: Allen and Unwin, 1934).

17

detailed examination of that school will implicitly cover what he holds in common with it. Some of the principal points in which he differs from other humanists will be discussed in Chapter VI.

Led by Professor Irving Babbitt and Dr. Paul Elmer More,[32] and starting as a criticism of naturalism, "literary humanism" probably first became widely known through its attacks on the demoralization of literature, which resulted from the havoc of the World War and a faulty assimilation of natural and social sciences and psychology. These humanists defend primarily the ethical standards of Plato and Aristotle, completed and refined by Christianity. They would raise men from imagining themselves to be puppets of irrational inner and outer forces to an effort to lead a temperate, civilized life firmly inspired by "sound" ideals. To this end they rely upon reason, science, ethics, art, and the more obviously beneficial features of religion, on the whole ignoring, like other humanists, but not rejecting, its supernatural side.[33] Their aim is to cultivate, in literature (since so far most of their members have been writers or literary critics) and in other departments of life, man's special capacity for restraint and balance. If they have not yet dealt thoroughly with social and economic conditions, it is perhaps owing to their conviction that improvement merely in those respects, unquestionably desirable as it is, will not automatically make men better and happier. They distinguish between the "progress" effected by multiplying conveniences and the necessity of checking inordinate affections for the sake of developing a character equal to ever changing circumstances—the difference, as Dr. L. J. A. Mercier (echoing Professor Babbitt) puts it, between self-control and social control.[34] From this arises their distrust of hu-

[32] Baron Ernest Seillière might be mentioned as doing similar work in France.
[33] "Shall we not bring to Your service all our powers
  For life, for dignity, grace and order,
  And intellectual pleasures of the senses?"
T. S. Eliot, *Collected Poems 1909-1935* (New York: Harcourt, Brace, 1936), p. 206.
[34] "Make perfect your will." *ibid.*, p. 181.
"If humility and purity be not in the heart, they are not in the home: and if they are not in the home, they are not in the city." *ibid.*, p. 195.

manitarian[35] promises of quick utopias attainable by mass movements and external means—"systems so perfect that no one will need to be good."[36]

Such, without indicating individual contributions, is the platform of this group. While commending religion, Professor Babbitt on the whole advocated leaving it alone in order to obtain an apparently more feasible humanistic level below it but above naturalism.[37] Here his intellectual and moral preoccupations seem to have slightly obscured for him the fact that, even from an empirical point of view like his own, religion exercises at least as strong a sway over the minds and the hearts of mankind as any urbane secularism is likely to do. Dr. More, when he stated that "literary humanism" is to be thought of less as a creative, self-subsistent force than as a means of directing and criticizing forces of that kind, and when he warned that, isolated from the realistic moral and religious faith that invigorates it, humanism would relapse into naturalism,[38] probably

---

[35] "Humanism [i.e. "literary humanism"] concerns itself with defining 'man as such' while the word 'humanitarianism' is reserved for the doctrines that 'benevolence or philanthropy forms the sum of man's duties,' that 'mankind may become perfect without divine aid,' and that 'Christ possessed a human nature only.'" L. J. A. Mercier, *The Challenge of Humanism* (New York: Oxford University Press, 1933), p. 44. For "literary humanists," the "humanism" of the mediating school is largely "humanitarianism."

[36] T. S. Eliot, *Collected Poems 1909-1935*, p. 197. cf. *ibid.*, p. 192:
   "O weariness of men who turn from God
   To the grandeur of your mind and the glory of your action,
   To arts and inventions and daring enterprises,
   To schemes of human greatness thoroughly discredited,
   Binding the earth and the water to your service,
   Exploiting the seas and developing the mountains,
   Dividing the stars into common and preferred,
   Engaged in devising the perfect refrigerator,
   Engaged in working out a rational morality,
   Engaged in printing as many books as possible,
   Plotting of happiness and flinging empty bottles,
   Turning from your vacancy to fevered enthusiasm
   For nation or race or what you call humanity."

[37] cf. T. S. Eliot's essay on "The Humanism of Irving Babbitt," in his *Essays ancient and modern* (London: Faber and Faber, 1936).

[38] "Do you need to be told that even such modest attainments
   As you can boast in the way of polite society
   Will hardly survive the Faith to which they owe their significance?"
                              —T. S. Eliot, *Collected Poems 1909-1935*, p. 196.

19

estimated the character of the movement more justly. Maintaining not that religion and morality always are, but that they rightly can be, the most fundamental and comprehensive aspects of human life, and that, when humbly, unselfishly, and honestly examined, they lead, despite countless practical and theoretical difficulties, to a sustaining faith that reality is capable of arousing and satisfying our most exacting demands, Dr. More, drawing generously from Buddha and Plato, guided what he called "humanism" towards its culmination in a free, catholic, Christian theism.[39]

"A Humanist [of the "religious" rather than the "literary" stripe—so misleading have the labels become] is not," according to Professor J. A. C. F. Auer, "one who necessarily denies the existence of God; he may deny it, he may doubt it, or he may accept it. . . . But all [humanists] insist that a true religious experience without belief in God in the theistic sense is possible."[40] Theists themselves recognize an experience genuinely religious (as far as it goes) in many who, for one reason or another, fall short of theistic theory. Generally uncorrupted by professional training in philosophy, literary humanists deny, doubt, or accept God as He is for ordinary Christians. The pessimistic naturalists frankly disavow Him. But about the middle-of-the-road "new naturalists" it is hard to make a general statement. Their confidence in human goodness and progress causes them to minimize the destructiveness of their negations, even to themselves. Not content (unlike, at one time or another, John Stuart Mill, William James, and Mr. H. G. Wells) with a finite personal Demiurge, or with his own former conception of God as a symbol of social values, Dr. E. S. Ames nearly consolidates the two in a limited cosmic tendency personified and idealized by human beings. Dr. John Dewey would call God that which is

[39] This sketch of "literary humanism" has not been substantially altered since the late Dr. More (not knowing his name was to be inserted in the last sentence) wrote of it in 1935 that it seemed to him "quite sound." For an account of literary humanism in relation to other types of humanism, see Mr. Lawrence Hyde's *The Prospects of Humanism* (London: Howe, 1931). Professor G. R. Elliott's book called *Humanism and Imagination* (Chapel Hill: The University of North Carolina Press, 1938) contains an account of Dr. More's and Professor Babbitt's views on religion.

[40] *Humanism States Its Case* (Boston: Beacon Press, 1933), pp. 79-80.

"inclusive and deep seated" enough to integrate human nature. Having rejected any supernatural, antecedent reality as inconsistent with moral effort, and yet not wishing the ideals that compose his divinity to be "rootless," he has them "generated" and "supported" by "forces in nature and society." Slightly more "emancipated," Dr. C. F. Potter discards any proposed object of worship and prayer, because humanism "is not interested . . . in any worship at all, but seeks, rather, the improvement of humanity"[41] by positivistic means. Among the new naturalists may be noted, then, a gradual dilution of the Christianity with which to some degree most of them started. They range from a small, relatively religious right wing still attached to certain aspects of the Christian God; through a large, ethico-philosophical center fumbling for a half-subjective, half-objective justification of ideals; to a socially-minded, secular left wing virtually immune to speculation. Hence it is not exact to assert, as some writers on the subject have done (both within and without the camp), that all humanists are atheists, although probably most of them are.[42]

This conclusion is strengthened by the way in which many of them combine their claim of modernity with an insistence that godless religion belongs to them as direct heirs of Lâo-tse, Confucius, and Buddha.[43] Lâo-tse, recommending humility, economy, gentleness, simplicity, and purity of spirit, as guides of life, reveals, apart from his lack of interest in religion as commonly understood, little affinity with humanists,[44] who rely chiefly upon aggressive, self-confident will and scientific technique. Believing that release from

[41] *Humanism, A New Religion* (New York: Simon and Schuster, 1930), p. 78.

[42] Nevertheless, "we must see in humanism, however misguided we may think it is, an attempt of earnest spirits to reach the supreme values that we find realized in God." W. A. Brown, *Humanism, Another Battle Line,* edited by W. P. King (Nashville, Tenn.: Cokesbury Press, 1931), p. 243.

[43] Dr. Curtis W. Reese tempers some of the more extravagant statements of humanist pedigree-makers by speaking of "early Buddhism and Confucianism" as "not in direct line but comparable" to humanism. *The Humanist Tradition,* p. 5, published, without date, by All Souls-at-Lincoln Centre, 700 Oakwood Blvd., Chicago, Ill.

[44] Unless otherwise qualified, the words "humanism," "humanists," etc., will be applied from here on to the mediating school of religious humanists or "new naturalists."

21

earthly misery and attainment of Nirvana can best be sought by resignation, asceticism, poverty, chastity, and abstract contemplation, Buddhism, in its marked other-worldliness, in its reverence for the immutable law of Karma transcending the changes of mundane existence, must suspect occidental humanism of being wrong in end and means. Though, allowing for differences between the ancient East and the modern West, the contrast between primitive Confucianism and humanism is slight compared to that between the latter and Buddhism, the new naturalists frequently forget, when they rejoice in the miscalled "atheism" of Confucius, that while he (like Lâo-tse) was "mainly concerned with ethical, political and social questions,"[45] instead of openly denying, he seems rather to have implicitly presupposed, that our ethical nature is conferred on us by Heaven or God. In spite of the fact that apparently he always referred to Heaven in an impersonal manner and, in his highly superstitious times, warned his disciples, in their religious rites, against intimacy with the gods, what allows the system that he transmitted to be called a religion instead of a noble way of life[46] is the presence in it of an urge towards the supernatural, exemplified by sporadic phases of polytheism among some of his followers. No matter how much, for intellectual, ethical, and practical reasons, one may sympathize with the original agnosticism or indifference of Buddha, Confucius, and Lâo-tse, towards establishing intimate personal relationship with what they believed to be ultimate, and no matter how unsatisfactory one may find the attempts of some of their admirers to effect such a relationship, for the sake of clarity one is obliged to conclude that in their agnosticism and indifference those three men were more secular than religious and that the systems to which their names have been attached are properly called

[45] Sir Reginald F. Johnston, *Confucianism and Modern China* (London: Gollancz, 1934), p. 85. cf. *ibid.,* pp. 88-92.

[46] "Whatever conclusion we may come to as to the right of Confucianism to be called a religion, we may safely say that it possesses two characteristics which most of us would agree are essential to religion—namely, a sound and workable system of ethics and an acknowledgment of the existence of a divine order. . . . Whatever else Confucianism may or may not be, it is certainly neither atheistical nor materialistic." *ibid.,* pp. 92, 96. cf. the rest of his Chap. VII, called "Is Confucianism a Religion?"

religions on grounds other than those particular traits of their chief proponents.

In looking back over history, humanists are inclined to associate themselves with any movement that magnifies the importance of man and minimizes the importance of the divine. Greek sophism and Renaissance humanism, at least in popular opinion, seem to be especially liable to such interpretation. Other forerunners of their own way of thinking humanists find, to a certain extent, in the Reformation and in subsequent, theological, philosophical, and scientific tendencies to individualism, social reform, secularism, free thought, subjectivism, naturalism, and atheism. To discuss these as fully as they deserve would require volumes. But even a fragmentary and impressionistic sketch of them may be of some use in bringing out salient features of humanism and of types of thought to which it is opposed.

Several family resemblances substantiate the claim of humanists that the Greek sophists of the fourth and fifth centuries before Christ may be numbered among their intellectual ancestors. It is probably not too fantastic to see a certain similarity in the philosophical situation then and now. The speculations of both the physical philosophers (Thales, Anaximander, Anaximenes, Anaxagoras, Empedocles, and Leucippus) and of what might be called, in the loosely fitting terminology of a later day, the logical and epistemological metaphysicians (Heraclitus, Parmenides, and Zeno) led to a momentary despair of human ability to know the physical world and truth. For sophists generally, as for Protagoras in particular, the proper study of mankind was man—the measure of all things, in the sense that anything beyond his immediate concern and common grasp was a matter of indifference and agnosticism. Hence science and cosmology tended to dwindle, as Plato suggests, into "courses" in arithmetic, geometry, astronomy, and music. Philosophy gave way to rhetoric, politics, civics, and oratory. A young man lucky enough to study under several sophists could get from them what might be described today as an undergraduate, liberal arts education, with special attention to successful salesmanship of whatever his wares happened to be.

23

The intellectual atmosphere is somewhat the same now. Though practical or applied science flourishes as never before, the nineteenth century dogma that science best pictures not only the physical universe but all reality has, except for a few lingering examples, dissolved in the current conflict of theories concerning biology, psychology, sociology, and physics. Ethics too, with neither religion nor science as a crutch, limps rather than strides along. The crumbling of the elaborate epistemological and metaphysical structures of Kant and Hegel, crushing their professional satellites and theological parasites, has added to a scepticism about the physical world and morality an amused contempt for philosophy and religion. Comparable to the sophistic disintegration of the philosophical search for truth into less ambitious undertakings is the rise of specialized studies of the structure of language and number, like mathematical logic, symbolic logic, and logical positivism. A natural reaction to idealistic intellectualism—resulting in suspicion of the quest for certainty; emphasis on the place of purpose and personal bias in matters of judgment and value; and a tendency not merely to test but to equate truth with practical consequences and efficiency not always envisaged as widely and profoundly as could be desired— has fostered pragmatism, instrumentalism, and humanism, all three of which stress, in one way or another, man as not only the measure but to an indefinable extent the master and the creator of reality. No matter how much the ancient sophists enriched subsequent culture and no matter how necessary and refreshing have been the contributions of contemporary pragmatism and humanism, nevertheless, viewed against the historical course of philosophy, both sophistry and humanism seem to be sectarian reactions or heresies, symptoms of temporary weakening in the central stream of metaphysics.

But perhaps that is not the chief thing humanists boast of in relation to their alleged ancestors, the sophists. Probably they would prefer to dwell on their forebears' free inquiry, interest in public affairs, and religious agnosticism, which are important elements of contemporary humanism, though equally common elsewhere. On the surface the sophists seem to have been innovators and freethinkers for their times, because, especially at first, they were frequently charged by the conservative elder generation with corrupting the youth, with novel ideas. But on the whole philosophers like Plato and Aristotle were the fundamental innovators, whereas the sophists generally reflected in but a superficially novel and clever way the thought and the morality of their age. They corrupted their pupils in so far as, with an indifference to ultimate intellectual, moral, and religious requirements, they let them rest content with facility, applause, and "success," apart from original work, integrity, and truth—in so far as they put high polish before high seriousness. Though members of the profession differed in character, manner, personal beliefs, and subjects of instruction, yet as a rule they tried to develop a style or form sufficient to impress others regardless of the material or content to which it was attached. They sought first-hand knowledge, accuracy, and right judgment less than the telling repartee of table and law court, the dramatic improvisation of stage and rostrum. They were not loath to exploit others, who, like themselves, lived "not upon bread alone, but principally by catchwords."[47]

Naturally, they often took an intense and sometimes beneficent interest in other public affairs besides literature and education. In particular, exponents of the Second Sophistic (founded by Aeschines in the fourth century before Christ and lasting until shortly after the death of Julian the Apostate in A.D. 363) played many important civic rôles. Antipater, for instance, was a friend of Septimius Severus and the empress Julia Domna, tutor of Caracalla and Geta, imperial secretary, consul, and governor of Bithynia; Lollianus and Prohaeresius, food controllers of Athens; and Herodes Atticus, consul and philanthropist on a vast scale.

It is sometimes asserted that sophists resemble humanists in being remarkably enlightened about religion. True, the Athenians outlawed Protagoras for saying that he did not know whether or not the gods existed. But that might be countered by the example of Gorgias, who played such "a distinguished part at the religious festivals of the Greeks," declaiming his *Pythian Oration* from the altar, that "his statue was dedicated in gold and was set up in the

[47] R. L. Stevenson, *Virginibus Puerisque* (New York: Caldwell, 1900), p. 53.

temple of the Pythian god."[48] Scopelian, of the Second Sophistic, was high priest of Asia. Under the reign of Julian the Apostate, the prominent sophist Prohaeresius never wavered in his Christianity. In short, sophism, while hardly a positive religious force, was not so agnostic or sceptical as current humanism is. There is no record of an official Sophistic Manifesto comparable to the Humanist Manifesto. A sophist's religious beliefs were an individual matter. The reformer's zeal, marked in humanists, in sophists usually gave way to making the most of the world as they found it. In the first three Christian centuries the sophists might even be called religious reactionaries, so tenaciously did their leaders, like Eunapius and Libanius, support dying paganism against the Christian revolution.

As the word "humanism" is especially associated with the Renaissance and, to a lesser degree, the Reformation, humanists do not fail to make the most of this verbal connection with a glorious age. After smouldering for centuries under medieval ecclesiasticism, dogmatism, and other-worldliness, the human, the natural, and the this-worldly blazed forth in the Renaissance with a magnificence scarcely rivalled since. Even so, certain resemblances and contrasts pertinent to our study exist between its humanism and the one with us now.

Most of the world's great religions began under essentially rural conditions. Their literature is permeated with reflections born of constant contact with nature. But when, as with Confucius (at least as compared with Christ), attention is directed more to the average actualities than to the finer possibilities of human relationships; or when, as now and as in Renaissance Italy, the tone of a civilization is set by cities, with concentration on human beings and human activities more in their external, economic, and social than in their internal, spiritual, and individual aspects, religion, taking on the colors of the secularism around it, tends to become humanistic. The humanism of one period, however, never fully repeats that of another. Today's humanism is quickened by faith in the natural goodness of man, in democracy, equality, humanitarianism, and progress

[48] *Philostratus and Eunapius: Lives of the Sophists,* translated by W. C. Wright, Loeb Classical Library (London: Heinemann, 1922), p. 31.

—ideas drawn from the eighteenth century and early theories of evolution rather than from the Renaissance, the Reformation, or Greece. Compared with the Reformation's insistence on man's depravity and the Enlightenment's sentimentality about his goodness, the intense interest of the Renaissance in everything human was more aesthetic and cultural than moral, more pagan than Christian. And though the liberation of the human spirit in the Renaissance and the Reformation later developed along humanitarian, democratic, and progressive lines, at first it was quite at home with despotism, aristocracy, and a partial return to the classical or the Christian past.

The humanism of the Renaissance exhibits, against a background of sinister shadows, a youth and exuberance, a delighted, spontaneous, and subtle appreciation of natural beauty and human nature, which contemporary humanism shows no sign of imitating. Though literary humanists have already in their brief course contributed more than their share to criticism, their moral and intellectual qualities, which account for most of the solidity and the keenness of their work, by a natural preference of the *frein vital* to the *élan vital,* seem to restrict their creative production. Besides, the energies of western mankind are currently more absorbed in science, practical inventions, industry, finance, and domestic and international politics, than in art and the humanities. The trend of the first group of interests is towards creation less through individual initiative than through the subordination of specialists to collective technique—as in Mr. Ford's method of manufacturing automobiles, or in many elaborate scientific experiments, or in the functioning of a large insurance company. Though at first such systems were often clearly envisaged, they grow according to hidden exigencies, which at times escape their would-be directors. And the growth of means and mechanisms frequently destroys or distorts the ends they serve or should serve. The American instrumentalists, who influence the new naturalists, apparently anticipate and recommend a similar collective technique in religion, philosophy, art, and most other fields. Whether this tendency to exalt technical corporate, over imaginative personal, creation will die young, or, taking from us what little self-sufficiency we have acquired since the Renaissance and the Reformation, will transform us into societies as rigid and indifferent to personality as those of "primitive peoples," or, by new motives and resources, will develop persons in proportion to their corporate solidarity, is a question for the Delphic oracle.

The humanists of today would lean on science and peer into the future. They stake their claims in "the world of tomorrow." For them the world of today is scarcely awake and the world of the past rests in the darkness of death. The explorations of Columbus, Vespucius, and da Gama opened to the Renaissance prospects more thrilling than any we may know again until we tame the arctic regions or domesticate the moon. Under the leadership of Nicholas of Cusa, Regiomontanus, Copernicus, Paracelsus, and Galileo, Renaissance science gained momentum. But, as the opposition not only of the Church but of public opinion proved, it was not a scientific era. Though Greek science was studied and developed, notably among the Mohammedans, scientists were relatively few and too often smacked of the occult. Ideals of established order, heirlooms of the Middle Ages, combined with aesthetic appreciation of what is, in the Renaissance largely occupied the place now held in humanistic attention by concern for progress and the future. The hopes and fears inspired in us by science, the rediscovery of the ancient world inspired in Renaissance humanists. There they beheld a pageant of man's greatness and his baseness, of his beauty and his wisdom and his power. The "realms of gold and many goodly states and kingdoms seen" were small and stale compared to this revelation of the vast expanses and the perennial vigor of the human spirit.

If the Italian Renaissance rejoiced in man, it tended, in reaction to the Middle Ages, to ignore God. And in so far as it ignored God its appreciation of man, growing superficial and erratic, weakened and decayed. Reason and morality alone, without the invigoration of religion, occasionally hold out long before lapsing into pessimism. But a combination of reason, sense, and imagination, without morality or religion, is seldom stable. Italian humanists, even if sometimes atheists at heart, like the sophists generally exhibited no more than indifference or scepticism beneath a cloak of conventional religion. A pontiff like Nicholas V could combine much that was best in Christianity and humanism. But, though no worse than their class and their epoch and merely following some of the precedents set by popes whom Dante assigned to hell, other humanistic bishops of Rome like Innocent VIII, Clement VII, and the infamous Alexander VI, corrupted religion for their own sordid ends, while at the same time adorning it with the construction or the decoration of St. Peter's and the Sistine Chapel.

Outside Italy humanism expressed itself more strongly in moral, religious, and social ways. Amidst all the changes and chances of life Erasmus and More, for example, preserved a noteworthy openness of mind, independence of spirit, and sympathy with liberal reform, which humanists today rightly vaunt as their own most cherished possessions. While admitting a certain likeness of motive, they would doubtless hesitate to call their own quest for a good life in a good world "utopian." It is, they think, too scientific to deserve such an old-fashioned name. Be that as it may, a deeper cleavage appears in the fact that whether with St. Thomas More, Erasmus, Reuchlin, and Colet, the humanists of northern Europe remained Catholics, or whether, like Melancthon and Œcolampadius, they became Protestants, at that time they usually professed something much more like Christian theism than like an embryonic new naturalism.

At the zenith of the Middle Ages, but rapidly disintegrating by the Renaissance, European civilization, despite great diversities, enjoyed a degree of coherence that it never knew before or afterwards. In theory, though (as proved by the Jacquerie and similar peasant revolts) often quite the opposite in practice, feudalism was not only an economic relationship between lord and vassal, owner and tenant, but a moral relationship involving mutual sacrifice, loyalty, and honorable service. Far outstripping in spiritual significance and social importance its classical archetype of patron and client, it gave Europe a more personal and intimate form of organization than that supplied by the military and the commercial bonds of the Roman empire and of later nations. But a source of unity greater than feudalism, relatively stable conditions, and reverence for custom, was the general acceptance of a religion that, at least in ideal, was catholic enough to deepen, purify, enrich, and bless every good, and to redeem every other, aspect of life.

With the growth of trade and travel, the crystallization of new classes and professions, the differentiation of administrative and juridical functions, the rise of modern states, and the friction between lay rulers and the Church, the unity achieved under simpler conditions, instead of successfully adapting itself to more complex circumstances, gradually fell to pieces. In almost every line of thought and action since the Middle Ages imperceptibly merged into the Renaissance, specialization, clarity, and an ever more limited expediency or efficiency have increased at the expense of unity, synoptic appreciation, and publicly accepted obedience to moral and religious motives and principles. But as humanism, except for its rather vague sympathy with liberal reform, is more an intellectual and religious than a social and economic phenomenon, it would be irrelevant to discuss here how the state and later industrialism and capitalism not only supplemented the personal relationships of medieval society but, notwithstanding the spread of political democracy, gradually supplanted them with those impersonal and amoral relationships which now, by hardening the hearts of those whom they profit and by goading to rebellion those whom they oppress, aggravate western social travail.[49]

The condition of the Catholic Church at the time of the Reformation fulfils the saying, *corruptio optimi pessima*. Almost all its faults and errors were—to put it as charitably as possible—virtues and truths spoilt nearly beyond recognition by the enervation of excessive power. That any attempt on the part of Christianity to introduce religious or moral principles into business, economics, and politics is today suspected by the public as selfish "interference" or contemptuously waved aside as futile derives largely from the fact that throughout their history both Catholic and Protestant Churches

[49] cf. *Religion and the Rise of Capitalism,* by R. H. Tawney (New York: Harcourt, Brace, 1926).

have used state and politics for brazenly sectarian ends. Though the Reformation itself was to some extent a political by-product, yet on simply religious grounds the contrast between the claims of the Church as the divinely right way of bringing man and God together and its condition—notwithstanding scattered strongholds of holiness and charity—as then perhaps the most unscrupulous, pernicious, and mighty, single institution in Europe was glaring enough to cause the pope to glow like antichrist in the eyes of many of the long-suffering faithful.

The remarkable thing is that the continental reformers found so much of Catholicism worth keeping.[50] Luther's intention to cleanse Christianity of what seemed to him to be unjustifiable accretions, or, in the words of Dr. John Dewey, "historic encumbrances," was mild compared with the new humanism's desire to sweep away theistic religion altogether. God, Christ, heaven, hell, and prayer remained vital concerns for the reformers. Indeed, even more than in the case of the Renaissance, mention of the Reformation in connection with contemporary humanism seems at first sight far fetched.

Over the significance of that sixteenth century crisis men still show such bitter partisanship that anybody trying to go his own "mugwumpish" way soon feels the plight of the maid "whom there were none to praise and very few to love." But that bitterness proves how alive the issues it clouds still are in Christianity. If a few characteristics or effects of the Reformation are touched on here, later the reader not already acquainted with humanism may see in them influences that moulded today's theism into an object of scorn for humanists and that helped to hasten the birth of humanism itself.

That Luther and Zwingli, while disagreeing about the eucharist, could concur on fourteen of the fifteen Marburg Articles and that Calvin, instead of initiating a new movement, virtually consolidated the one launched by Zwingli suggest, despite important differences of emphasis and spirit, enough common ground among those re-

---

[50] Because the Reformation in England involved no break with the past so drastic as that made by Luther and Calvin, discussion of it is omitted.

formers and their disciples to warrant discussing them roughly as a whole. They wished to remain orthodox about the creeds, the Trinity, the Incarnation, and the postulate that the Bible is inspired by God. Though Calvin was almost pre-Christian in reviving much of Old Testament ecclesiasticism, the general intention of the reformers was to brush away the mercenary and spiritually enslaving devices of priestcraft and to find again the ultimate verities and pure springs of Christianity in the Bible. They sought to liberate the individual soul from mechanisms that had become its master, from a Church that had become more its prison than its home. Had the Church been in good spiritual health, it might have met without schism most or all of the needs for reform, so elastic and buoyant was its best theology. Marriage of the clergy, communion in one or both kinds, indulgences, invocation of the saints, veneration of relics, and the regulation of monastic orders—these sources of conflict in the Reformation (and sources of irritation or jest for humanists today) are matters of discipline that the Catholic Church in its more gracious moments and especially when dealing with peoples for one reason or another unsympathetic to the Latin rite (like the Uniat Oriental Churches) has been able to adapt to the satisfaction of those concerned.

To prune the diseased parts of the Church (which the hierarchy notoriously failed to do, until, too late, in the Counter-Reformation), the reformers laid the axe to the roots of the institution as it had developed over a thousand years. Finding protests against the misuse of papal power unavailing, they denied the pope's right to any allegiance at all. Though in some countries Lutheranism retained an episcopal form of church government, most Protestants, as much because of Swiss democratic influence on Zwingli and Calvin as because of Biblical promptings, turned to presbyterianism and congregationalism. The general effect, even with the façade of episcopacy, was to minimize the importance that "valid orders" had hitherto had—and to some extent still have—for Catholic theologians. Though many Lutherans regard sacraments as "means of grace," in Protestantism as a whole anything more than a "subjective," "psychological," or commemorative value in sacraments, which might equally well or better be obtained by other and quite secular means, seems to verge on the "magical," the "materialistic," the "mechanical," and the "mystical." The distinction between clergy and laity became in Protestantism one of office rather than of class. Instead of priests and bishops set aside with special "supernatural" privileges and powers transmitted through ordination and consecration by a self-perpetuating class, Luther emphasized the natural priesthood of all Christians, among whom some choose, or are chosen, to become ministers to the rest, from whom they differ no more than other officeholders differ from their constituents.

This excision of the sacramental and the priestly, which until then the Church at its best had believed to be the heart of the institutional Body of Christ and His designated way of diffusing divine grace and which at its worst it had utilized as a means of monopolistic control of the superstitious, led to various results. Among Protestants it led to less and less appreciation of the value of priests and of institutional forms not only in Catholicism but in any world religion. So well have they and their more radical descendants, the humanists, weaned themselves from the sacramental and the institutional that they are almost unaware they have lost anything at all. In mere opposition, some Catholics have receded to a traditional position formulated before the development of Biblical exegesis and "higher criticism" and resting more on the authoritarianism of medieval and Roman law than on the spirit of Christ or of the New Testament. Ultimately, however, the requirements of such a position are generally acknowledged as secondary, institutional, external criteria or desiderata subordinate to the truly religious and practically convincing (but far more difficult and less convenient) test of the true priest and of the true Church, namely, the effective presence and working of God.

Two important fruits of the Reformation might be telegraphically described as the sanctification of the secular and the secularization of the sacred. Having sought salvation in vain by out-monking the monks, Luther swung to the other extreme of virtually repudiating monasticism and the supposed claims of the absolute in religion. His own enjoyment of the pleasures of life and sympathy

33

with daily labor helped to make business, marriage, family, and nation natural fields for religion. It would be preposterous to say that Catholicism had previously overlooked this. But it is a fact that the ark of salvation, as pictured in medieval painting, sculpture, illumination, and stained glass, overflowed with priests, prelates, and religious. The laity as a rule were sadly unrepresented. Reverence for the religious life, in the specialized sense, had tended to make the rest of life irreligious.

But the process of sanctifying the secular gradually blurred into the secularization of the sacred. Even with the best will people came to feel that religion asked of them nothing more than respectable adaptation to the common environment—complacent conformation rather than godly transformation. In the first half of the last century, Kierkegaard, observing the way in which Luther's "corrections" of abuses had become "norms" for religious life, was scathing in his denunciation of Danish Lutheranism. He charged it with so forgetting Christ's counsels of perfection that the ordinary precepts of religion, its minimum requirements, were exalted as its highest ideals.[51] The secular had become the only religious way and was becoming steadily more secular and less religious all the time. The cycle neared completion; for the serious practice of religion had shrunk into a profession, a specialty, a hobby, to an even sadder extent than in the Middle Ages, and among most men it was difficult to distinguish Christians from pagans. Denmark had no exclusive possession of that state of affairs then, nor has it now. The situation gives humanists their strongest reason for despising theism and explains in part their own, possibly rather inconsistent, ground for asserting that there can and should be no invidious distinction between the sacred and the profane.

So far we have considered chiefly the negative work of the reformers, what they protested against in the Church as an institution. But also they brought with them new or modified doctrines of grace, original sin, salvation, faith, and predestination. These encouraged direct and loving relations with God, without sacramental

[51] *Kierkegaard,* by Walter Lowrie (London: Oxford University Press, 1938), pp. 332-4, 428, 529-30, 546-7.

mediation. The formulation of the doctrines was questionable from the first. Were one constitutionally melancholy, like Cowper, one might be depressed by the possibility of not being one of the elect; one's helplessness before God, one's lack of faith, which only He can give, instead of leading to peaceful surrender might drive one to despair. Any doctrine has its danger if taken too literally. But a healthy man is seldom cowed by logic. Calvin, Knox, and Cromwell, for example, acted as though their wills were God's and heaven their home. That attitude may menace civilization but it disproves a frequent humanistic charge that the worship of God makes for servility and paralyzes initiative.

If we put on one side God's omnipotence, holiness, and omniscience, and on the other side man's nothingness apart from Him, our brutish depravity, our platant ignorance, and quite credible original sin (or, as humanists might prefer to call it, our room for improvement), and the superficiality of our external works as a substitute for, and apart from, spiritual transformation effected by living in, by, and for God—if we thresh these doctrines and are not too discouraged by the toughness and the strangeness of their husks, a tiny kernel of truth rolls out of the chaff. A tiny kernel but a foundation truth of theism: God first and everything else as He wills; love God and do as you please; the best one can do is to give oneself to God, who does the rest. Such expressions, apart from their context in a well balanced religion, are absurd, though they express a religious fact found in the Psalms, in the life and the teaching of Christ, in St. Augustine, in St. Thomas Aquinas (especially in his more intimate writings), in Catholic devotional literature from Thomas à Kempis through St. François de Sales to Père Grou, in Protestant hymns, and in the religions of Mohammed and Buddha. Doctrines, dogmas, practices, and so on, seem to be at bottom symptoms, varying with circumstances, of this religious malady, as humanists like to think of it, or of this peculiarly and preeminently human struggle to apprehend the Divine and to act accordingly.

A reason why it seems far fetched to mention the Reformation and today's humanism in the same breath is the latter's inability to understand, much less to sympathize with, the former's conviction of the reality of God. No matter how obviously defective one's own religion may be, perhaps in direct proportion to its imperfection, one is tempted to complain that the new naturalists have very little religious sense. Though not tone-deaf, they are—one is tempted to say—religion-deaf. But the tone-deaf do not claim that there is no such thing as music. They merely observe that they do not enjoy it. Humanism, however, has a music of its own. In its most idealistic form, in the special and honored place that the new naturalism (reversing the procedure of earlier naturalism) gives to ideals, above all to scientific and social ideals, as alone worthy of man's complete devotion, humanism may be unconsciously moving towards the same goal as theism but from a different angle. Perhaps the sameness of the end, and not practical reasons alone, accounts for humanism's otherwise odd insistence that it too is a religion—a "purer" religion, it would maintain, against the charge that it was cleansed of almost all religion. And if that were so, it might be a clue to the constant quarrel between humanism and theism; for only where the end is virtually the same and somehow felt to be so, though the conception of it and the means to it are bristlingly different, do rivalry, recrimination, and jealousy usually enter.

As it is impossible to assume that people a few centuries ago differed much from ourselves, who recognize the authority of different ideals in different situations, so it is merely a *façon de parler,* though perhaps a useful one, to suggest that ultimate authority for the reformers was ethico-religious, and for humanists today is ethico-scientific. One might say with momentary plausibility, that Luther, for example, was a rationalist, because it seemed more reasonable to him to put the authority of the Bible above that of the Church. But the fact that he takes the authority of the Bible more for granted than as a result of analysis; that he does not investigate to any extent the range of Biblical authority over fields other than religion and ethics; and that, contrasted with Zwingli's broader appreciation of the New Testament, he casts his lot almost exclusively with St. Paul—these facts suggest

36

more the working of spiritual intuition, right or wrong, than the exercise of discursive reason.

A surer example of such exercise is furnished by one whom humanists hail as a notable ancestor, Faustus Socinus. Two things concerned Luther: a genuine desire to preserve religious truth, even if he himself could not fully grasp it; and a fear lest the success of his labors be compromised by political and religious "cranks," or "anabaptists," as many persons putting their own individual inspiration above the Bible and social customs were (even apart from their views on baptism) then called about as indiscriminately as we now term some people "reds." Socinus, however, was provided with neither profound religious insight nor the responsibilities of a great party leader. His interest in religion was almost exclusively moral and intellectual. While accepting the authority and the inspiration of the Bible, much more freely than most of the learned men of his day did he rely on individual reason to determine the relative degree of inspiration or value of different parts of it. Any doctrine not clearly developed in the Bible itself, like the doctrines of the Trinity and of the deity of Christ, he felt bound to reject if they struck him as being contrary to reason. By using reason not merely to interpret but to criticize Scripture and by recognizing its authority as virtually ultimate in everything outside Scripture, he paved the way for rationalism. The Racovian Catechism, which includes his point of view, expressly makes room, in sharp contrast to the dogmatic spirit then prevailing in similar Catholic and Protestant documents, for development of thought and freedom of individual opinion. In this it seems to be a forerunner of similarly liberal Unitarian, Ethical Culture, and humanistic statements of belief.

It is no derogation of Socinus, however, to suppose that in one respect Luther delved deeper than he. How reason and religious faith or insight are defined and what each reveals are largely matters of chance and style. Many people, however, betray the presence of one more than of the other, and a few the presence of both in an extreme form. Recklessly speaking, religion and morality tend to affirmation, and reason to criticism and even negation, so-called

37

"constructive reason" being a hybrid. Pure "spiritual affirmation" —to use Dr. Paul Elmer More's terminology—almost free from the acids of reason, might be exemplified in Jesus. And pure reason ending in "intellectual scepticism," in Hume. But in Hume the philosopher, of course; not in Hume the historian; for the negative process—and *mutatis mutandis,* the affirmative one too—might well end in madness, did it not wisely cultivate counterbalancing interests, or did it not, as in F. H. Bradley's puncturing of the specious perfection of Hegelianism, ultimately fall back on some sort of "spiritual affirmation," intuition, or plain "animal faith." Now, these single-string men are not much bothered by the string not in their bow. Jesus, for example, rises above philosophical problems; at least, in schoolboy slang, they get no "rise" out of Him. And nobody goes to Hume to "get" religion. For a one-string man, like not so much Socinus as a present day rationalistic humanist, everything is on one plane, in one dimension, or subject to one test, that of reason or of whatever his string happens to be. His "solution" of problems is like fitting together a jigsaw puzzle, or like "harmonizing" the Gospels by putting somewhat similar texts in corresponding parts of four columns down a page. His earth does not shudder with the subterranean warring of principalities and powers. But Luther's does, though his intellectual string is shorter than his religious string. And Socrates's does, though he is just the other way round. And Pascal's and Kierkegaard's do. These double-string men try to perfect both their spiritual and their intellectual natures to the fullest extent and with complete confidence. They usually arrive at a strange and fascinating combination of "spiritual affirmation" and "intellectual scepticism." Humanists have the same elements in them, led by science and morality, but they fear to race one or the other as fast as it will go. The result is a state of confusion, vacillation, and ineffectiveness, which, unlike Socrates and Kierkegaard, they do not see in themselves or will not admit, and thus cannot overcome. Luther sought to "strangle" reason, because he feared it might overwhelm his faith. It might well have eroded the formulae of his faith, but it is hard to imagine that anything could have made him an out-and-out atheist. In Socrates, however, and on a smaller scale in Kierkegaard, "spiritual affirmation" recognizes, by a sort of "double vision," that it looks "paradoxical" and "absurd" to the critical intellect.[52] But faith is no more discouraged by that than is reason humiliated by the realization that, in the well rounded conduct of life, it must accept support from some sort of "spiritual affirmation." Bergson's "anti-intellectualism" is ponderous and wooden compared with Socrates's irony towards the working of his own mind. For him the intellect itself, which, compared with its pretentions, is ignorance, is as absurd for itself as are the amusing but divine flutterings of the soul. In these two-string men we are in the presence of powers or functions—faith and reason—that grow and are effective only in continual conflict and cooperation. It is true and trite to say that our whole personality, and not only one or two "parts" of it, must work and work together. The attitude of humanists, however, who would chose either science or ethics, or, more typically, who would not really choose at all, is like an old bachelor's. Reason must ward off "petticoat government," and when faith resigns her maiden name to become reason's better half she must retain her submissive independence. Like man and wife, as the old saw has it, they cannot get along well with one another and they cannot get along well without one another. Or, in the less banal words of von Hügel, they form a "fruitful tension."

Though in his own case what he thought was reason and what he believed was revelation continually fought within him, Luther used to say that anyone can interpret the Bible easily. Much too easily for comfort, the reformers soon agreed, when they saw their disciples wandering away in the imaginations of their hearts. From the time of Melancthon's *Loci Communes* and Calvin's *Institutions of the Christian Religion* a Protestant scholasticism grew up, expressing itself in a *corpus doctrinae* for almost every Protestant state and in innumerable confessions to which different Protestant groups subscribed, often with fear and trembling.

[52] Walter Lowrie, *op. cit.,* pp. 265, 337-8.

If scholasticism be defined as reasoning on premisses that have come to be accepted as true and that are therefore virtually exempt from examination, it can appear in any phase of thought or action. What is "done" or not "done" reflects the social scholasticism of one's caste. "Business procedure" and "legal procedure" rest on a mass of premisses that are seldom overhauled. A too certain acceptance of "laws" and "facts" in science, usually accompanied by indifference to their hypothetical and relative nature, is a sure sign of hardening of the scientific arteries. Granted that scholasticism is as inevitable in all kinds of social life as habit is in all kinds of individual life, one must be careful that scholasticism and habit are as good as possible and that each is occasionally turned inside out and inspected for moths. Catholic scholasticism was based on the Bible, the fathers, and the living tradition and interpretation of the Church; it incorporated much religious material, philosophical acumen, and ordinary practical shrewdness, based on vast and long experience. Of these, Protestant scholasticism retained almost nothing but the Bible and had little more to add than the bitter experiences of the Reformation. It seemed possessed by the notion that the Bible alone afforded not merely a norm for faith but a complete and consistent encyclopedia of salvation, from which religion might be logically deducted and systematized. More like the scribes and the pharisees than like Jesus, it made what it took to be logic the master of man, rather than his tutor. The new quality of life that Christ brought into the world and that the Reformation tried to revive was almost stifled under theological bric-a-brac. Instead of "travelling light," as on any other enterprise requiring free movement and exertion, men were weighted hand and foot by doctrinal propositions.[53]

[53]
"That Love is all there is,
Is all we know of Love;
It is enough, the freight should be
Proportioned to the groove."

—Emily Dickinson. From *The Poems of Emily Dickinson*, edited by Martha Dickinson Bianchi and Alfred Leete Hampson (Boston: Little, Brown, 1937), p. 262. Reprinted by permission of Little, Brown and Company.

On behalf of scholasticism it should be said that "a new quality of life" must have particular material and intellectual embodiments lest it evaporate into an abstraction. If it does not bother to transform the material, the logical, and the institutional in a material, somewhat logical, and still institutional world, it is doomed. Also for any sort of order and consistent advance standards must be formulated and revered. But standards themselves aspire to a standard, that of ever becoming better and truer. Whenever creeds and confessions (scientific, religious, economic, etc.) are revered for their own sakes, regardless of the standard to which they implicitly aspire, regardless of the standard (supposing it to be more than a convenient compromise) in the light of which they were originally formulated, and regardless of new knowledge and experience, they oblige some of the best adherents of the cults, or of the practices, or of the schools in which they are enshrined, who will not abandon a good cause merely on account of its flaws or because they must sometimes act with "mental reservations," to bide their time, as Kierkegaard put it, in open and honest dishonesty.[54]

As the scholastic type of Christianity was strongly developed when Galileo, Kepler, and Newton appeared, the beginning of the scientific era did not greatly affect it. But when men like Priestley, Lavoisier, Laplace, and Darwin undermined it in its declining years, it could no longer hold its own. The theism characteristic of our age is not that of the sixteenth and seventeenth centuries. It has spent the last hundred years and more trying to catch up with and to assimilate the discoveries made while it was still dominated by Catholic and Protestant scholasticism. To attack that scholasticism under the impression that one is annihilating the Christianity of today has its rewards, like other kinds of shadow boxing. But when one notices that, on the whole, the new naturalists oppose a dying variety of Protestant and Catholic "fundamentalism," with rusty naturalistic weapons reinforced by nineteenth century bits of positivism and utilitarian social idealism similar to John Stuart

[54] Walter Lowrie, *op. cit.*, pp. 522-3.

41

Mill's view of religion, all lightly polished with generally pre-Einsteinian science, and that most of them show little or no acquaintance with the works of such recent religious thinkers, Catholic and Protestant, as Rudolf Otto, Édouard Le Roy, Friedrich Heiler, Karl Heim, Søren Kierkegaard (whose works have only recently begun to exercise much influence in English-speaking lands), Nathan Söderblom, Ernst Troeltsch, A. E. Taylor, and Friedrich von Hügel: when one considers these things, one is inclined to doubt whether humanists are as up-to-date as their praise of modernity might casually lead one to suppose.

And although they speak again and again of "the scientific view of the world," even cursory reflection on the history of science and perusal of the works of Professors É. Meyerson, Henri Poincaré, Abel Rey, Dr. A. N. Whitehead, and Sir Arthur Eddington, may well lead one to doubt whether there is such a thing. With the increasing departmentalization of knowledge, the methods and the goals of the different sciences, which confine each to special aspects of reality, are not merely disputed in the privacy of their own domains but, when wrongly applied to the universe as a whole, often contradict one another. When thus used they become sectarian speculations expressing the prejudices of the science from which they started and which they have left well behind. Much Victorian materialism, for example, against which the new naturalism reacts, was an unjustified extension of the physics of the day to subjects intrinsically beyond its scope. Even now when, according to Sir Arthur Eddington, physics modestly offers only "pointer readings" of certain features of the world, the ghost of a cold, black, impersonally determined universe haunts popular thought, the pessimistic humanists, and the mediating school (as far as the last interprets the fact that physics does not deal with moral values as proof that such values are more subjective than the external world).[55] But while other and incompatible views derived from science exist—like Professor Alexander's impressive scheme of emergent evolution, springing from biology and appar-

[55] "We are alone in a terrifying and uncaring universe," J. H. Dietrich, "The Advance of Humanism," p. 47.

42

ently opposed to current speculations about the second law of thermodynamics as involving a gradual, inevitable diminution of physical energy—none of them can claim to be *"the* scientific view of the world."[56]

Modern specialization has always been counterbalanced by a desire for unity, but, where the genius of science prevailed, the synthesis itself—rendered ever more complicated by new materials, discoveries, and means of analysis—has been effected on constantly more abstract lines. This is obvious when one compares not merely petty philosophies that would cramp all reality into some momentarily popular scientific pattern, or movements (like neo-Kantianism, phenomenology, and mathematical logic) deliberately restricted to special sorts of philosophic criticism, but the central tradition of philosophy itself, with the synthesis of the major interests of their day achieved by St. Thomas Aquinas and his colleagues. Despite its inadequacy under present circumstances, probably no other synthesis has ever met the problems of its age with as much breadth, balance, and success. If idealism is generally recognized even by its foes as the predominant or native strain of metaphysics, and if post-Hegelian absolute idealists like T. H. Green, F. H. Bradley, and Bernard Bosanquet, may fairly be called eminent representatives of recent idealism in its direct line, much contemporary philosophy has come into being as a protest against failings in what was nevertheless the most closely organized and synoptic outlook then available. Thus Green's intellectualism led Bradley and Bosanquet to seek richer ranges of experience and consciousness. But even that—Bergson, the pragmatists, and the instrumentalists think—does not do justice to the unconscious forces influencing life and thought. Nor do the various realists feel that absolute idealism fully appreciates the objectivity of the external world. The numerous varieties of spiritual pluralism arose in part to protect personality, ethics, and religion, from being swallowed up in an absolutistic pantheism. This tendency to ignore or to distort great stretches of experience and to correct ex-

[56] Incompatibility here occurs when other "levels" of reality are assumed to behave like the level to which physical energy belongs.

43

cessive affirmations by impoverishing negations seems to be fostered less by personal failings of philosophers than by a simplifying spirit which, having escaped from scientific laboratories, where it was a recognized methodological necessity, is fêted everywhere like an irresistible débutante.

The descent of humanism, in one of its many ancestral lines, from a continually diluted Protestantism reveals some of the effects of such a process of simplification. Though in popular medieval practice the supernatural, for example, frequently became almost indistinguishable from magic and anything contrary to usual experience, nevertheless, orthodox theology, as represented by St. Thomas, never radically opposed nature and supernature. On the contrary, it considered supernature to be the completion, the perfection, the culmination of nature, so that everything created involves the joint action of both. But as soon as one goes beyond a tentative, conceptual isolation of those two forces of thought and being (or regulative, although ontologically well founded, processes), one tends to decompose active, concrete reality into arbitrary abstractions. The power of God can be so magnified (as was done by some of the reformers) that man's will becomes insignificant, and relations between God and man, supernature and nature, become strained, apparently extrinsic, mechanical, and so irreconcilable that one is almost driven in desperation to choose between them. That this matter, far from being an outworn quibble, is still alive today appears from the manner in which Professor J. H. Leuba (in his *God or Man*) rejects supernatural religion on the ground that human morality and divine grace are mutually exclusive and contradictory. Dr. C. F. Potter betrays a similar inclination to identify the supernatural with magic or anything that runs counter to, instead of drawing out the full potentialities of, the natural.

While accepting a crude supernaturalism and while magnifying, like most Christians of their day, the authority of the Bible, the Socinians emphasized the rights of the individual and the importance of the rational and the moral. On these grounds they rejected the doctrine of the Trinity and several Protestant tenets about the depravity of man, predestination, and justification by faith. In spite of increasing freedom of interpretation, their Unitarian successors clung to the Bible as the supreme revelation of God, until about the time of Channing. This was perhaps well for their church, because reason (which they later put before the Bible) in the meanwhile danced to tunes of thought not consoling to religion. Modern philosophy, starting with the rationalism of Descartes, passed by way of Locke, Hume, Kant, Comte, and Spencer, through various shades of sensationalism, empiricism, scepticism, phenomenalism, and agnosticism. The growing religious toleration of the seventeenth century led, in the eighteenth, to the deistic compromise between science and orthodoxy. Nature was pictured as a mechanism, as a clock that God, the First Cause, made, wound, and left to run by itself. Because it ran so well, some concluded that God was superfluous and that the universe was self-originating and self-sustaining. Transcendent deism and mechanistic materialism fell in their turn before evolution, dynamism, and the immanent deity of the nineteenth century. The idea of progress encouraged social reform in place of yearning for a "static" heaven. Reason, no longer the one and only key to reality and truth, found itself often treated as merely a tool of instinct, will, and emotion, to be used for purposes beyond its ken. Logic working itself out in historical events and institutions, overshadowed logic as a dissection of ideas and propositions. Everything seemed richer, more complex, more full of tensions. The living process of apprehending reality called for the use of all faculties and all experience. Through these centuries of storm and stress, the Unitarians, despite their notable work in education and the presence on their rolls of a name like Joseph Priestley's, on the whole stayed by themselves away from the philosophic arena. Not until the relatively peaceful, prosperous, and polished reign of Victoria did Unitarianism fully flower. Then there was some temptation to turn (with Parker and Martineau) from an unwieldy Bible to the gracious reason and the delicate conscience of the polite. They became the measure of deity; nothing that ruffled them could be divine. The more "refined" the worshipper, the more

45

rarefied his God. Reason and conscience, at first His interpreters, became His creators. "But why create Him?" asked some who thought themselves "advanced," "superior," and "emancipated." "Why not depend, as He does, upon ourselves?" And they called themselves "humanists," not because their point of view remarkably resembled anything previously known as humanism, but simply to distinguish themselves, believers in men without God, from those who believe in God as well as men.

So far as earlier interpretations of miracles and revelation as intrusions of an order contrary to nature were either hyperbolical or else compatible with natural explanations, Unitarians followed the understandable course of rejecting the supernatural altogether. They were doubtless right in rejecting a conception of the supernatural which, despite a rough apologetical force, was of little religious, moral, or scientific worth. But that does not dispose of the further question of the character of that reality which is ever urging men and nature to attain heights they might otherwise never dream of. Whether that reality can be more vividly apprehended with the aid of Platonic Forms, or Thomistic God and supernature, or some theory of emergent evolution, or any of the other countless ways in which it has been approached in thought and action, not yet has any philosophy or religion gone far without being obliged to admit its existence under one form or another. But to date the majority of humanists consider that instead of necessitating further inquiry into the mystery of its being, the power and the scope of nature make such investigation pointless.

Another instance of simplification (common in humanism, liberal Protestantism, some types of Roman Catholic modernism, advanced Judaism, and Ethical Culture) is that of confounding religion with what has usually been one of its most important concomitants but never its whole nature—morality. Luther's perception of the spiritual importance of daily life, together with a natural reaction from medieval ways, probably contributed something, as has already been remarked, to the eclipse of the sacred, the clerical, and the other-worldly, by the secular, the lay, and the this-worldly. Kant with his scorn of divine "court duties" and with his bent for keeping or rejecting aspects of religion solely according to their rational and moral merits doubtless added impetus to the movement. But though Kant approached religion through ethics, ethics for him reached farther into the nature of things than it does for present-day humanists, and did so without being mistaken for religion. Whereas he could accept God, immortality, and many features of the Lutheranism of his time (all indeed considerably modified by criticism), most recent humanists look upon religion as exclusively concerned with improving moral and material conditions of humanity, without reference to God, religious institutions, or the hope that this life is not the only phase of our existence. Like Kant they feel that pure or scientific reason cannot establish the validity of conscience or duty. But unlike him they waver continually between a view of science as a means of dealing with certain limited features of reality and a view of it as the only adequate source of true knowledge. In the first case, the mediating school inclines to admit the existence of moral influences greater than social conventions or merely human characteristics. Other types of humanists, like Professor Hartmann and Dr. More, then do not hesitate to conclude that the ultimate structure of reality involves dominant moral elements or Ideas. From the recognition of the supremacy of a spiritual order it is only a step, as Kant and Dr. More have shown, to theism. The serious attention literary humanists pay to "the inner check" suggests that they are as impressed by certain negative and intuitive implications of conscience as Kant was by what he believed to be the positive, rational aspects of the categorical imperative. But whenever "new naturalists" timidly betray any such faith in the ultimate significance of their consciences and religious stirrings, belief in science as the only way to reality commences to paralyze them. They suspect that anything as perfect as God is but a dream and that moral ideals are simply properties—one might almost say eccentricities —of the human race. Then swinging in the other direction, they add that for us those ideals are the most important interests in life and the real and only constituents of religion. The fact that science shows them to be fragile social productions referring to nothing beyond themselves should, they argue, more strongly induce us to protect them than does the belief that, although at least for our own sakes we must do everything possible to realize them, their full existence and significance are not entirely dependent upon the efforts of a few, passing, featherless bipeds.

So much—or rather, so little—for the site, the extent, and the ancestry of humanism. If sixteen quarterings have not been displayed, at least the relationship of humanism to some of the movements and tendencies with which, in East and West, it is commonly compared have been indicated. We are now ready to examine the movement itself in closer detail.

CHAPTER II

SYNOPSIS OF CHAPTER II

The Humanist Manifesto. The spirit of the Manifesto compared with Comte's. The tone of humanistic "literature" towards its opponents. Some of the primary postulates of humanism about the self-existence of the universe, the relation of man to nature, of mind to body, of life to immortality, of value to existence, of religion to other aspects of life, and of nature to supernature. Humanists object to, and seem to believe that theists hold, a "gap" conception of the supernatural. This misunderstanding exposed. Dr. Potter's substitute for the Christian notion of the supernatural. The "new naturalism" of humanists distinguished from the older naturalism, which it would correct and replace. Three general attitudes (not quite corresponding to the three "schools") towards the world of the new naturalists: the "disinterestedness" or "indifference" of Mr. Lippmann, the cheerfulness of Professor Haydon, and the gloom of dramatic despair in Bertrand Russell and of sophisticated disillusionment in Mr. Krutch. Observations on the appropriateness of calling anything short of theism a "religion."

CHAPTER 11

AMERICAN HUMANISM

PROBABLY the most carefully pondered official statement of what humanism means to its votaries appeared in the May-June 1933 issue of *The New Humanist*. At the time the editor of the periodical, Mr. R. B. Bragg, observed: "The Manifesto is a product of many minds. It was designed to represent a developing point of view, not a new creed. The individuals whose signatures appear, would, had they been writing individual statements, have stated the propositions in differing terms. The importance of the document is that more than thirty men have come to general agreement on matters of final concern and that these men are undoubtedly representative of a large number who are forging a new philosophy out of the materials of the modern world." Generously, impartially, *The New Humanist* also published criticisms of the Manifesto from humanists and theists. Both seemed to conclude that, if not treated too carpingly, the Manifesto is about as exact a summary of humanism by humanists as could be expected at present.

"A Humanist Manifesto

"The time has come for widespread recognition of the radical changes in religious beliefs throughout the modern world. The time is past for mere revision of traditional attitudes. Science and economic change have disrupted the old beliefs. Religions the world over are under the necessity of coming to terms with new conditions created by a vastly increased knowledge and experience. In every field of human activity, the vital movement is now in the direction of a candid and explicit humanism. In order that religious humanism may be better understood we, the undersigned, desire to make certain affirmations which we believe the facts of our contemporary life demonstrate.

"There is great danger of a final, and we believe fatal, identification of the word *religion* with doctrines and methods which have lost their significance and which are powerless to solve the problem of human living in the Twentieth Century. Religions have always been means for realizing the highest values of life. Their end has been accomplished through the interpretation of the total environing situation (theology or world view), the sense of values resulting therefrom (goal or ideal), and the technique (cult) established for realizing the satisfactory life. A change in any of these factors results in alteration of the outward forms of religion. This fact explains the changefulness of religions through the centuries. But through all changes religion itself remains constant in its quest for abiding values, an inseparable feature of human life.

"Today man's larger understanding of the universe, his scientific achievements, and his deeper appreciation of brotherhood, have created a situation which requires a new statement of the means and purposes of religion. Such a vital, fearless, and frank religion capable of furnishing adequate social goals and personal satisfactions may appear to many people as a complete break with the past. While this age does owe a vast debt to the traditional religions, it is none the less obvious that any religion that can hope to be a synthesizing and dynamic force for today must be shaped for the needs of this age. To establish such a religion is a major necessity of the present. It is a responsibility which rests upon this generation. We therefore affirm the following:

"*First:* Religious humanists regard the universe as self-existing and not created.

"*Second:* Humanism believes that man is a part of nature and that he has emerged as the result of a continuous process.

"*Third:* Holding an organic view of life, humanists find that the traditional dualism of mind and body must be rejected.

"*Fourth:* Humanism recognizes that man's religious culture and civilization, as clearly depicted by anthropology and history, are the product of a gradual development due to his interaction with his natural environment and with his social heritage. The individual born into a particular culture is largely moulded by that culture.

"*Fifth:* Humanism asserts that the nature of the universe depicted by modern science makes unacceptable any supernatural or cosmic guarantees of human values. Obviously humanism does not deny the possibility of realities as yet undiscovered, but it does insist that the way to determine the existence and value of any and all realities is by means of intelligent inquiry and by the assessment of their relation to human needs. Religion must formulate its hopes and plans in the light of the scientific spirit and method.

"*Sixth:* We are convinced that the time has passed for theism, deism, modernism, and the several varieties of 'new thought.'

"*Seventh:* Religion consists of those actions, purposes, and experiences which are humanly significant. Nothing human is alien to the religious. It includes labor, art, science, philosophy, love, friendship, recreation—all that is in its degree expressive of intelligently satisfying human living. The distinction between the sacred and the secular can no longer be maintained.

"*Eighth:* Religious humanism considers the complete realization of human personality to be the end of man's life and seeks its development and fulfillment in the here and now. This is the explanation of the humanist's social passion.

"*Ninth:* In place of the old attitudes involved in worship and prayer the humanist finds his religious emotions expressed in a heightened sense of personal life and in a cooperative effort to promote social well-being.

"*Tenth:* It follows that there will be no uniquely religious emotions and attitudes of the kind hitherto associated with belief in the supernatural.

"*Eleventh:* Man will learn to face the crises of life in terms of his knowledge of their naturalness and probability. Reasonable and manly attitudes will be fostered by education and supported by custom. We assume that humanism will take the path of social

53

and mental hygiene and discourage sentimental and unreal hopes and wishful thinking.

"*Twelfth:* Believing that religion must work increasingly for joy in living, religious humanists aim to foster the creative in man and to encourage achievements that add to the satisfactions of life.

"*Thirteenth:* Religious humanism maintains that all associations and institutions exist for the fulfillment of human life. The intelligent evaluation, transformation, control, and direction of such associations and institutions with a view to the enhancement of human life is the purpose and programme of humanism. Certainly religious institutions, their ritualistic forms, ecclesiastical methods, and communal activities must be reconstituted as rapidly as experience allows, in order to function effectively in the modern world.

"*Fourteenth:* The humanists are firmly convinced that existing acquisitive and profit-motivated society has shown itself to be inadequate and that a radical change in methods, controls, and motives must be instituted. A socialized and cooperative economic order must be established to the end that the equitable distribution of the means of life be possible. The goal of humanism is a free and universal society in which people voluntarily and intelligently cooperate for the common good. Humanists demand a shared life in a shared world.

"*Fifteenth and last:* We assert that humanism will: (a) affirm life rather than deny it; (b) seek to elicit the possibilities of life, not flee from it; and (c) endeavor to establish the conditions of a satisfactory life for all, not merely for the few. By this positive morale and intention humanism will be guided, and from this perspective and alignment the techniques and efforts of humanism will flow.

"So stand the theses of religious humanism. Though we consider the religious forms and ideas of our fathers no longer adequate, the quest for the good life is still the central task for mankind. Man is at last becoming aware that he alone is responsible for the realization of the world of his dreams, that he has within himself

54

the power for its achievement. He must set intelligence and will to the task."[1]

Perhaps humanists think of their Manifesto as a "clarion call"; to issue "clarion calls" for this or that is one of their fortes. Others will find in it resemblances to Comte's solemn, prophetic solicitude for mankind. Utilitarian in spirit, both stress the necessity of social feeling, which in itself, though indispensable, seldom solves specific problems. As positivism would construct a new social order on the foundations of the French revolution, so humanism would synthesize into a new world the conflicting forces born of the industrial revolution. Though in reality neither is more scientific or religious than, say, Spencer's evolutionary philosophy, both would start from science and would culminate in religion. Progress,

[1] The Manifesto was signed by the following: J. A. C. Fagginger Auer, Parkman professor of church history and theology, Harvard University; professor of church history, Tufts College; E. Burdette Backus, Unitarian minister; Harry Elmer Barnes, general editorial department, Scripps-Howard Newspapers; L. M. Birkhead, The Liberal Center, Kansas City, Mo.; Raymond B. Bragg, secretary, Western Unitarian Conference; Edwin Arthur Burtt, professor of philosophy, Sage School of Philosophy, Cornell University; Ernest Caldecott, minister, First Unitarian Church, Los Angeles, Calif.; A. J. Carlson, professor of physiology, University of Chicago; John Dewey, Columbia University; Albert C. Dieffenbach, formerly editor of *The Christian Register*; John H. Dietrich, minister, First Unitarian Society, Minneapolis; Bernard Fantus, professor of therapeutics, College of Medicine, University of Illinois; William Floyd, editor of *The Arbitrator*, New York City; F. H. Hankins, professor of economics and sociology, Smith College; A. Eustace Haydon, professor of history of religions, University of Chicago; Llewellyn Jones, literary critic and author; Robert Morss Lovett, editor, *The New Republic*, professor of English, University of Chicago; Harold P. Marley, minister, the Fellowship of Liberal Religion, Ann Arbor, Mich.; R. Lester Mondale, minister, Unitarian Church, Evanston, Ill.; Charles Francis Potter, leader and founder, The First Humanist Society of New York, Inc.; John Herman Randall, Jr., Department of Philosophy, Columbia University; Curtis W. Reese, dean, Abraham Lincoln Centre, Chicago; Oliver L. Reiser, associate professor of philosophy, University of Pittsburgh; Roy Wood Sellars, professor of philosophy, University of Michigan; Clinton Lee Scott, minister, Universalist Church, Peoria, Ill.; Maynard Shipley, president, The Science League of America; W. Frank Swift, director, Boston Ethical Society; V. T. Thayer, educational director, Ethical Culture Schools; Eldred C. Vanderlaan, leader of the Free Fellowship, Berkeley, Calif.; Joseph Walker, attorney, Boston, Mass.; Jacob J. Weinstein, rabbi, advisor to Jewish students, Columbia University; Frank S. C. Wicks, All Souls Unitarian Church, Indianapolis; David Rhys Williams, minister, Unitarian Church, Rochester, N.Y.; Edwin H. Wilson, managing editor, *The New Humanist*, Chicago, Ill., minister, Third Unitarian Church, Chicago, Ill.

55

adored by both, for both rests on order, and order, on "the whole series of natural laws,"[2] best dealt with by science. A certain similarity exists between Comte's hierarchy of sciences—mathematics, astronomy, physics, chemistry, biology, and sociology—and the stages of emergent evolution usually accepted by humanists—space-time, matter, life, and consciousness. Just as thought, moreover, working with objects of the highest kind (human nature and its aspirations) is (though in Comte's opinion it should not and will not long be) most tainted by non-positivistic metaphysics and theology, so, according to emergent evolution, the highest quality, level, or stage we can dream of—namely the level of deity, the next level beyond what we now know—must be enjoyed, if at all, in a non-scientific fashion until dream dissolves into daylight, which itself engenders new dreams. Scientific spirit, the master of thought, must serve goals and ideals exceeding its grasp—the development of our moral nature, especially (for Comte) of sympathy, energy, and active love. Humanism and positivism would thus realize "the highest aspirations of medieval Catholicism."[3] Humanism, perhaps rather against its will; for its references to religion are usually based on outworn types of American Protestantism and conceptions of Catholicism derived from hearsay more than from intimate experience and practice. If Comte, imbued with Catholic traditions, almost lost sight of Catholic mysticism—of devotion to God as well as to man—could one expect better of humanism?

Since the tone of a document reveals the ambitions and the limitations of its authors and since the tone of humanistic writings—far more restrained in the Manifesto than usual elsewhere—has generally been passed over in silence, it may not be irrelevant to notice it. In their individual, less formal productions humanists do not hesitate to admit that they are "novel," "modern," "forward looking," "mature," "frank," "social," "clear-eyed," "dynamic," "intelligent," "radical," "democratic," "vital," and "unfet-

[2] *A General View of Positivism,* by Auguste Comte, translated by J. H. Bridges (London: Routledge, no date), p. 116.
[3] *ibid.,* p. 120.

tered" by any authority other than the latest speculations of science as interpreted by themselves and their "fresh," "fearless," "torch-bearing" colleagues. Their "explicit," "manly" "candor" not infrequently hints that those who disagree with their "brave" and "winsome naturalism" are prevented from exhibiting or admiring the same qualities by the misfortune of being "pre-modern," "prescientific," "sick souls," hopelessly caught in a "static" tradition that lulls them to sleep with "supernatural," "magic" "guarantees" and "consolations" of "wishful thinking."[4]

Humanists incline to describe contemporary Christians as either hidebound and orthodox or intelligent and heretical. Expressions like "developing point of view, not a new creed," "mere revision of traditional attitudes," "complete break with the past," and the implication that "traditional religions" cannot be "shaped for the needs of this age," all suggest that Christianity is a fixed, finished body of antiquated, unchanging dogmas and institutions rather than a living spirit of truth and goodness. Dr. David S. Muzzey[5] represented that position clearly when he wrote: "The Church, in its official pronouncements, has never allowed freedom, except the freedom to accept its doctrines. . . . The creeds are not liberating. They bring you into a 'fold,' a little confined place of safety. You may not wander freely. But we who face the future rather than the past do wander freely. We set no limit to our intellectual search or to our historical criticism; we look with an historical eye on all forms and confessions; and we are free to take whatever good we find in them, and to leave whatever does not conform with our own spiritual demands. . . . Religion is fundamentally

[4] cf. "The humanist . . . can appreciate why sensitive souls, or men with an inferiority feeling, or gentle hearts, sick with the anguish and chaos of a ruthless civilization should flee for refuge to the security of some system of final truth. The humanist cannot flee but he can sympathize with those who do. . . . In the societies of yesterday there were sick souls who needed otherworldly opiates." A. E. Haydon, "What Is Humanism?", *The University Review* (University of Kansas City, Kansas City, Mo.), summer 1937, Vol. III, no. 4, pp. 238, 240. cf. also his review of M. C. Otto's *Things and Ideals* in *The American Review,* March-April 1925, pp. 224 *ff.*

[5] In 1938 a leader of the New York Society for Ethical Culture, the leader of the Westchester Society for Ethical Culture, and one of the editors of *The Standard.*

a matter of sanction. Where does the authority lie? Where is the compelling thing? Now for the fundamentalist or even for the liberal Christian or Jew the authority lies in some compelling thing that is outside of man, in some revelation or tradition. For us it lies within. For us, all these outward forms and sanctions are historical events. They may or may not appeal to us. I am not arguing for or against (for example) the belief in the existence of a God or Providence, or for or against the belief in the existence, say, of effective sacraments. It is simply that whether or not you believe in these things depends on one of two alternatives—either you accept what somebody tells you about them, and take it on faith, or you arrive at your belief through your own intellectual processes."[6]

Though nobody can deny that certain interpretations of authority and of the Church have had on many people in the past and today the bad effect described by Dr. Muzzey, nevertheless he here refers to only one aspect of historical Christianity and does so in an abstract fashion that makes contrasts and frictions appear to be more sharp than they normally are in the economy of institutional religion. It is equally true that since Christianity began there have been churchmen in good standing for whom the fold was not merely "a little confined place of safety" but a house of many mansions, a living, growing organization, the unity and the permanence of which lie not so much in its developing doctrines and institutions as in a Christ-like search for the kingdom of God and His righteousness. Though they believe that certain features of that kingdom are best revealed in Christian tradition and life, they do not assume that that exhausts the kingdom or that anything called Christian is worthy of acceptance on grounds other than its intrinsic merit and its harmony with the broadest, deepest, and fullest truth, beauty, and goodness available from all sources and times.

This point deserves to be mentioned, because by keeping laudatory adjectives for themselves and by giving disparaging ones to those with whom they disagree humanists often create the impression of insinuating that their opponents are intellectually and mor-

[6] *The Standard,* issued by the American Ethical Union, April 1935, pp. 171-2.

ally retarded. Some theistic writers err against humanists in the same way. Doubtless the method has its reward as propaganda or entertainment. But more fruitful discussion would seem to require, at least as an ideal, the recognition by each side that the other is inspired by an equally honest desire for truth, that the major capacities and limitations of both sides in this matter are about the same, and that the differences in another's equipment and training are worthy of respect not because they blind him to what one sees but because they enable him to see things to which one is blind.

If they could use "humanism" to mean giving human nature its due (as they understand it) and could maintain that God, in the richest and most fundamental sense of the word, is the highest abiding value of life, many Christians, if they did not know the source of the Manifesto, might mistake its three opening paragraphs for a collection of fervent generalities compiled from their own religious publications. Humanists may doubt whether, even with those provisions, the Roman Catholic Church (commonly considered to be the most rigid group in Christendom) could truly admit that mere revision of numerous traditional attitudes is insufficient.[7] But if not only intelligence but worldliness, sophistry, and timidity occupy on the whole about the same place in any Christian or humanistic denomination, it may be possible for people to have the same fundamental outlook and sympathies and yet (because of different conditions and opinions about proper time, place, method, and extent) to express them with equal sincerity and justness in antagonistic ways.

[7] cf. "If, for instance, he is dealing with Christ's descent into Hell or His ascension into Heaven, the Baron points out that, under the pressure of science, the figurative imagery has gradually fallen away, leaving the doctrine itself untouched. Stripped of the coverings which concealed it, it has come to form an even more integral part of the organic unity of Christianity. . . . Von Hügel seems to hope that the future will show a similar purifying of other dogmatic imagery; such as that of the Virgin Birth and of the Resurrection. . . . Frankly, it is difficult, if not impossible, to imagine the kind of 'purification' of the dogmas of the Virgin Birth and of the Resurrection which would be acceptable to the [Roman Catholic] Church, and we prefer to think that the [Roman Catholic] Church will always continue to teach in the future that which on these points she has taught in the past." Maurice Nédoncelle, *Baron Friedrich von Hügel, A Study of His Life and Thought,* translated by Marjorie Vernon (London: Longmans, Green, 1937), p. 190.

A perusal of the numbered items of the Manifesto proves that its full significance is obscured by any attempt to read it in the light of the provisions just mentioned or on the assumption of a fundamental similarity in outlook and sympathy, except the desire for truth common to all men of right mind. The affirmations fall roughly into two groups, one of primarily naturalistic import reflecting the influence of science, the other primarily humanistic and a by-product of the refinement of civilization by Christianity. The naturalization of the universe (item one), man (items two, three, and eight), and religion (items four, five, and six) belongs to the first group. The second group includes the humanistic view of religion (items seven, nine, and ten) and of the individual and society (items eleven, twelve, thirteen, fourteen, and fifteen).

The postulate that the universe is self-existing and not created (item one) probably draws its plausibility from exaggerated notions of science and from disgust at the acceptance of primitive legends as literally true. No one science demonstrates, nor all of them together, that the universe was or was not created. The nature of the sciences makes the question of creation for them an idle fancy.[8] Their purposes of investigation require the assumption of

[8] Bertrand Russell writes, apropos of the second law of thermodynamics: "It seems that the world was created at some not infinitely remote date, and was then far more full of inequalities than it is now, but from the moment of creation it has been continually running down, and will ultimately stop for all practical purposes unless it is again wound up. . . .

"We must, I think, admit that there is far more to be said for the view that the universe had a beginning in time at some not infinitely remote period, than there is for any other theological conclusions which scientists have recently been urging us to admit. The argument does not have demonstrative certainty. The second law of thermodynamics may not hold in all times and places, or we may be mistaken in thinking the universe spatially finite; but as arguments of this nature go, it is a good one, and I think we ought provisionally to accept the hypothesis that the world had a beginning at some definite, though unknown, date.

"Are we to infer from this that the world was made by a Creator? Certainly not, if we are to adhere to the canons of valid scientific inference. There is no reason whatever why the universe should not have begun spontaneously, except that it seems odd that it should do so; but there is no law of nature to the effect that things which seem odd to us must not happen. To infer a Creator is to infer a cause, and causal inferences are only admissible in science when they proceed from observed causal laws. Creation out of nothing is an occurrence which has not been observed. There is, therefore, no better reason to suppose that the world was caused by a Creator than to suppose that it was uncaused; either equally

some sort of existence for the objects observed but may ignore the question of their ultimate origin. Centuries of argument have not silenced the debate about the extent to which objects of science are "self-existing." As a matter of method and efficiency it is frequently useful to treat triangles or mathematical relations as if they existed in and for themselves and were not to some extent products of our minds, or to study botany or biology regardless of the way in which colors, magnitudes, and teleological concepts are conditioned by our physical and psychical constitution. But restricted procedures like that reveal little about the manner and the degree of the self-existence of objects. If it is asserted that though no object within the universe is fully self-existent, since at least part of its being consists of its relations with other things, nevertheless the universe as a whole is self-existent, one may wonder how the universe as a whole escapes roughly the same difficulties concerning the nature and the extent of the self-existence of any object of thought. Perhaps it escapes because methods and theories adapted to objects and relations within the universe are inapplicable to the universe itself, which by definition is a being of a different order. But the sciences, to which humanists appeal, have been designed to cope with special fields within the universe and not to describe the universe itself.

If humanists protest against the adequacy of Biblical or Platonic myths of creation, they can find sympathizers among theists from at least the time of St. Thomas Aquinas. Whether it be called an evasion, a normal advance of theological thought, or both, the doctrine of creation now common in theistic circles claims that the element of truth in those myths lies in maintaining the supremacy and the priority of the spiritual, or God, as they believe to be the conclusion when all other relevant considerations are taken into account. The relations of designer and material and of

contradicts the causal laws that we can observe." *The Scientific Outlook* (New York: Norton, 1931), pp. 91, 117, 118.

Professor Haydon seems to have reached about the same conclusion when, four years after signing the Manifesto, he wrote: "Regarding ultimate origins and ultimate ends the humanist preserves a proper scientific humility." "What Is Humanism?", *The University Review,* summer 1937, p. 239.

cause and effect are recognized as less ultimate than that of ground and consequence, or of the reason (scientific, moral, aesthetic, etc.) for an event and the event expressing that reason. The fundamental question becomes, is there an ultimate reason for the existence of the universe? If there is such a reason, it is of secondary importance whether its total or partial expression is temporally later or concomitant, since the ordinary expression of human thought and will offers us analogies by which to try to imagine those possibilities. But should the reason be both temporally later and a chance by-product of existence, that situation would be harder for us to conceive. We should have to presuppose a brute fact, something existing without any reason. "Reason" is here used not in a narrowly rationalistic or merely logical sense but as meaning that which in some way—scientific, emotional, volitional, perceptional, etc.—can be no matter how faintly appreciated or acted upon by human experience and thus cannot be deemed utterly alien to us. Healthy religion, in spite of doubt and difficulty, is persuaded of our affinity with, and home in, the ultimate nature of reality. While our knowledge remains so insignificant that challengingly brute facts and apparently insoluble questions (like this one of the creation and the self-existence of the universe) abound, philosophy and science have to admit that there is no proof of a reason or spiritual principle in everything, no matter how incommensurably superior to our experience that reason or affinity may be. Yet not only religion but science, morality, art, every serious human enterprise, presuppose the essential truth of that unproved assumption and attain their greatest success in proportion to their confidence in it. Either that is one of the most reliable of human characteristics or we have been on the wrong track since life began.

This bare minimum of what creation now means for many theists looks slight compared to the elaborate tradition of the average Christian. But, not to mention the pessimistic humanists, this trifle in some ways staggers even the moderate school. Most of them postulate the universality of natural, physical, material, or scientific laws, but will not allow moral and religious presuppositions and convictions to hold good far beyond society, the race, or some influence greater than either but not ultimate. To what extent scientific thought essentially differs from ethical, religious, or artistic thought and impulse, and how far it can exist apart from and unaffected by them so as to deserve such deferential treatment, may be questioned. As almost any object of experience has more facets than its scientific ones, it is arbitrary to reduce nature as a whole or in part to its physical or scientific elements alone. By its emphasis on the importance of morality, the new naturalism expressly tries to avoid this. But one may suspect that it wavers concerning the absolute worth of morality and religion as compared to science because it has not outgrown the anthropomorphisms that it attacks in theism. If goodness means only something that makes us comfortable and contented as we are, or if the essence of personality is an easygoing, easily grasped sympathy and understanding, not merely science but common experience protests that the universe cannot be, and ought not to be, good or personal in that sense. Because most of us in our average moments think of reasonableness, goodness, and personality on a plane not much higher than that, it is no wonder that we and humanists feel that religion and morality as often heedlessly conceived and practised are shown by the best hypotheses of science to be petty, narrowly human, and of no cosmic importance and stability. But instead of being discouraged we should be glad to realize that the better we appreciate the universe the more exacting are its demands on our minds, feelings, conduct, and faith. We have no tribal God now, no national one, and none that satisfies our wants except in the best way of showing how small they are (if taken as final in their present stages) and thus ever spurring us on to something better. If the universe is such as (even in its evils and obscurities) to evoke our best in every way in order to live truly and fully, it is essentially what theists claim when they say, in one fashion or another, that God is behind and in it all.

The affirmation (number two) that man is "a part of nature" and has "emerged as the result of a continuous process" might suggest that everything human can be completely explained in categories applicable to objects of natural science or that our consciousness can be "reduced" to something physical or other than itself. But in insisting that our spiritual nature, while possessing laws and characteristics of its own, is on the same general plane of reality as our physical nature, the new naturalism wishes to escape the materialism of older naturalisms and the crude supernaturalism of early theistic and idealistic systems. Recognizing, as Professor S. Alexander does in his *Space, Time, and Deity,* the factors that make for naturalism, in the phrase "continuity," and, in the word "emergent," the facts suggesting some sort of idealism, creationism, or supernaturalism, humanists have not yet shown how the two are united. To say that both are parts of "nature" simply casts a verbal veil over them, so that their differences are less apparent though none the less there.

The same is true about the rejection of "the traditional dualism of mind and body." Which traditional dualism? That of a simple, substantial, immortal soul interacting with its passing, material body?[9] In spite of recent advance in details, probably Plato and sages of the ancient East were as well aware as modern psychologists of the general ways in which our minds are conditioned by our bodies and yet are not the same but in several respects[10] transcend them. Their descriptions and explanations fail to meet the exigencies of increased knowledge, but the fundamental relations remain unchanged. It is hard to know exactly what humanists mean by their "organic view of life." When we say that we have an organic view of the relation between mind and body, we usually mean that somehow they form a whole apart from which neither exists. There seems to be no distinctively humanistic study of this problem that really goes beyond such a common assumption. Expressions like mind-body, if mistaken for satisfactory answers

---

[9] In rejecting this dualism, one fostered largely by Descartes, humanists seem to forget that the prevailing tradition before him was much more "organic," namely, the Aristotelian tradition of the soul as the form of the body.

[10] Professor W. E. Hocking has discussed some of these in his *Types of Philosophy.*

rather than cues for further investigation, mask ignorance with a hyphen.[11]

Theism too "considers the complete realization of human personality to be the end of man's life and seeks its development and" at least its partial "fulfillment in the here and now" (item eight). But, unlike humanism (as far as terminology is concerned), it believes that communion with God is, in one form or another, the chief goal of man and essential to complete realization of personality. The realization, however, is an effect or a concomitant of that communion and, like pleasure, comes from absorption in suitable objects and interests. Sought for and by itself alone, it turns out to be as disappointing and artificial as a stage smile. Not all kinds of theism, as the Psalms show, necessarily involve belief in personal immortality. But though Christian theism cherishes the hope of everlasting life (and thus admits vistas and possibilities that, as far as evidence one way or the other goes, humanism not quite arbitrarily but with too much assurance denies), it is interested in the temporal side of life primarily as a corollary of its qualitative side. Since for Christians the possibility of a tolerable future life of ever fuller action and opportunity depends largely upon their seeking the best in everything here and now, their belief in immortality, so far from rendering this life insignificant or contemptible (as humanists frequently charge, but with effect only as regards aberrations of Christianity, like quietism), makes it profoundly important. As well as anyone else they know

> "The sweeping up the heart,
> And putting love away
> We shall not want to use again
> Until eternity."[12]

[11] "The humanist takes the living, intelligent organism as the basic reality and follows psychology in revising the notion of mind from immaterial substance, or stream of ideas, to functional activities which are conscious." (R. W. Sellars, "In Defense of the Manifesto," *The New Humanist,* November-December 1933, p. 11.) But the dualism between "functional activities which are conscious" and those that are not is no less mysterious and profound than the old dualism described as existing between an immaterial substance and a material one.

[12] Emily Dickinson, *op. cit.,* p. 166.

The devastating finality of death and the difficulties of any theory of survival after it make them wonder, too, whether "until eternity" is more than a phrase. And they are taught by their religion that he who would save his life—who would put his selfish will before God's, who would expect favors incompatible with the spiritual principle of the universe—will lose it; hence their scepticism towards their own motives and beliefs in so far as they diverge from disinterested devotion to God. Baron von Hügel used to say that Christianity is a heroism. That does not necessarily involve rigorism and recklessness. But it means that the lethargy of a complacent parish is not the whole of Christianity. The Christian God is, in part, a goad, a source of the strain and the pain of expansion. The repose of heaven lies not in absence of strain but in the peace of functioning as perfectly as circumstances permit.

In the first (item four) of the three affirmations leading towards a naturalization of religion nothing unacceptable to present day theists seems to lurk, apart from the ambiguity of "natural environment." Until humanism made its improvements in philosophical terminology, such a phrase would probably suggest the environment depicted by the natural sciences and by social sciences and psychology in their most naturalistic spirit. The new naturalism, however, recognizes that the chief facts of religion, morality, and art—the power of certain spiritual forces and values—are as real, natural, and observable as sticks and stones. Hence it now calls "natural" facts that in the past had to rely for defense on idealists, supernaturalists, and intuitionalists. The heavy hand of supposedly scientific authority, however, prevents humanists from accepting these facts as, according to theists, they naturally clamor to be accepted. Thus belief in God may be called natural, but, from a humanistic point of view, such belief is explicable on almost any other ground than the apparently most appropriate one of some sort of apprehension of divine reality. In the matter of "natural environment," then, humanists after accepting probably most of the facts substantiating theism seem by their theories to empty them of almost all theistic significance.

66

From their fifth assertion, that "the nature of the universe depicted by modern science makes unacceptable any supernatural or cosmic guarantees of human values," humanists generally infer that there are no supernatural or cosmic guarantees for any kind of values. But since when have the speculations of astrophysics or psychology, for example, both of which humanists would probably admit as sciences, become infallible or even weighty authorities in matters of morality and religion? Though "religion must formulate its hopes and plans in the light of the scientific spirit and method," it cannot help realizing that that is only one side of "intelligent inquiry" and that ethical and religious values are primarily affairs of religion and morality. To date at least, the sciences have shown themselves constitutionally adapted to other things. Their pronouncements on moral and religious values are usually irrelevant and inadequate, because instead of belonging strictly to science they reflect opinions that scientists have adopted, often hastily and uncritically, from other sources. Long before modern sciences developed, people were as strongly convinced as they are now that most merely human values (for example, fashions in clothes and speech) and different manifestations of even fundamental human longings perish. The seeming impersonality of science and the splendor of its discoveries and inventions attained without reference to, or apparent dependence on, religion and morality, reinforced that perennial conviction. But, like religion, morality, and art, science itself, so far from being utterly impersonal, expresses human interests, values, and motives. In their frequent attacks on cosmic guarantees of values, humanists oppose the notion that ideals exist already realized and preserved in celestial cold storage (to use one of Dr. Dewey's expressions about Platonism),[13] whither, instead of toiling to realize them here below, we may direct our raptured gaze, or from which supply an

---

[13] Yet Plato seems to have had a richer, warmer view capable of coalescing, as it did centuries later, with Christian theism. cf. *Sophist,* p. 249, Jowett's translation: "And, O heavens, can we ever be made to believe that motion and life and soul and mind are not present with perfect being? Can we imagine that being is devoid of life and mind, and exists in awful unmeaningness an everlasting fixture?
"That would be a dreadful thing to admit."

indulgent God may dole them out to us when we renounce our efforts so that His grace may abound. But certainly most theists and Christians today maintain nothing like that. They ask, not for the minimization of human effort, nor for the realization of every casual desire, but for the recognition as a reasonable working belief, rather than as an abstractly demonstrated fact (no matter how firm may be their personal conviction), that reality on the whole favors, even in chastening, those aspirations and values in devoted and unstinting, or begrudgingly obligatory, realization of which we find the truest satisfaction. That the universe is of such a nature, the painfully slow, confused, uneven progress of civilization in its major lines suggests. If theism thus presupposes a "guarantee" postulated by all human endeavors and one that stimulates rather than stultifies humanity, perhaps, in spite of the sixth affirmation, its time is not yet passed.

Items seven, nine, and ten, in spite of superficial hostility to Christianity, represent a profound though elementary Christian apprehension in a form distorted by the acceptance of common but inadequate approximations as substitutes for that religion at its best. Not merely "those actions, purposes, and experiences which are humanly significant"—if "humanly significant" (which might cover all our experience indiscriminately) means existing primarily for the sake of humanity—but almost anything can contribute to religion. Disinterested admiration of the perfection with which something realizes its nature and possibilities, frequently passes into religious awe and gratitude. This feeling of the fundamental rightness of things in so far as they truly are; this joy in their exhibition of a perfection more appealing to us than any ordinary subservience to our lesser needs; this appreciation of objectivity in and for itself and, only as an afterthought, because it enhances and supplements our incomplete and parasitic being: all this "dim and dumb religiosity"—just as experience in other lines will express itself in poetry, inventions, or deeds of valor—takes on definite, developed, and effective forms in beliefs, doctrines, institutions, and practices, of historical religions—though certainly not there alone, even if there especially. But as forms of poetry, ordinarily means of leading it to greater achievement, can assume an existence of their own sometimes destructive to poetic power and insight, so likewise can forms of religion function awry. "Any activity pursued in behalf of an ideal end against obstacles and in spite of threats of personal loss because of conviction of its general and enduring value is religious in quality."[14] Such a statement from Dr. Dewey, stressing the search if not consciously of God at least of something beyond the ordinary "natural" state of affairs, irresistibly recalls numerous passages about the "anonymously supernatural" written by the saintly Roman Catholic thinker Baron Friedrich von Hügel, who here relied on St. Thomas Aquinas. No reputable Christian theologian today (and which of them in the past?) denies that what humanism here describes as being "religious in quality" is essential to theism. But the dignity of the man (or of the system) that seeks the best, with meager notions of what he is seeking and of the universe that permits such a search, is in no wise lessened by recognizing other men (and systems) equally sincere and broader and deeper. Because, from the point of view of religion, Christ, for instance, surpasses Socrates, and most of the Psalms Greek polytheism, it need not be concluded that Socrates and polytheism have no religious merit or that Greek philosophy and civilizations different from our own cannot in many ways improve our culture and religion.

Human smugness, pedantry, and sloth, rather than any special defect in Christianity, often lead those who profess it to treat as secular anything not immediately connected with its peculiarities, or to identify the divine (and the supernatural) with only the Christian forms in which, as many impartial students believe, it has so far most intimately and satisfactorily manifested itself, forgetting that since faith partly conditions the success of such manifestations a narrow faith will not only hinder the work of God in its finest expressions but will fail to recognize it in the simpler and sometimes more vigorous states indispensable to re-

[14] John Dewey, *A Common Faith* (New Haven: Yale University Press, 1934), p. 27.

ligious growth. Not only the young, who want things clear, straight, and true, who are impatient with blendings and over-lappings, nor those who in later years have found no key to Christian treasures, but Christians of unquestionable loyalty find the Church, on account of staid restrictions of doctrinal and institutional custom, oppressive, a "hair shirt," a purgatory. With several modifications to be mentioned later, they do not think Dr. Dewey greatly exaggerates when he writes: "It is widely supposed that a person who does not accept any religion is thereby shown to be a non-religious person. Yet it is conceivable that the present depression in religion is closely connected with the fact that religions now prevent, because of their weight of historic encumbrances, the religious quality of experience from coming to consciousness and finding the expression that is appropriate to present conditions, intellectual and moral. I believe that such is the case. I believe that many persons are so repelled from what exists as a religion by its intellectual and moral implications, that they are not even aware of attitudes in themselves that if they came to fruition would be genuinely religious.[15] . . . If I have said anything about religions and religion that seems harsh, I have said those things because of a firm belief that the claim on the part of religions to possess a monopoly of ideals and of the supernatural means by which alone, it is alleged, they can be furthered, stands in the way of the realization of distinctively religious values inherent in natural experience. . . . Just because the release of these values is so important, their identification with the creeds and cults of religions must be dissolved."[16]

When one remembers the jealous exclusiveness and arrogant authoritarianism of many Christian sects, the rigorous treatment of pleasure, worldliness, and human nature in some strict Prot-

[15] *A Common Faith,* p. 9. cf. "Religion is in a confused state because its conventional forms are still bound up with the values of the past, with submissive faith, otherworldliness, and the symbols which these have generated; while the newer interests of scientific knowledge, social welfare, and their appropriate symbolism have not yet sufficiently permeated the popular mind to make them generally religiously significant and commanding." *Religion,* by E. S. Ames (New York: Holt, 1929), p. 33.
[16] John Dewey, *op. cit.,* pp. 27-8.

estant and Catholic circles, and a tendency occasionally present in the past to think of the monastic or ascetic life as the full ideal for many rather than as the highest vocation for a few, one understands how much ground there is for Dr. Dewey's attack on the alleged ecclesiastical monopoly of ideals and callousness to the religious significance of nature. If those are some of the "uniquely religious emotions and attitudes of the kind hitherto associated with belief in the supernatural" (tenth affirmation), no wonder Dr. Dewey dismisses them so brusquely that "it sometimes seems as if he were saying that there is only one kind of activity in which a man cannot be religious, namely, the activity of religion."[17]

But what Dr. Dewey attacks are occasional travesties and perversions of Christianity or things often good in certain circumstances but sometimes applied beyond their bounds. He mentions hardly an evil that Christian popes, clergy, theologians, and laymen have not stigmatized and fought against far more fiercely. Here again it is a defect not of Christianity but of a simplifying attitude common to all men—the tendency to make so much of a good thing (discipline, for example) that it becomes bad (inhumanity). For Christianity as a whole, as eminently for its Founder, the God of nature and the God of supernature has always been the same God. Possible exceptions might seem to be some of the "exclusive" mystics, like St. John of the Cross, in the most ascetic moments of their *via negativa*.[18] But, not to mention the fact that their practice (their often profound love of nature and humanity, expressing itself in effective action) frequently counterbalanced the excesses (of other-worldliness) of their theories, their usual recognition of their calling as a highly specialized function within the greater life of the Church testifies to a comprehensive corporate ideal of Christianity, which, though elaborated by St. Paul and as matter of course as the seasons to countless Christians, seems to be barely divined by humanists. Christian art, architecture, music, literature, above all Christian philanthropy on a scale and with a

[17] M. C. Otto, *Things and Ideals* (New York: Holt, 1924), p. 42.
[18] Mystics like Boehme and Wordsworth (so far as he may be called a mystic) reveal a contrary tendency.

71

depth of love and sympathy rare if known at all before Christ, not only show a normal appreciation of nature and mankind but one rendered stronger and more intense by relating both to God. The distinction between the sacred and the secular,[19] so meticulously specified in the Old Testament and in primitive religions, is in practice for most sincere Christians a fluctuating indication of how far they have progressed with their religion and of how far there is yet to go. They feel that there is nothing, not excepting evil, that God's grace working in man and nature cannot permeate and change for the better.[20] So far from excluding (as item nine might suggest) "a heightened sense of personal life" and "a cooperative effort to promote social well-being," "the old attitudes involved in worship and prayer," as known to earnest Christians, have been the surest sources and protections of both and, through their diffused though frequently misunderstood, disparaged influence, remain indispensable to the vitality of humanism and other partial offspring of Christianity.

Our gregarious nature and the ever present need of making society more tolerable has led millions of well disposed people of different times, places, and schools of thought, to affirmations at bottom the same as the last five in the Manifesto. That man "alone is responsible for the realization of the world of his dreams" overlooks facts that make chance, providence, and fate, or at least

[19] Just as humanists incline to dismiss the supernatural altogether when they have shown a particular theory of it (mistakenly attributed to Christianity) to be untenable while at the same time emphasizing the validity of the facts that make some sort of distinction between nature and supernature inevitable, so (in item seven) the realization that certain things called secular in the past can nevertheless have religious value seems to prevent them from discerning beneath the ever-changing guises of the sacred and the profane the permanent truth that some things (the sacred) are on the side of religion and that other things (the secular) are, under the circumstances of the moment at least, indifferent or antagonistic to it. The "humanly significant" becomes the sacred for humanists, and the anti- or non-humanistic, the secular. The appearance of the distinction changes but its essence remains.

[20] George Herbert expressed this in his well known poem beginning:
>"Teach me, my God and King,
>In all things thee to see;
>And what I do in anything
>To do it as for thee!"

our limitations, always things to be reckoned with.[21] Ever since Adam ate bread in the sweat of his face, the overwhelming bulk of mankind, not excluding Christians (except a few quietistic "heretics" and their like, to prove the rule), realized that, God or no God, men must help themselves. As a matter of history, so far from weakening human beings, probably nothing has fired them to greater action than an awful love of the living God. Although Christians recognize His presence in (as it seems to them) the thin, occasional pools of humanism, the bulk, the complexity, and the antiquity of the Christian sea, together with overhanging, always changing mists of scientific theories, seem to make it difficult for humanists to find the power that moves it. Means and methods alone, even if incredibly better than those of modern science, cannot save us but, without the right spirit, are more apt to destroy us. Nor are the humanists' exalted ideas of personality and ethics—drawn from Christianity—likely to improve or even to survive, should, with the encumbrances of religion, the world's most highly developed type of communion with God be ignorantly and impatiently destroyed in the name of a morality, science, and art, which it continually enlightens and sustains.

To understand exactly what humanists oppose and exactly what reforms they offer, the vaguely expressed official utterances of the Manifesto must be supplemented by more detailed discussions of special points as humanists have treated them. What, more fully, is the idea of the supernatural that they attack? What would they put in its place? As every humanist's substitute cannot be outlined here, only those of two leaders, Professor Leuba[22] and Dr. Potter, will be noted. But as even their substitutes are less appreciated by others than by their authors, it will be necessary to regard the broader tendency, represented by Professor Sellars, to do away with the awkward supernatural altogether, by identifying its best features with the natural. Provided then with at

---

[21] "It is the part of manliness to insist upon the capacity of mankind to strive to direct natural and social forces to human ends. But unqualified absolutistic statements about the omnipotence of such endeavors reflect egoism rather than intelligent courage." John Dewey, *op. cit.*, pp. 24-5.

[22] Professor emeritus of psychology at Bryn Mawr College.

least a rough idea of humanism, we shall pause a moment to observe the attitudes of humanists towards the world as they see it—the disinterestedness of Mr. Lippmann,[23] the irrepressible cheerfulness of Professor Haydon,[24] the picturesque spleen of Bertrand Russell, and the cultivated despair of Mr. Krutch.[25] Before taking off for the next chapter we may wonder, as loitering travellers question billboards, why humanism advertises itself as a religion.

Their idea of the supernatural—generally a sort of "gap" conception—is one of the things that drive humanists to naturalism. They talk of "dependence upon the supernatural" and "the use of natural agencies" as though they were mutually exclusive alternatives,[26] rather than interpenetrating, inseparable aspects and tendencies of thought and reality. Professor Leuba's book called *God or Man* rests on the assumption that if, for purposes of scientific explanation, he can point to anything physical or psychical known to ordinary experience, that automatically rules out God and the supernatural. On such a basis he no more finds God than he could find human personality apart from any of its physical and psychical manifestations. If "personal divine intervention"—which Professor Leuba calls "the cardinal belief of the churches"[27]—cannot, by hypothesis, act in or through nature, any investigation of it seems doomed to futility by the way the question is begged from the start. Even if "by the supernatural we" should "mean miracle working,"[28] as Dr. C. F. Potter proposes, all alleged miracles, in spite of their strangeness, have at least enough connection and interrelation with natural objects to be somehow described and recorded. "Theism," Dr. Potter informs us, "regards the supernatural as beyond the comprehension of man and therefore to be worshipped."[29] The supernatural is certainly beyond our clear,

[23] Formerly a magazine editor; now special writer for the *New York Herald Tribune* and other papers, and author of numerous books.
[24] Professor of comparative religions at the University of Chicago.
[25] Dramatic editor of *The Nation* and author of many books.
[26] John Dewey, *op. cit.,* p. 81.
[27] *God or Man* (New York: Holt, 1933), p. 190.
[28] *Humanism, A New Religion,* p. 53.
[29] *ibid.,* p. 33.

complete, logical comprehension, but theists do not maintain that it is totally insignificant even so or that it cannot be vividly though obscurely apprehended in other ways—which seems to be true of all rich, complex realities. Why "therefore"? Theists do not insist upon worshipping anything of which they are ignorant. But, because Dr. Potter apparently believes that they do, he denies "the existence of any realm outside the field of cause and effect" and holds "that what is called the supernatural is only the not-yet-understood natural."[30] The restriction of reality to the field of cause and effect, large as it is, reveals the influence of the older naturalisms and materialisms. Neo-realists have done much to emphasize the importance of other relations commonly overlooked, to indicate the small part played by causality in logical and mathematical spheres of reality, and by their doctrines of emergent evolution either to deny the spanning of causation over the "breaks" between "levels" (inorganic, living, conscious) or else to enrich the former physical (and even spiritual and creative) connotations of causality beyond recognition. The "not-yet-understood natural" is one of the forms of the "gap" theory that the supernatural is to be sought and found only where the natural fails or is absent. In various degrees of explicitness it haunts humanistic writers, as in Dr. Dewey's suggestion that "the religious element in life has been hampered by conceptions of the supernatural that were imbedded in those cultures wherein man had little control over outer nature and little in the way of a sure method of inquiry and test."[31]

Though such a view of the supernatural could perhaps be matched in some ignorant Christian circles, and though the grounds mentioned doubtless had much to do in the framing of such an idea, certainly that conception of the supernatural is today as alien to educated Christians as it is to humanists. Where in the works of Anglicans like the present Archbishop of York (William Temple), Professor A. E. Taylor, Dr. W. R. Inge, Dr. C. C. J. Webb, and Dr. A. C. Bouquet, or in those of Protestants like Dr. J. Oman, Professor J. F. Heiler, and the sometime Archbishop of

[30] *ibid.*
[31] *op. cit.,* p. 57.

Upsala, Nathan Søderblom, or in those of Roman Catholics as different as Baron von Hügel and the neo-scholastic Professor Jacques Maritain, is that idea of the supernatural accepted? As long as humanists ignore the works of recognized representatives of contemporary theism, which are read in almost every Christian seminary and by those of the laity that think religion is worth studying, thoughtful Christians will probably find humanism often too "forward looking" to see much around it.[32]

Almost all humanists recognize, with Professor Leuba,[33] an irresistible desire to go beyond scientific descriptions and to learn why they are as they are. The primitive idea of the supernatural and the divine, indicated above and rejected by theists and humanists, is not the only one. People may and still do wonder whether ultimate reality, regardless of its intermediate appearances, is in some sense spiritual or not. Professor Leuba believes that he can detect an "energy of life" that seeks "the perfect." "In so far as the moral life is concerned, the aim is the realization of a social ideal. Civilized humanity exhibits a stupendous and heroic effort, outside as well as within the ethical religions, to establish a 'Kingdom of God' upon earth. . . . They do not do what the biologist says the animal world does: seek adaptation to its surroundings. This striving away from adaptation to the already existent, and towards a social ideal is, it seems to us, the most noteworthy characteristic of the urge that is in humanity. Science is aware of the presence of this urge, creative of knowledge, goodness, and beauty; and so it may recognize, even as do the religions, that there is in the universe something mysterious, greater than the individual."[34] Leaving aside doubts as to whether this subject especially belongs to any science or combination of

[32] Professor Edwin Arthur Burtt may be welcomed as an exception. In his recent book called *Types of Religious Philosophy* (which did not come to the attention of the author of these pages until they had reached final form) he outlines, among other things, several kinds of current Christian theology. Also he mentions communism as a form of humanism. And while classifying Santayana as a humanist, he shows how fundamentally that philosopher differs, except in his naturalism, from other humanists.

[33] *op. cit.*, p. 200.

[34] *ibid.*, pp. 247-8.

sciences; whether the urge for the perfect could be satisfied with but a this-worldly social ideal and with a mysterious something only greater than the individual but not necessarily the infinite and the ultimate towards which all finite and conditioned things point; and whether Professor Leuba's psychological method, with its assumptions about the adequacy of natural causes and with its apparatus of wish-fulfillment, projection, auto-suggestion, and so forth, could ever justify the existence of such a mysterious, "anti-materialistic" reality as he believes in, without thereby jeopardizing the validity of his naturalistic contentions about the illusoriness of religion and his humanistic fears that belief in any god greater than man must paralyze human effort and responsibility: leaving all these doubts aside, we cannot help feeling that the admission of even such an embryonic spiritual principle in the universe is a first step towards theistic religion, which humanism not so much contradicts as falls short of.

But when humanism tries to describe its "something mysterious" by exalting scientific abstractions not exhausting even sub-human realities into explanations of personality and of the universe as a whole, it ends in results more grotesque than any speculations of Christian theology. We might here note in passing Dr. Potter's personal version of ultimate reality, not only because he is the influential founder and leader of the First Humanist Society of New York but also because "explanations" of the universe by some unknown, sub-personal force or energy are prevalent in the ever increasing number of those that mistake the peripheral fancies of science for the central postulates of philosophy. "Humanists may differ among themselves," Dr. Potter acknowledges, "concerning the forms and manifestations of the primal energy and its *modus operandi,* but that it exists must be conceded. That this energy operates scientifically through natural laws and not through supernatural means, all intelligent people admit. The Humanist believes that this power cannot be personal, that man himself is the greatest manifestation of this [impersonal] energy, and that it [unconscious, by hypothesis] reaches full consciousness only in the personality of man. . . . The Humanist does not believe that this

77

energy is a sort of spiritual electricity that vibrates around us in a pure form, to be apprehended mystically, but that it is latent in all forms of material in the universe. There is energy 'sleeping in matter, dreaming in animals, waking in man.' "[35]

Conflicting currents trouble the new naturalism that humanists have been obliged to construct on account of the failure of previous science to include their primal energy and the search for the perfect. Dr. E. S. Ames charges "many advocates of modern 'humanism' " with committing the "fallacy of supposing that one term of a dualistic conception may be dropped while retaining the other. Convinced that the empirical values are the only values discoverable, they conclude that this justifies their naturalistic, humanistic interpretation of the world. They are therefore compelled to devote much of their strength to denying the existence of God and the supernatural. But as a result, they are left with a truncated world, and the lower half of the old dualistic order. They have unwittingly separated man from nature by the same stroke, and have left their humanistic realm suspended between the void of matter on the one side and the vacancy left on the other by the removal of the old supernaturalistic deity."[36]

Humanists, as a rule, protest that their *new* naturalism is *not* convinced that empirical values are the only ones discoverable, yet they deal with the whole matter confusedly. Although God is

[35] *op. cit.,* p. 58. Dr. Potter is not responsible for the interpolations in square brackets. One can hardly avoid being struck by the similarities between his primal energy (neither scientific nor religious) and the notion of mana among peoples of undeveloped religion and science. " 'Mana,' . . . in the opinion of the majority of modern anthropologists, is the most primitive conception of the supernatural which we have yet discovered. It is a conception which is universal among savage peoples. It is known by the name of 'Oudah' among the Pygmies in Africa. The Sioux call it 'Wakan.' Among the Iroquois it is called 'Orenda.' The Shoshone tribes name it 'Pokunt,' and among the Algonquin it is called 'Manitou.' In Melanesia this conception is known as 'Mana.' Anthropology has taken this term . . . to denote that diffused, amorphous, ubiquitous power which the Melanesian authority, Codrington, says 'is a power or influence, not physical and in a way supernatural; but it shows itself in physical force, or in any kind of power or excellence which a man possesses. This Mana is not fixed in anything, and can be conveyed in almost anything. All Melanesian religion consists, in fact, in getting this Mana for oneself, or getting it used for one's benefit.' " (A. R. Uren, *Recent Religious Psychology* [Edinburgh: Clark, 1928], p. 186.)

[36] *op. cit.,* pp. 174-5.

a Being "whom no man hath seen nor can see," Professor Leuba, in his *Psychology of Religious Mysticism,* Dr. C. C. J. Webb says, ultimately makes "lack of verification by 'sense-perception' " the ground for his denial of the validity of any "sense of divine presence."[37] Such a gross type of empiricism inevitably prejudges the bulk of religious experience as illusory. On that basis, which was essentially the foundation of the older naturalism, only objects of sense perception are real. The method caused no particular alarm so long as it was confined to unusual facts concerning which no mystics could be shaken and about which few "average people" would care. But applied to art, morality, ordinary religion, and daily feelings and emotions, to say nothing of abstract and *a priori* sides of science itself, the method devastated almost everything men live for.

It became obviously imperative to enlarge the sphere of the natural, the real, and the scientific, so that our major demands might be blessed by those designations. The old empiricism which graded "down actual differences into the blind motions of inert particles"[38] was decried. Professor Sellars, for example, indicated from the point of view of emergent evolution some of the limitations of a supposedly all-inclusive spatio-temporal system and of "the desire for explanation in terms of objects which can be handled and studied in accordance with scientific methods," as the older naturalism understood those methods. But he had no hesitation in dubbing as "mythology and supernaturalism" "explanations in terms of superhuman agencies of a generally invisible and unlocalizable sort."[39] Although his "new naturalism asserts that nature is actually heterogeneous and that heterogeneity is intrinsic," the universal spatio-temporal standardization and homogeneity of the old naturalism has such a hold on him that he "would point out," apparently as a weighty objection, that "theism has

[37] *Religion and Theism* (London: Allen and Unwin, 1934), pp. 112-17. cf. Chap. XI of *Psychology of Religious Mysticism* (London: Kegan Paul, Trench, Trubner, 1925).
[38] R. W. Sellars, *Religion Coming of Age* (New York: Macmillan, 1928), p. 243.
[39] *ibid.,* p. 141.

usually had difficulty in the location of its deity."[40] But if local-izability is a criterion of reality, human personality, truth, good-ness, beauty, mathematical and logical relations, and any sort of universal, are left in a precarious position. Humanists often tend to speak of these things as merely human (and in no way trans- or super-human) characteristics, as if they could be pointed to and localized in certain parts of the brain, regardless of the fact that personality itself and none of the objects of our experience would have any reality at all were they not to a certain extent ob-jectively conditioned by more of external nature than our brains. Though somehow manifested in spatio-temporal objects, which one can handle, point to, and localize, they themselves seem to be essentially non-spatial, non-temporal aspects of reality, on a level and with a character quite different from anything that naturalism or the continually relapsing "new naturalism" of Professor Sellars whole-heartedly recognizes.

Needless to say Professor Sellars does not apply his require-ment of localization to everything. It seems to occur to him chiefly in his attacks on God and the supernatural. Ordinarily he follows other humanists in taking the natural as synonymous with "all that is experienced" (in the words of Dr. Ames), so that "it includes the ideal, the mental and the spiritual, as well as the so-called physi-cal and material. . . . In these ideal aspects of experience God is immediately possessed through human insight and feeling. God is not supernatural, but wholly natural, just as ideals are natu-ral."[41] If everything can be accounted for by "natural processes," one might suppose that humanism had firmly established the validity of divine existence. But it turns out that in simply calling every-thing "natural" one changes names only; so "the word 'natural' may be dismissed, for it came to have significance at the point where an order of nature was distinguished as the experienced op-posite of the supernatural."[42] Generally continuing, however, to call all the real by the word "natural," which originally applied to those

[40] "In Defense of the Manifesto," *loc. cit.,* p. 9.
[41] *Religion Coming of Age,* p. 174. Order of sentences altered without changing essential meaning.
[42] *ibid.*

aspects of it approved by naturalism, humanism undermines not everything that the older naturalism did (for humanism exempts a certain amount of morality)[48] but some of the latter's chief *bêtes noires,* like God and the supernatural, by (as will be shown in Chapter IV) a psychical, or psychological, instead of a physical, "reduction."

Towards the world they have conjured for themselves humanists display three major attitudes—indifference, cheerfulness, gloominess. Though these moods naturally fluctuate in individuals and though they do not coincide exactly with the three "schools" of humanism (for cheerfulness, rather than indifference, is almost as marked in the mediating as in the optimistic school), nevertheless the fact that what one believes affects one's general attitude towards life is substantiated by the glumness that invariably tinges the thought of the pessimistic school and by the brighter colors that illumine other humanists as they move towards the optimistic school.

If external nature is merely a screen on which we project our values and ideals, Mr. Walter Lippmann's indifference to it is not out of place. He calls it "disinterestedness," a word having for him, as Professor W. M. Horton observes, three meanings. When "Mr. Lippmann faces towards nature, he appears to take an attitude which is 'disinterested' in the sense of being imperturbable, indifferent, free from frustration because entirely free from hope and faith. When he turns to consider the large concerns of business and politics, he recommends that the statesman adopt an attitude which is 'disinterested' in another sense: free from prejudice and self-seeking, but certainly not wholly free from faith in human nature or hope of a happier human destiny. When, finally, he comes to the intimate personal relations of men and women, he finds the word 'disinterested' more or less of an incubus (try, if you can, to imagine a 'disinterested' lover) and in a burst of frankness . . . he agrees with Dean Inge that *not* cool disinterestedness,

[48] Some of the earlier naturalists, Spencer, for example, found in their theories a defense of morality; but this was hardly the rule.

but 'personal affection for man,' is the path that leads to moral salvation."[44]

Luckily for mankind personal affection and a reasonable interest in others is so much a spontaneous delight and a natural necessity that they do not depend upon arguments. But Mr. Lippmann's "faith in human nature" transcends sympathy with his species regardless of their pathetic insignificance to anything but themselves, in so far as he claims that a high degree of unselfishness, courage, honor, temperance, veracity, faithfulness, and love, are necessary for the happiness and the survival of humanity.[45] Though more virtue than society is ready for leads individuals to martyrdom, and though "civilizations die from philosophical calm, irony, and the sense of fair play quite as surely as they die of debauchery,"[46] nevertheless heroic examples spur us on, and the better the group, as others besides Plato have observed, the more stable it is. If the world is so ordered that in the long run, on the whole, and for duly developed people, selfishness, timidity, deceit, excess, carelessness, and other vices, lead to misery and ruin, it can hardly be called indifferent. Good men, rather, appear to be in what Mr. Lippmann calls "a mature and disinterested partnership with the world."[47]

Probably because he did not go far along that line of thought, Mr. Lippmann in general preserves his indifference to the end. Professor A. Eustace Haydon, on the other hand, is perhaps the most sanguine humanist alive. Although he holds that values and ideals are our own subjective fabrications and projections, he believes that the universe happens to tolerate them in several different ways. For one thing, man is a part of nature, is in harmony with it, and has an ever increasing control over it, which promises more power and longer survival to him than to any other creature.

[44] W. M. Horton, *Theism and the Modern Mood* (New York: Harper, 1930), pp. 81-2. Since 1926 Dr. Horton has been the Fairchild professor of theology at the Oberlin Graduate School of Theology.
[45] W. Lippmann, *A Preface to Morals* (New York: Macmillan, 1929), p. 227.
[46] J. W. Krutch, *The Modern Temper* (London: Cape, 1930), p. 45.
[47] Quoted by W. M. Horton, *op. cit.*, pp. 78-9.

Moreover he is not alone, but is moulded and protected by society.[48] Indispensable as society is, collective morality (resulting from the sorry fact that a man's sense of responsibility decreases as he shares it with others) is usually inferior not only to that of its best members but to that of its average members when they can move away from the madding crowd and listen to the voice of conscience. Possibly this high price for protection is what Professor Haydon refers to when he writes of the individual that "he is wrapped about with an environment of social security. If there is any complaint, it should be registered against the too great security and bondage involved."[49] It might be unfair to cavil at such a rosy statement made before the extent of the American financial crisis of 1929-1932 was apparent or before perennial barbarism revived in Europe. But memories of the World War, the poor we have ever with us, and the whole history of humanity, ought at least to whisper that the bondage from which most people suffer is not that of security but of insecurity.[50] His appeal to the natural and the social sciences, however, to develop a better material and spiritual world and to overcome evil itself, shows that he realizes the badness of the present situation. If his ideal of "a good life in a good world" is a twentieth century version of the Abbey of Thélème,[51] and if he, whose infatuation for "science" can hardly be equalled, believes that nothing better than a disappointingly meager realization of that ideal lurks "just around the corner" of the unguessed future, his general position may strike others as an unwitting prelude to pessimism rather than as a well founded optimism.[52]

Since Bertrand Russell evolves on every other page with unpredictable versatility, the person referred to here as exempli-

[48] A. E. Haydon, *The Quest of the Ages* (New York: Harper, 1929), pp. 111-14.

[49] *ibid.*, p. 116.

[50] Eight years later Professor Haydon admitted that "the new world is bleak with despair for millions." *Man's Search for the Good Life* (New York: Harper, 1937), p. 234.

[51] "A society of free, creative, cultured persons in harmonious cooperation would know life's noblest happiness." *The Quest of the Ages*, p. 174.

[52] cf. *ibid.*, pp. 114, 117, 118, 121, 140, 141, 147, 148, 196, 198.

fying another humanistic attitude is the author of "The Free Man's Worship." Whether or not he has later recanted, the mood of his essay is still a living force. A "free man" then (as now) recognized that only science finds objective facts and that moral values and God are subjective creations. Deity, he discovered, was a dilapidated construction to be condemned. But he devoted himself with passionate impersonality to truth, education, social reform, mathematics, and logic. The last two opened to him a realm of eternal, orderly relations, which appear to subsist without special connection with anything else. Although he found refreshment from this source, he did not rashly claim it as an indication of rapport between man and reality. On the contrary, resolutely remembering what scientists had told him, he pictured the human race as on a raft in mid-ocean. Perhaps on quiet days we might see our gaunt reflections in the waters, or the waves might even echo our laments. The captain never yielded to such sentimentality. The more the winds howled and the sea roared, the more calmly he bade us live nobly before we drowned. Considering that there was no land to go to, no boats to pick us up, nothing to expect from death, and nothing for our plucky little band to do but to try to be comfortable and intelligent, it was all quite exalted and impressive. Every now and then our captain, and often humble members of the crew, would feel called upon to shake his fist and defy the sea, to show how free and worshipful he was.

That may seem melodramatic to the so-called "futilitarian," Mr. Joseph Wood Krutch.[53] Not particularly infatuated by logic and mathematics, he describes the modern temper as one of sophisticated ennui. Milder humanists frequently fail to find in him any family resemblance. He is, according to Dr. C. F. Potter,[54] " 'too radical religiously and scientifically to be an Academic Humanist[55] and too pessimistic for the future of man to be a Religious Humanist.' . . . In fact he is not really a humanist at

[53] He may feel inclined to exclaim, as Mr. Logan Pearsall Smith did at a strikingly similar attitude towards the universe, "By Jove, that is a stunt!" cf. *All Trivia* (London: Constable, 1933), p. 81.

[54] *Humanism, A New Religion*, p. 112, quoting Mr. Wakefield.

[55] i.e. a "literary humanist."

all." Regardless of how he is classified, Mr. Krutch starts with the same ingredients as other humanists and from them concocts a cordial too sharp for his fellow experimenters. Though our physical and biological continuity with nature may, as Professor Haydon notes,[56] substantiate a sentiment of union with it, the ethical indifference of the universe—for it is essentially indifferent as long as it is unaware of our existence or merely happens in part to tolerate rather than foster it—makes us feel alone and strangers in the world.[57] That our moral and religious aspirations should be as "natural" and necessary to us as our arms and legs, while yet receiving no answer from the universe better than an echo, causes our ceaseless "projection" to oppress us with a sense of futility and mockery. Science, Mr. Krutch apparently believes, alone reaches reality and shows it to be but intellectually satisfactory, if even that.[58] "It is better . . . for those of us who have grown up in an age of scientific thought . . . to rest content with the admission that, though the universe with which science deals is the real universe, yet we do not and cannot have any but fleeting and imperfect contacts with it; that the most important part of our lives—our sensations, emotions, desires, and aspirations—takes place in a universe of illusions which science can attenuate or destroy, but which it is powerless to enrich."[59] Realizing how little necessary connection there is between scientific and mechanical advance and the improvement of character, "we no longer believe that the millennium presents merely a problem in engineering."[60] The growth of civilization (and here Mr. Krutch seems to be influenced by Dr. Freud) involves a development of spirituality and virtues which, in their claims to objective reference beyond ourselves, are largely illusory and artificial and the cultivation of which "renders us progressively unfit to fulfill our biological duties."[61] That is not surprising, if psychology has

[56] *The Quest of the Ages,* p. 119.
[57] *The Modern Temper,* pp. 8, 10, 14, 20. Man "is of all living creatures the one to whom the earth is the least satisfactory." *ibid.,* p. 20.
[58] *ibid.,* pp. 17, 19, 69, 81.
[59] *ibid.,* p. 72.
[60] *ibid.,* p. 61.
[61] *ibid.,* p. 248.

dissolved our personality, wills, and ideals "into an unstable agglomeration of sensations and impulses which we cannot recognize as ourselves."[62] "The more we learn of human nature, the less sure a foundation it seems to be upon which to build; and the more we know of the origin of the arts and faiths which have made the human race seem heroic, the less we see how they can be carried on to any perfection."[63] With a courageous penetration unmatched in this respect by other humanists, Mr. Krutch has turned upon humanism itself the methods and the assumptions that it ordinarily reserves exclusively for its opponents. The effect is as unwelcome there as elsewhere. "Distrusting its thought, despising its passions, realizing its impotent unimportance in the universe, it [i.e. "a too sophisticated society" such as ours would be, if we accepted the negative implications of humanism] can tell itself no stories except those which make it still more acutely aware of its trivial miseries."[64] Nevertheless "we should rather die as men than live as animals."[65]

Most outsiders see no reason why the philanthropy of humanists, with its naturalistic background softened by moralism, should be named religion. Social service, as one of the countless ways in which religion, sympathy, economic prudence, or all three, manifest themselves, is so excellent that it need not, in defiance of usage, defend itself as the essential and complete nature of religion. It would seem appropriate to term atheists the new naturalists that reject belief in God and the supernatural.[66] One of them, Professor Sellars, does not hesitate to say of two of his fellow humanists, "Dewey and Ames are pious, socially minded atheists who are constructive in that they stress social values."[67] Clearly he uses "atheist" to signify a verbal rather than an actual denial of God;

[62] *ibid.*, p. 65.
[63] *ibid.*, p. 63.
[64] *ibid.*, p. 128.
[65] *ibid.*, p. 249. cf. "Mr. Krutch and Ideal Values in Literature," by J. W. Beach, *Ethics*, July 1938, pp. 487 ff.
[66] cf. C. F. Potter, *op. cit.*, p. 7; W. M. Horton, *op. cit.*, p. 46; and D. C. Macintosh, *Humanism, Another Battle Line,* edited by W. P. King (Nashville, Tenn.: Cokesbury Press, 1931), p. 55.
[67] *Religion Coming of Age,* p. 216.

for nothing could be more misleading than to call humanists atheists in the sense of deliberately detesting ideals and values that theism finds in God. As theists themselves insist, true devotion to Him, regardless of its cut,[68] and not merely a saying of "Lord, Lord," rightly determines the extent to which a person should be called (as far as men may guess what only God knows) a theist. Professor Haydon maintains "that there are no specifically religious values, that there is no need for specifically religious education, that scientific quest for human values can make no room for specifically religious behavior."[69] If religion and theism are so far gone, why do humanists shun the word "atheist" and try to pass off their opinions as a religion? According to Dr. D. C. Macintosh,[70] "Professor Sellars reveals the fact that he himself debated in his own mind whether or not he should continue to use the term 'religion' for devotion to human ideals without belief in God, and admits that his final decision was based almost wholly upon practical considerations." "A world which is still fundamentally respectful of religion" is more likely to swallow something called religion than atheism.[71]

Whether religion strictly speaking is to include its elementary non-theistic stages is largely a matter of definition, which in turn depends upon religious insight. In support of humanism Professor Sellars writes that there is nothing absurd about a non-theistic religion in countries where religion is chiefly a matter of custom and social position. "In India," he asserts extravagantly, "all social dogmas and customs *are* religion."[72] In so far as any of those customs and dogmas have become meaningless, simply external, or obstacles to true advance, humanists would reject them as irreligious encumbrances. The ideals that humanism stands for are those that have gradually become to a large extent self-justifying and automatically obligatory for men in their civilized moments. The craving for goodness (though it does not

[68] Nevertheless too deep a difference between thought and action is unhealthy.
[69] D. C. Macintosh, *op. cit.*, pp. 58-9.
[70] Since 1916 Dwight professor of theology at Yale University.
[71] *ibid.*
[72] *Religion Coming of Age*, p. 117. Italics his.

always rise above mere velleity) and the obligation to be good (whatever the content of that idea turns out to be) is, for a man in his right mind, as intimate and inescapable as his own being of which it is a part. At the same time it exhibits an absoluteness and transcendence of himself even at his best, which sometimes calls upon him to sacrifice if necessary all that he has and is. With its treatment of ideals as of not merely partial but of entirely social construction, convention, and convenience, humanism fails to do justice to the characteristic note of absolute obligation in moral goodness and, to a closely comparable extent, in truth and beauty.[73] It offers no reason for the call to follow an ideal, sometimes in spite of social disapproval and earthly gain. When theism claims that these ideals are in some way backed by the existence and the power of ultimate reality, that for us they express its nature better than anything else, it means not to nullify man's efforts but to justify them to the limit. Yet that is not the highest experience common to man. The intimacy and the ultimacy[74] of these lower stages reach their culmination not in this or that value nor in all of them, not in moral consciousness, nor intellectual vision, nor in any mixture of these experiences,[75] but in an apprehension of God, who, as any religious person can ascertain by experiment, cannot be described apart from these nor adequately by them.

[73] cf. Chaps. VI and VII of W. Temple's *Nature, Man and God* (London: Macmillan, 1934) for a discussion of the different senses in which truth, goodness, and beauty may be called "absolute values."

[74] cf. C. C. J. Webb, *Religion and Theism* (London: Allen and Unwin, 1934), pp. 15 *ff.*, 136 *ff.*, and "The Nature of Religious Experience," *Hibbert Journal*, October 1933.

[75] cf. A. R. Uren, *op. cit.*, pp. 193, 221-2, 226.

CHAPTER III

SYNOPSIS OF CHAPTER III

The idea that science is free, forward-looking, and empirical, whereas religion is cramped, hidebound, and *a priori*, arises from contrasting the spirit of science with the shell rather than the spirit of religion. That the faults as well as the merits of religion have their counterparts in science is illustrated by reference to Bertrand Russell. To ascertain what scientific method means to humanists, how they employ it, and the kind of world it reveals to them, the opinions of Professor Haydon, Professor Huxley, Bertrand Russell, and Professor Sellars, on these subjects are reviewed. Professor Sellars's struggles with causation, order, organization, purpose, and consciousness, are typical of the more searching kind of humanistic philosophy.

HUMANISM AND SCIENTIFIC METHOD

HUMANISTS as a rule assert that science has invalidated theistic religion. "The physical world has crystallized into a tremendous system whose ways seem foreign to theistic traditions and hopes. Cause stands out where purpose once shone through; miracles retreat before the advance of law; immortality becomes increasingly doubtful."[1] Where criticism fails to prove the legendary nature of religious documents heretofore accepted as historically true, anthropology aids humanism by tracing higher religions back to instincts and primitive superstition. The idea of God finds itself eclipsed by the fascination of an evolving universe. Bertrand Russell, indeed, holds that the evidence for evolution discovered by biology, geology, and astronomy, which apply only to "an infinitesimal fragment of space and time" (probably "not an average sample of events in the world at large"), cannot be scientifically generalized so as to cover the whole universe. Even to call the earthly process from protozoan to philosopher "progress" is, he alleges, dubious and immodest.[2] So too Professor Sellars writes, "Time is but another word for change and that is always local and within the world.[3] . . . *Time is in the world, and not the world in time.*"[4] But Professor Sellars is so strongly influenced by the theory of emergent evolution that he remains singularly uncommunicative concerning trans-temporal

[1] R. W. Sellars, *Religion Coming of Age*, p. 203.

[2] *Mysticism and Logic and Other Essays* (London: Longmans, Green, 1925; quoted by permission from Allen and Unwin, Ltd.), p. 106; cf. *What I Believe* (London: Kegan Paul, Trench, Trubner, 1928), p. 23.

[3] *Religion Coming of Age*, p. 164.

[4] *ibid.*, p. 171. Italics are his. cf. Plato's *Timaeus* (37D-38D) and St. Augustine's *Confessions* (XI, xiii).

or eternal aspects of the universe. The spell of time, creative evolution, immanence, and dynamism, doubtless accounts for much of the moderate school's resistance to any transcendence of spatio-temporal categories. They are encouraged likewise by difficulties introduced into theology by recent theories of physics and astrophysics. Just as theism was beginning to feel at home in an absolute system with immutable laws and deterministic causality, rumors spread that the universe was "expanding," that its available energy was "running down," that everything was relative to the observer, and that indeterminism was as undeniable as determinism.[5] Remarks like those of Sir Arthur Eddington's about the lack of scientific verification for universal determinism inflated speculations on the freedom of the will, only to be followed by horrified recoils from a haphazard chance worse than any form of order no matter how impersonal or mechanical it might be.

Probably psychology and psychoanalysis dealt the most shattering blow to older views of religion. The advances of the other sciences might have been more easily assimilated had man retained confidence in his own integrity. The wavering of the moderate humanists and the disillusionment of the pessimistic school increase with their belief that the ideals and the values exalted by Christian tradition have been proved to be deceptive "projections" or expressions of our "lower" nature.

In these circumstances science—which for most humanists apparently designates a vague ensemble of attitudes and opinions like those just indicated—seems to have all virtues, and religion, all vices. The former is lauded as modern, disinterested, universal, compared to which the latter looks old, biased, narrow. Religion is supposed to be essentially *a priori*, deductive, and dogmatically authoritarian, whereas science rejoices in experiment and induc-

[5] Such were some popular notions. The confusion of the principle of indeterminacy with a denial of causal determination was prevalent enough to justify Bertrand Russell's attention to the error. "The Principle of Indeterminacy has to do with measurement, not with causation. The velocity and position of a particle are declared by the Principle to be undetermined in the sense that they cannot be accurately measured. . . . There is nothing whatever in the Principle of Indeterminacy to show that any physical event is uncaused." *The Scientific Outlook,* p. 105.

tion. When religion becomes empirical, experimental, and free, it courts the charge of preferring intuitional, private experience to public, observational, cooperative evidence and record. If it then obligingly develops its institutional and social aspects, it is blamed for materialism and formality. The truth, however, seems to be that neither religion nor science is all of one piece or of one mood. Both have elements conducive to freedom and empiricism, and both, elements favoring dogmatism and the *a priori*. Although these "virtues" and "vices" may appear in religion in a more intense form, an impartial survey of religious and scientific history would probably show that the average proportion of the good and the bad qualities mentioned above are about the same in both; for they are characteristics not so much of religion or of science, as of men and women, who behave in about the same way under similar circumstances. Only by overlooking this can one believe, as apparently humanists frequently do (thus reversing an equally one-sided view of other times and places), that to worship in a church, synagogue, mosque, or temple, makes man little better than a brute, whereas to work in a laboratory opens the door of heaven.

In the following passages Dr. John Dewey reveals why humanists feel as they do about theistic religion in comparison with science. "Science is not constituted by any particular body of subject-matter. It is constituted by a method, a method of changing beliefs by means of tested inquiry as well as of arriving at them. It is its glory, not its condemnation, that its subject-matter develops as the method is improved. There is no special subject-matter or belief that is sacrosanct. The identification of science with a particular set of beliefs and ideas is itself a hold-over of ancient and still current dogmatic habits of thought which are opposed to science in its actuality and which science is undermining.[6] . . . The scientific-religious conflict ultimately is a conflict between allegiance to this method and allegiance to even an irreducible minimum of belief so fixed in advance that it can never be modified.[7] . . . Faith in the continued disclosing of truth

[6] *A Common Faith*, pp. 38-9.
[7] *ibid.*, p. 39.

93

through directed cooperative human endeavor is more religious in quality than is any faith in a completed revelation. It is of course now usual to hold that revelation is not completed in the sense of being ended. But religions hold that the essential framework is settled in its significant moral features at least, and that new elements that are offered must be judged in conformity to this framework. Some fixed doctrinal apparatus is necessary for *a* religion. But faith in the possibilities of continued and rigorous inquiry does not limit access to truth to any channel or scheme of things. It does not first say that truth is universal and then add that there is but one road to it. It does not depend for assurance upon subjection to any dogma or item of doctrine."[8]

The essential motif in those quotations, and one as much the desire of religion as of science, is the free quest of truth wherever and however it may be found. So native is that to religious people of any stripe that probably only the differences between religion from the outside and religion from the inside could have led Dr. Dewey to confound the latter with certain features of the former. Though a person has many phases, now one and now another predominating, generally a man is supposed to be most himself when, without undue external constraint, he can exercise his various faculties peacefully according to their nature. So too any religion or church appears in public and on its battle fronts quite different from the way it looks and lives at home. Under what circumstances does religion seem to involve an unmodifiable, irreducible minimum of belief oppressively imposed as the exclusive way to truth? Probably under roughly the same conditions as those in which pedagogical or polemical introduction to a science or an art, the routine of laboratory experiment or creative work, the first years (and often later ones) in business or professional struggle, and similar preliminaries and means, lead, when exaggerated out of proper perspective, to impatience and revulsion. For purposes of elementary instruction, external transmission, discipline, and self-defense, religion, like any other human interest, objectifies itself

[8] *ibid.,* p. 26.

in a limited way to meet limited demands, and builds up a wall, or gives an account of itself, which inadequately suggests its full nature.

The informed Christian today does not cling to his faith in God because he is unscientific, if that means wilfully opposed to truth. His belief springs from personal religious experience (which he shares with, and recognizes in, countless others), to which some scientists and humanists, either through feebleness of that experience in themselves or through mistaking the present restricted methods and ideologies of science for the beginning and the end of truth, fail to do justice. Although Dr. Dewey realizes more clearly than most humanists that momentary scientific dogmas must be subordinated to the method of science, he does not emphasize how narrow and always verging on mere empiricism and positivism the means of tested inquiry so far developed by scientific method appear when that method is in turn subjected to the spirit of truth, which is confined to no science, art, or action, but is a common stimulus and ideal of them all.[9] The success of certain methods of experimenting in the natural sciences has apparently so intoxicated most humanists that far from seeing how inadequate such methods are in their original fields they extol them in matters to which they are suited even less.

Dr. Dewey would doubtless admit that not only "a religion" but every major human interest and notoriously science itself, requires (as an implication of the "apperceptive mass" indispensable to knowledge and action) a minimum of belief or "doctrinal apparatus" the "essential framework" of which is stable enough to assimilate what conforms to it and elastic enough to

[9] At times he seems to appreciate this fully, as when he writes: "For were we to admit that there is but one method for ascertaining fact and truth—that conveyed by the word 'scientific' in its most general and generous sense—no discovery in any branch of knowledge and inquiry could then disturb the faith that is religious." (*ibid.*, p. 33.) In that sense science as the only "avenue of access" to truth is unobjectionable, because it bursts its bonds and becomes identical with an open-minded search for truth by all means and all experiences and not merely by those now peculiar to the natural and the mathematical sciences. But generally Dr. Dewey uses "science" not in that equivocal sense but as more closely conforming to the present practices of those sciences.

adapt itself to what does not. Nothing pops into the world without any connection or coherence with what has gone before. Even emergent evolutionists recognize the necessity of a certain degree and kind of organization before a new level of reality appears. Though the desire for certainty and definiteness is naturally stronger in the ultimate questions of religion than in less vital matters, so that rigidity, without being less repellent, is more understandable in religion than elsewhere, dogmatic fixity instead of being an exclusive peculiarity of religion is a personal characteristic common to certain men whether they are engaged in religion, science, or anything else. Much Victorian science, for example, and recent psychology parading as philosophy, to say nothing of political fanatics whose conceits continually menace the world, suffer from a bigotry akin to that of the Inquisitors'.

Yet at their best, both Christianity and science condemn this fault: Christianity, because any narrow, monopolistic attitude towards God and the world runs counter to the love and the inexhaustible richness with which He manifests Himself in creation; science, because perpetual self-criticism is of its essence. In neither genuine Christianity nor real science is any doctrine held to be fixed except in so far as truth has chained it. The most rigid form of ecclesiastical authority (papal infallibility, for example) is accepted—where it is honestly and knowingly accepted at all—to the extent and in the manner that it is believed to be true. The continual testing and improvement of every item of faith and practice in the light of goodness, beauty, and truth, which leads to transforming this or rejecting that, constitute the normal course of religious, as of any other thoughtful, development. The spirit is the same as that which animates art, science, and practical action. As science has reached certain convictions about the existence and the nature of the external world and about the appropriate ways of dealing with it, so Christianity is convinced that Christ offers, among other things, the best religious norm applicable to communion with God. So far from excluding or competing with other values, ideals, and means of realizing God and appreciating nature, this conviction hallows everything for Christians and makes them long to bring every process to its appropriate or divine culmination. Though in religion (as anywhere else) no two people have exactly the same attitude towards, or agreement as to what are, "fundamentals and accessories," the firmest believer in the validity of the general framework of religion is the most avid for improvement no matter how drastic. Remembering that a better apprehension of God has always involved the painful transcendence of one previously supposed to be the best, such a person is ever eager to repeat the necessary effort, if the new prize is more attractive than the old.

Humanists may object to this as an idealization or a diminution of religion, which, they at least hint, is intrinsically "static." But the above remarks are meant to indicate only that rigidity is not a necessary or special trait of religion and that although it manifests itself easily there it does so under circumstances leading to its evocation almost anywhere. We are so accustomed to noting the militant, self-preserving aspects of Old Testament religion, the hostile mien of a generally outgrown, scholastic type of Mohammedanism, the armed frontiers of Christian sects—in brief, the rough shell of any cult not our own—that we overlook a fact daily verified in intercourse with friends of different faiths and recorded in saintly literature the world over, namely, that when one of the higher religions is free to be practised at its best, it combines conviction with self-criticism, charity, and a desire for truth as untrammelled and exacting as that of any science. One would expect something of the sort from lives with God. Only when the sources of such lives are in danger of poison from within or of destruction from without does fixity or intransigence serve as a shield that defends by partially concealing. As Wilfrid Ward suggests, present Roman Catholic views about authority, dogma, and discipline belong to over three hundred years of domestic strife aggravated by a formidable Protestant and intellectual siege.[10] At the beginning of this century the normal spirit of freedom, revolting against protracted suppression, asserted it-

[10] cf. M. Ward, *The Wilfrid Wards and the Transition* (London: Sheed and Ward, 1934), Vol. I, Chap. XIX.

self prematurely and headily in Modernism. A long-suffering, less claimful, though equally courageous independence, more considerate of the failings and the difficulties of others, still animates the inner life of the Roman Church. But owing to historical circumstances, a contrast and tension probably still exist there between inner spiritual realities and external exigencies, which can be approximated only in certain "fundamentalistic" Christian bodies. Were they less indiscriminate in their condemnation of its outward forms, perhaps humanists might foster better the spiritual buoyancy they admire but often fail to detect outside their own ranks.

Bertrand Russell illustrates, here not in religion but in science, how the conditioned and the absolute, the fixed and the fluid, operate as supplementary tendencies of thought. One might suspect that he was about to "limit access to truth" to a special "channel or scheme of things," when he avows of his own particular Weltanschauung that "only within the scaffolding of its truths, only on the firm foundation of unyielding despair, can the soul's habitation henceforth be safely built."[11] But if one may assume that fixity in philosophy tacitly challenges and welcomes correction, Bertrand Russell does not divulge whether the same is true also for physics. He seems to feel, in his little book called *What I Believe*, that, because space is finite and matter is composed of electrons and protons, physics has reached its end and become uninteresting. Since he maintains that "from science, rather than from ethics and religion . . . philosophy should draw its inspiration";[12] that "scientific philosophy comes nearer to objectivity than any other human pursuit, and gives us, therefore, the closest constant and the most intimate relation with the outer world that it is possible to achieve";[13] that ultimately philosophy is "indistinguishable from logic";[14] and, presumably, that of all the sciences the most logical is pure mathematics: it is likely that there the opposing tendencies of his preeminently abstract mind (ever focusing reality into

[11] *Mysticism and Logic and Other Essays* (London: Longmans, Green, 1925; quoted by permission from Allen and Unwin, Ltd.), p. 48.
[12] *ibid.*, p. 98.
[13] *ibid.*, p. 32.
[14] *ibid.*, pp. 111-12.

98

smaller and clearer concentration—the counterpart of the urge to "monopoly" that Dr. Dewey deplores in religion) should stand out most definitely.

The first of his two tendencies—that towards the fixed and the absolute—reveals an intellectual mysticism reminiscent of Pythagoras and Plato. The same note of exaltation, the same inordinate claims for their absorbing objects, others record, who in any serious undertaking have gone through the ordinary shafts of experience and wandered far enough to sense the fascination of "caverns measureless to man." Provoked at a sort of metaphysical pusillanimity, Bertrand Russell, as quoted below, commences in a disputatious vein, warms to moral fervor, and glorifies a magnificent experience with a sweep that later seems exaggerated in "the light of common day."

"Too often it is said that there is no absolute truth, but only opinion and private judgment; that each of us is conditioned, in his view of the world, by his own peculiarities, his own taste and bias; that there is no external kingdom of truth to which, by patience and discipline, we may at last obtain admittance, but only truth for me, for you, for every separate person. By this habit of mind one of the chief ends of human effort is denied, and the supreme virtue of candor, of fearless acknowledgment of what is, disappears from our moral vision. Of such scepticism mathematics is a perpetual reproof; for its edifice of truths stands unshakable and inexpugnable to all the weapons of doubting cynicism.[15] . . . Mathematics takes us . . . into the region of absolute necessity, to which not only the actual world, but every possible world, must conform; and even here it builds a habitation, or rather finds a habitation eternally standing, where our ideals are fully satisfied and our best hopes are not thwarted. It is only when we thoroughly understand the entire independence of ourselves, which belongs to this world that reason finds, that we can adequately realize the profound importance of its beauty."[16]

[15] ibid., p. 71.
[16] ibid., p. 69.

99

Then, like religion, he turns the guns upon himself. He remembers that Weierstrass proved many of the "most cherished propositions" of mathematics to be "in general false."[17] He acknowledges that in "the world of time and space" the "certainty and precision" of that science err and stray "among approximations and working hypotheses."[18] And doubt as to whether mathematics builds or finds a habitation—the possibility, nay, the likelihood, that we construct our beliefs and choose their materials— leads him to admit regretfully that under such circumstances "the true dignity of reason is very greatly lowered; it ceases to be an investigation into the very heart and immutable essence of all things actual and possible, becoming, instead, an inquiry into something more or less human and subject to our limitations."[19]

Though it should now be clear from even those disconnected passages that the faults and the virtues ascribed by Dr. Dewey exclusively to religion and science respectively, inhere in science, as personified in Bertrand Russell, to about the same degree and under roughly the same circumstances as they inhere in religion, we have yet to ascertain what humanists mean by the scientific method and how they understand and employ some of the major scientific postulates upon which, according to their representations, humanism rests. Let us turn, therefore, to the principal humanists who have dealt with the subject—Professor Haydon, Professor Julian Huxley, Bertrand Russell, and Professor R. W. Sellars.

Nobody can deny that Professor A. Eustace Haydon is one of the leaders of American humanists or that his *Quest of the Ages* is one of their major productions.[20] It appears, under the examination of Dr. G. Rombotis, to be, not so much in its facts as in the treatment and the interpretation of them, scientifically, historically, and religiously insubstantial, except as an expression of a "twen-

[17] *ibid.*, p. 95.
[18] *ibid.*, p. 69.
[19] *ibid.*, p. 68; cf. pp. 69, 70, 71.
[20] As far as his humanism is concerned, his later book *Man's Search for the Good Life* (New York: Harper, 1937) shows no marked improvement.

tieth century naturalistic practical idealist."[21] Insisting that "the method of science . . . is the only authority which may hope to command the loyalty and cooperation of thinking men,"[22] Professor Haydon describes it as "simply a deliberate and objective way of thinking."[23] "It must be remembered that 'the scientific method knows only a democracy of facts.' Therefore 'no data can be snubbed, submerged, dismissed, or taken uncritically without challenge.' Finally, it should be realized that . . . the scientific method . . . is 'a bond of union among thinking men,' because it 'is the same in all fields. . . . The use of it varies with the material.' "[24]

Here again we meet the difference between the scientific spirit and scientific methods. Everybody wants exposure to and experience of reality, at least in those aspects of it that he enjoys and admires. The measure of his genius lies in the catholicity, the quality, and the harmony of his experience—in the degree to which reality reproduces itself in him. This craving for an ever better relation to reality through (among other things) deliberate and objective thinking is certainly a bond of union among men. As circumstances direct, they seek that relation in art, religion, society, science, politics, and other ways. They may neither understand nor sympathize with many roads to it, but, if they wholeheartedly pursue their own, they recognize and appreciate the same motives and influences in otherwise alien wayfarers. Each

[21] See Dr. Rombotis's articles called "Haydon's Philosophy of Religion and his Method" and "Scientific Method in Haydon's Religion," in, respectively, the July-August and the September-October 1933 issues of *The New Humanist.* Dr. Rombotis ends his second article with the following words: "Where are then the merit and the value of this philosophy? They are to be found in the sentiment and vision, zeal, enthusiasm, and the unconquerable will of the author to make clear to everyone who cares to hear him, that times have changed; that the people must profit from the evidences offered by the indefatigable efforts of the seekers of truth who unveiled the legendary sides of the religions of the world; that to hold to such legends and unhistorical tales is to perpetuate one's fears, hinder one's sense of freedom and the advance of mankind in many respects."

[22] Professor Haydon as quoted by Dr. Rombotis, "Scientific Method in Haydon's Religion," *The New Humanist,* September-October 1933, p. 33.

[23] *The Quest of the Ages,* p. 198.

[24] G. Rombotis, "Scientific Method in Haydon's Religion," *op. cit.,* p. 33. "Can" in the quotation above has been changed from "could" in the original text.

man also becomes thereby partially aware of the degree to which he grows more attached to his way than to the common goal—of the extent to which he ceases to be a man and becomes merely a politician, a scientist, a theologian, or an artist. So far as the desire for, and the increasing apprehension of, reality exist and so far as they may be called science, science snubs, submerges, dismisses, nothing, and becomes "the only authority which may hope to command the loyalty and cooperation of thinking men." In that sense everyone of single eye and not exclusively the chemist, the physicist, the mathematician, and their colleagues, is scientific. And only in some such sense could Professor Haydon's appreciation of science be more than panegyric.

But study of *The Quest of the Ages* and of Dr. Rombotis's criticisms of it reveals that Professor Haydon bases his idea of science, as might be expected, upon the procedures and the limitations of current methods in the natural sciences, and that he then concludes, as he need not have done, that that is the only valid type and source of all experience ("the only authority") for thinking men. Once that is granted, it follows that religion, like anything else, to deserve a hearing must keep within the bounds of science thus understood. Professor Haydon is driven to this also by his anthropological investigations of the origin of religion. *The Quest of the Ages* (and its successor, *Man's Search for the Good Life*) leaves the impression that until recently[25] religion was entirely a matter of emotion and superstition, "pre-scientific" and hence (so Professor Haydon everywhere implies without ever attempting to prove the assumption) illusory. Dr. Rombotis has no difficulty in showing the artificiality of Professor Haydon's conception of primitive man and the arbitrariness with which the author of *The Quest of the Ages* snubs and dismisses as "pre-scientific techniques" anything incompatible with his naturalistic description or simplification of religion. In accepting "hunches"

[25] Scientific method and its authority are, for Professor Haydon, "a new thing under the sun . . . growing out of a modern understanding of the nature of religion in the history of the race." Quoted by G. Rombotis in "Scientific Method in Haydon's Religion," *op. cit.,* p. 33.

and "flashes" Professor Haydon virtually admits that intuition and insight are and must always be as essential to life and knowledge as the deliberate thinking from which they can be distinguished but not separated.[26] His regard for music, art, and moral conduct, all of which involve emotions and taste, proves how inadequate his idea of science is when it is taken not merely as applicable, in different ways and to different degrees, to all experience but as including and being the norm of all experience and of humanism in its richest sense.[27]

This has been so often repeated and is so obvious by now to most students of science and philosophy that it would seem to be an imposition on the reader's patience to rehearse such platitudes, were it not for the fact that in humanistic writings scientific cant plays roughly the same persuasive and corrupting rôle that commercial advertising does in ordinary life. In both spheres the phrase "scientifically approved" (regardless of the truth or the falsity of the allegation, of the ability and the disinterestedness of the scientists, and of the qualifications of the approval) acts as an opiate, lulling those addressed into a misleading sense of security, catching them, as Bertrand Russell suggests in another context, "in their intellectually relaxed moods."[28]

Professor Julian S. Huxley also asserts "that the scientific method, although slow and never claiming to lead to complete truth, is the only method which in the long run will give satisfactory foundations for beliefs."[29] More cautious in his statement

[26] cf. "Analysis is the evocation of insight by the hypothetical suggestions of thought, and the evocation of thought by the activities of direct insight." A. N. Whitehead, "Harvard: The Future," *Atlantic Monthly,* September 1936, p. 264.

[27] In a valuable article ("Authority and the Normative Approach," *The Journal of Religion,* University of Chicago Press, April 1936) Professor H. N. Wieman adduces other reasons for criticizing those who "have hailed the scientific method as the final and the only authority for judging the merit of any religious way of living."

[28] The words were originally used in a quite different setting in *The Scientific Outlook,* p. 102. "Since science now enjoys prestige, because technology is so important to our productive pattern, we find advocates as different as Dr. Dewey and a toothpaste firm recommending their products under the aegis of science." Kenneth Burke, *The New Republic,* February 5, 1936, p. 371.

[29] *Religion Without Revelation* (London: Benn, 1926), p. 27.

of faith than Professor Haydon, he is also more detailed in his description of scientific method: "It consists in demanding facts as the only basis for conclusions; and of consistently and continuously testing any conclusions which may have been reached against the test of new facts and, wherever possible, by the crucial test of experiment. It consists also . . . in full publication of the evidence on which conclusions are based, so that other workers may have the advantage of the facts, to assist them in new researches, or, as frequently occurs, to make it possible for them to put a quite different interpretation on the facts."[30]

This continual stress on the necessity of dealing only with facts and of testing them in every conceivable way is less a definition of the particular manner in which modern sciences express the desire for reality than a description of that desire, or of the attitude of honest, intelligent inquiry, an attitude that has existed throughout history and that has found not its birth but one of its most definite exemplifications in the sciences. For several reasons we are apt to overlook this: authority in the past, if not actually stronger than today, was recognized and deferred to as much as it is now generally unperceived and popularly ridiculed; former experiments were crude and casual, compared with contemporary techniques. Even the last, especially in the newer sciences (as, for example, in some psychological experiments on the sense of divine presence), betray such ignorance of their objects and such clumsiness in their treatment of them that no break appears in their continuity with similarly undeveloped aspects of earlier times. The chief difference between ancient thought and modern science is not, as humanists often maintain, that thought outside natural science is emotional, deductive, and authoritarian, whereas science alone is rational, experimental, and free, but that in at least the well established sciences thought and emotion are so disciplined or stylized that, with the exception of rare spirits like Galileo, Darwin, and Einstein, experiment becomes steadily more the expression of dogma or the routine baptism of facts the character of which are predetermined in their major scientific aspects by the postulates and

[30] *ibid.*

104

the nature of the science that describes them. Thus science and standardization advance hand in hand. If increasing ability to elaborate spheres of knowledge and action flatters us into supposing it to be a sign of our increasing adaptation to reality, we can sober ourselves with the thought that too exact and rigid adaptation to immediate environment has usually been a prelude to extinction.

Professor Huxley recognizes that civilization has moulded theologians and fitted them with spectacles so that, barring a great wrench, they cannot see things except in an ever more prescribed way. He freely acknowledges that James Martineau "had not emancipated himself from the theistic views which surrounded him."[31] But he never seems to worry whether scientists as such need be saved from viewing the world "through the distorting medium of their own desires."[32] Hence he can write blandly of "the dispassionate gaze of an anthropologist,"[33] but would probably avoid "the dispassionate gaze of an orthodox theologian." Yet, if science is what Professor Huxley has outlined, both anthropologist and theologian may be equally dispassionate and scientific in searching for fact, consistency, experimental verification or refutation, and in keeping facts publicly available for continual use and revision. "The only possible solution" of the feud between theology and science, according to Professor Huxley, "save an indefinite prolongation of the conflict, is for religion to admit the intellectual methods of science to be as valid in theology as everywhere else, while science admits the psychological basis of religion as an ultimate fact."[34]

But religion today does admit science in Professor Huxley's sense of the desire for fact, truth, reality.[35] Indeed Christianity at

[31] *op. cit.,* p. 152.
[32] Bertrand Russell.
[33] *op. cit.,* p. 154.
[34] *ibid.,* p. 167.
[35] "Any appeal to considerations of value is rigidly eliminated in the exact sciences. Why? Not because the nature of logic or of 'disinterested' inquiry requires it, but because, on the basis of existing knowledge, values appear in this instance irrelevant to the facts that we wish to know. And this irrelevance is itself a fact about the particular subject-matter in question, not a presupposition

its best has always championed that, at least as far as religion is concerned; for it has sometimes been indifferent on other points. The difficulty is to ascertain what facts,[36] consistency, experiment, and verification are in and for religion. If "the intellectual methods of science" invariably meant for Professor Huxley the spirit of science, as distinguished from what Dr. Dewey calls "a particular set of beliefs and ideas" characterizing some highly restricted phase and methodological convenience of that spirit, then it should be more obvious in *Religion Without Revelation* that the real conflict is not between religion and science but between a fairly scientific, moderately critical religion and a few, young, over-confident trends of thought struggling, at the moment less critically, to be scientific. That this is not at all obvious derives from the fact that, as Dr. C. C. J. Webb has shown, Professor Huxley suffers from "a misapprehension of what is meant by Theism as a philosophical theory,"[37] and also constantly confuses science as the desire for truth with science as expressed in changing hypotheses valid under conditions that he is apt to ignore. What does he mean by the suggestion that science admit "the psychological basis of religion as an ultimate fact"? Looking over the field at large and not confining oneself to the dominant school of any particular place, one must acknowledge that so far no proposed basis for religion has met with anything like unanimous consent of psychologists. Professor Huxley's own belief that religion is subjective projection of our feelings of the sacred, and nothing more,

of 'disinterested' thinking in general. To suppose, as some 'humanists' do, that if we are to be rational in religion we must apply to it 'scientific methods' presupposing criteria of relevance and fruitfulness derived from our dealing with physical nature is not to be particularly enlightened, it is merely to be logically muddleheaded." A. E. Murphy, "Reason, Logic, and Scientific Method," *The New Humanist,* December 1934, pp. 21-2.

[36] "The word 'facts' is, in some ways, crucial. I have spoken with Jesuits and Plymouth Brethren, mathematicians and poets, dogmatic republicans and dear old gentlemen in bird's-eye neckcloths; and each understood the word 'facts' in an occult sense of his own." R. L. Stevenson, *op. cit.,* p. 20.

[37] *Religion and Theism* (London: Allen and Unwin, 1934), p. 41; cf. pp. 46-8. This may explain why, even though Professor Huxley portrays Christianity at a higher level than Bertrand Russell does, he paints it as more mediocre and ignorant than it commonly is.

is, as we shall see later, one of the least secure of psychology's fancies. He is in the position of a man who tastes an apple and finds it good but is persuaded by a zealous though bungling "specialist" on fruits that he has really been eating an indifferent pear. Personally aware of elements that have long been recognized as religious, even among people of diverse creeds, he has no emptiness to hide with some specially devised substitute for religion. "The consciousness of sanctity in existence" (which to a Christian suggests the immanence of God), he maintains, is a fact which "must" be basic to the "religion of the future."[38] As "*facts of the spiritual life*," he admits also "the conviction of sin, the desire of righteousness, the sense of absolution, the peace of communion."[39] Yet if those facts are to escape having their fullest meaning explained away, are they not, "if not necessarily, at least more naturally envisaged with a theistic background, in which there is a righteous God, against whom we have sinned, from whom we seek forgiveness, in reconciliation with whom we find our peace, than with the background of a [according to Professor Huxley] chaotic Nature which owes whatever unity it possesses to the 'organizing power of the human mind' "?[40] Does not Professor Huxley's disgust with common misrepresentations of God, rather than any adequacy of his own incoherent metaphysics, lead him to suppose that the facts of the spiritual life seek explanation less in terms of something ultimate and personal (in as rich a sense as possible) than in terms applicable primarily to things, mechanical relations, and exclusively human psychical peculiarities? His disintegrating interpretation of religious facts seems to suggest that on the whole for him science never leads to complete truth. Apparently he believes this not because there are sources and aspects of truth other than those now and perhaps always best managed by natural sciences, but because he assumes that in case of conflict the uncorrupted or otherwise acquired significance of facts must be subordinated to current hypotheses of psychology and natural

[38] *op. cit.*, p. 326.
[39] Quoted by Dr. C. C. J. Webb, *Religion and Theism* (London: Allen and Unwin, 1934), p. 46. Italics his.
[40] *ibid.*

107

sciences, which, though never complete as long as new material awaits their stamp, are yet virtually the only authoritative censors and organs of knowledge. This ignoring of subtle and difficult claims, presumably on behalf of scientific efficiency, is less consonant with his chance theoretical protests than with the general spirit and practice of what he has called—alas, too truly—*Religion Without Revelation.*

Although most humanists concede more authority to contemporary natural science than their theories warrant, it would be unfair to suppose that they have not analyzed its constitution further than this. Were there among them some outstanding man in the field, he could be studied as a representative. The nearest approach to this ideal is Bertrand Russell, who, although he differs from moderate humanists in his pessimistic deductions from science, has treated most of the principal points that they as a group consider relevant to its essence.

"The scientific attitude of mind," he writes, "involves a sweeping away of all other desires in the interests of the desire to know —it involves suppression of hopes and fears, loves and hates, and the whole subjective emotional life, until we become subdued to the material, able to see it frankly, without preconceptions, without bias, without any wish except to see it as it is, and without any belief that what it is must be determined by some relation, positive or negative, to what we should like it to be, or to what we can easily imagine it to be."[41]

In view of similar passages in their own publications, these remarks probably suffuse most humanists with a glow of approval. But since he wrote those words Bertrand Russell has passed, in regard to science, from enthusiasm through discrimination to disillusionment. It has become obvious, probably to him and certainly to others, that the attitude of mind which he described above as scientific is either the desire to know conceived as abstractly as possible or else a manner of dealing with reality, which is charged

[41] *Mysticism and Logic and Other Essays* (London: Longmans, Green, 1925; quoted by permission from Allen and Unwin, Ltd.), p. 44. cf. "The kernel of the scientific outlook is the refusal to regard our own desires, tastes, and interests as affording a key to the understanding of the world." *ibid.,* p. 42.

with prejudiced suppressions and preconceptions determining that what can be "known" must be so unrelated to the important expanse of experience called "the whole subjective emotional life" that scientific knowledge taken by itself and as the norm of thought, becomes, as Bertrand Russell strikingly shows in *The Scientific Outlook,* trivial, treacherous, repellent, so much the antithesis of wisdom that it clamors for correction "if a balanced view of human life is to be achieved."[42] "A scientific society in its pure form"—in other words, the unchecked domination of science as now usually understood— ". . . is incompatible with the pursuit of truth, with love, with art, with spontaneous delight, with every ideal that men have hitherto cherished, with the sole exception of ascetic renunciation."[43] It is incompatible with the pursuit of truth (and hence of many of the other things mentioned) as far as it denies and minimizes means of assimilating reality, other than its own special methods. Not emotion as such (for no profound thinking is unprompted or unaccompanied by emotion) but misplaced emotion is misleading. Duly recognized and treated, emotion in other forms is as revelatory of reality as are scientific curiosity and scientific lust of power. Failure to recognize its own emotions prevents science as metaphysics from appreciating the significance of other emotions and from relegating scientific ones to their proper place among them.

A scientist as such, Bertrand Russell asserts, is interested not (like an artist) in the particularity or (like a philosopher) in the totality, of a fact, but only in that aspect of it which is significant in making it an instance of a general law.[44] "Science, in its ultimate ideal, consists of a set of propositions arranged in a hierarchy, the lowest level of the hierarchy being concerned with particular facts, and the highest with some general law, governing everything in the universe."[45] Science as full and unbiased knowledge thus steadily gives way to science as "power of manipulating nature."[46]

[42] *The Scientific Outlook,* p. x; cf. pp. 260-9.
[43] *ibid.,* p. 264.
[44] *ibid.,* p. 58.
[45] *ibid.*
[46] *ibid.,* p. viii.

This power is obtained by the abstraction[47] of causal laws.[48] First —according to Bertrand Russell's scheme—"significant" facts are observed, i.e., those suspected of revealing the causal connections sought. An hypothesis is next advanced, "which, if it is true, would account for these facts." Finally the consequences of the hypothesis are deduced and tested by observation.[49]

Certainly this is a shrunken version of what in itself is a highly selective epitome of science. Not so much the actual words (for the phrases are general enough to include almost anything) as the contexts in which they appear tend, for the sake of showing science as power, to ignore categories dear to science as speculation. But the summary serves the purpose of revealing both the trend of the times and the gist of scientific method as described by humanists. Since, instead of following the psalmist in urging us to "taste and see that the Lord is good," they appeal to our vanity as "thinking men" and glory in the fact that humanism rests on science,[50] we must observe how the method of science is employed in the support of humanism.

If for them science has become more a power to manipulate nature than a communion with reality, humanists act as might be expected in regarding causation, or the determinism of the natural sciences, as of fundamental importance. "Humanism denies the existence of any realm outside the field of cause and effect and holds that what is called the supernatural is only the not-yet-understood natural."[51] This statement by a humanist leader, linking determinism with denial of supernaturalism, might well be a favorite text for the average run of his coreligionists. Bertrand Russell apparently shared the same view, when he asserted that "we are subordinated to nature, the outcome of natural laws, and their victims in the long run."[52] Man's "thoughts and his bodily

[47] *ibid.*, p. 84.
[48] *ibid.*, p. 83.
[49] *ibid.*, p. 57.
[50] Other bases of humanism are officially recognized, but, if they are not strictly scientific, they must be either compatible with science or, allegedly, of no ultimate significance.
[51] C. F. Potter, *Humanism, A New Religion*, p. 33.
[52] Bertrand Russell, *What I Believe*, p. 23.

movements," he maintains, "follow the same laws that describe the motions of stars and atoms."[53]

Being a victim seems to appeal to humanists. To believe things hated, feared, or at least indifferent, comes to them as a relief after Victorian propaganda for things true, honorable, just, pure, lovely, or of good report. Pringle-Pattison used to say that the reply to the remark, "It's too good to be true," was, "Only the good can be true." But humanists call that "wishful thinking." To avoid such a metaphysical variety of the pathetic fallacy, they indulgently "project" what they like upon the world, but—developing a pseudo-scientific obscurantism as a means of combating its religious counterpart—they maturely and frankly reserve the title of "fact" for things in proportion to their unpalatableness and incomprehensibility.[54]

One expects, therefore, that most humanists would insist on the ontological reality and the universal sway of an impersonal and sufficiently disagreeable determinism borrowed from mechanics and physics. And, after the passages just quoted from Bertrand Russell, one would suppose that he would concur with the others. But an ever-growing mind like his continually throws aside the childish things of earlier thought. "Academic philosophers," he observes, "ever since the time of Parmenides, have believed that the world is a unity. . . . The most fundamental of my intellectual beliefs is that this is rubbish.[55] I think the universe is all spots and jumps, without unity, without continuity, without coherence or orderliness or any of the other properties that governesses love."[56]

[53] *ibid.,* p. 9.

[54] ". . . without any belief, that what it is must be determined by some relation, positive or negative, to what we should like it to be or to what we can easily imagine it to be." p. 108, *supra,* cf. L. P. Smith's "trivium": "I like my universe as immense, grim, icy and pitiless as possible." *op. cit.,* p. 154.

[55] cf. *Mysticism and Logic and Other Essays* (London: Longmans, Green, 1925; quoted by permission from Allen and Unwin, Ltd.), p. 98: "I believe the conception of 'the universe' to be . . . a mere relic of pre-Copernican astronomy."

[56] *The Scientific Outlook,* pp. 94-5. "The idea of disorder objectifies for the convenience of language, the disappointment of a mind that finds before it an order different from what it wants." Bergson, quoted by Walter Lippmann in *The Phantom Public,* which in turn is quoted by L. M. Birkhead, Little Blue Book no. 1447 (Haldeman-Julius Publications, Girard, Kan., 1929), p. 25.

Without noticing that the phrase "the same laws that describe the motions of stars and atoms"[57] is, according to defamatory idiom, merely "literary," because measures and concepts appropriate to the very large or to the medium must be so altered before becoming properly applicable to the very small that they can hardly be called the "same,"[58] one may nevertheless wonder how any laws, sciences, governesses, or even naughty boys, could survive in such a jumpy mish-mash as Bertrand Russell despairingly gloats over. His, though, is the pen of a ready writer. "Order, unity, and continuity," he explains, "are human inventions just as truly as are catalogues and encyclopedias. But human inventions can, within limits, be made to prevail in our human world, and in the conduct of our daily life we may with advantage forget the realm of chaos and old night by which we are perhaps surrounded."[59]

It was nice of him to say "perhaps"; for if chaos and old night exist science will be the last to discover them. So far no one has run across an instance of chaos. The wildest dream, the most agonizing pain, the most grotesque freak of nature, far from being bolts from a mysterious old night, are miserable shreds of daily experience. If chaos were the dominant feature of reality, how, either with or without advantage, could we forget it? The maddest fact of all, then, would be our existence and ability, within any limits whatsoever, to prevail upon what is by definition beyond our power and understanding. But the meaninglessness of chaos, except as an epithet to hide our weakness and ignorance, and its inconsistency with even the minimum of order and ordering required by

[57] p. III, *supra.*
[58] For considerations concerning the limits and the conditions of the validity of scientific concepts see "Ce que la Microphysique apporte ou suggère à la Philosophie," by Édouard Le Roy, in the April and July 1935 numbers of the *Revue de Metaphysique et de Morale.* Though not to permit the mass of his knowledge from interfering with a momentary effect is a characteristic of Bertrand Russell's style, perhaps when he wrote about the same laws for stars and atoms he had not yet learned what he later maintained, namely that "the older laws of mechanics which governed the movements of bodies large enough to be seen remain true to a very close approximation as regards such bodies, but are found to be not applicable to single atoms, still less to single electrons and protons." *The Scientific Outlook,* p. 103.
[59] *ibid.,* p. 98.

Bertrand Russell's philosophy are minor matters compared to the rigor with which he drives humanistic logic to its end. He "projects" not merely morality and religion but science itself—in fact everything. "In all things," he says, "it is well to exalt the dignity of man.[60] . . . Let us preserve our respect for truth, for beauty, for the ideal of perfection which life does not permit us to attain, though none of these things meets with the approval of the unconscious universe."[61] If even a major part of the universe rolled "on its relentless way"[62] indifferent to human values, it could be borne. But the acme of humanistic delight is the realization of the illusoriness of any faintest trace of unity, continuity, coherence, or order, which might produce the mirage of a universe.

Moderate humanists do not reach this nirvana presumably experienced now and then by Bertrand Russell. Although they do not agree on every point, their position is probably on the whole best represented by Professor R. W. Sellars, who, more than most of them, has sought a systematic philosophical basis for humanism. In his *Religion Coming of Age, The Philosophy of Physical Realism,* and his articles in *The New Humanist,* he has investigated with special care the idea of causation, which colors the humanistic conception of nature. "We can know"—if he is right —"only the things which cause sensations in us and those which we must infer as connected with such causal things."[63] Without arguing "that we mysteriously intuit an external something called force or necessary connection,"[64] he believes "we can justly say that we perceive causal relations, if we realize that such perceptions are empirical and may be mistaken, if we rid ourselves of any intuitional notion of perceiving, and if we leave it to analysis to discover the meaning of causality."[65] "True causes must be localized and observed; they must be parts of nature in intimate

[60] *Mysticism and Logic and Other Essays* (London: Longmans, Green, 1925; quoted by permission from Allen and Unwin, Ltd.), p. 49.
[61] *ibid.,* p. 50.
[62] *ibid.,* p. 56.
[63] *Religion Coming of Age,* p. 167.
[64] *The Philosophy of Physical Realism* (New York: Macmillan, 1932), p. 211.
[65] *ibid.,* p. 212.

relations with other parts."[66] A cause "is a specific and localizable antecedent.[67] It is a natural event which we have good reason to believe conditions a later event. It is something measurable and observable, something which is a part of nature. Thus nature stands on its own feet and explains itself. It is a domain of events and changes which are connected together. It is a vast system in space and time."[68]

That sounds like the materialism that humanists claim to have outgrown. But in the following passage Professor Sellars hints that science and causation are primarily instruments for the manipulation of certain features of reality our best knowledge of which comes from personal experience: "To reduce nature to abstract symbols of quantitative knowledge is to do it injustice. Things are fields of action with a reality-content which eludes our measurements. It is the pattern and mode of working of things which we can comprehend in this external way. And it is not until we come to ourselves that we are confronted with the fact that our living experience is real."[69]

[66] *Religion Coming of Age,* p. 160. Spatial or temporal proximity, or both, no matter how close, is by no means an "intimate" relation. Intimacy in its fullest sense applies only to persons. In a truly close-knit cosmos personal relations would underlie impersonal ones.

> "Distance is not the realm of Fox,
> Nor by relay as Bird;
> Abated, Distance is until
> Thyself, Beloved!"   —Emily Dickinson, *op. cit.,* p. 265.

[67] "The causal relation involves continuity and contiguity, and in this respect demands more than regular sequence of a merely temporal sort." *The Philosophy of Physical Realism,* p. 380.

[68] *Religion Coming of Age,* p. 146. Whether a given cause is one natural event or many depends not only upon what we are investigating but upon our purposes and patience.—"In space and time" does not imply, for Professor Sellars, absolute space and time or Kantian forms of perception. "Space means the measurability and localizability of things. This physical world is not *in* space; it is spatial. Physical space is simply the extended physical world." (*ibid.,* p. 168; italics his. Similarly for time; cf., e.g., *ibid.,* p. 171.) How this can be and what it presupposes (the more advanced questions which Kant attacked) do not seem to disturb Professor Sellars. Psychical causes—like a thought provoking tears—though they may be experienced by the weeper at a given time are not, and probably never will be, observable and measurable in the same way as causes in "the external world," on which Professor Sellars's idea of causation seems to be based and to which it is chiefly pertinent.

[69] *ibid.,* p. 195.

To Professor Sellars's account of causation as far as it is a rough, practical device no objection is here taken. But, like most humanistic writings, his books suffer from a perpetual vacillation between and confusion of an impersonal, valueless picture of the world and a humanistic appreciation of consciousness, purpose, and quality. His honesty in grappling with these different points of view does not hide the fact that he does justice to one only at the expense of the other. Though difficulties remain in the theistic subordination of the impersonal to the personal, that nevertheless offers, at least in the form given it by Baron von Hügel and Professor A. E. Taylor, a solution fairer to both than anything yet proposed by humanists.

If "nature stands on its own feet and explains itself" by disclosing one thing as conditioned by another, causation might be regarded as science's means of explanation. Yet "I am quite aware," Professor Sellars protests, "that the origin of a set of beliefs does not determine their truth or falsity.[70] . . . I want now just to point out that the physical sciences have nothing to say about values because it is their task to *know* external things and not to discuss what they mean to human life with its needs."[71] Though the passages quoted are widely separated, they belong together in Professor Sellars's idea of causation. Science's method of explanation, therefore, or better its type of knowledge, has according to Professor Sellars, nothing to do primarily with truth, falsity, or the meaning of things to human life. In fact it has very little to do with what we commonly call knowledge.

What makes it so shy? It fears that some plan, purpose, value, or meaning may be found in nature, which will open the door for religion. This appears in Professor Sellars's attempt to outwit any theological deductions possible from relations existing between reason and its object. "A rational world is a world that reason can grasp; and, because of this, it is associated in our minds with reason and thought of as akin to it, but, as a matter of fact, the relation between intelligence and order is just the reverse of the

[70] *ibid.*, p. 16.
[71] *ibid.*, p. 143. Italics his.

115

one the idealist suggests. It is intelligence which presupposes order and not order which presupposes intelligence. Without order in the world, the human reason could neither have risen nor could it have got leverage upon the world. An orderly world is rational only in the sense that it is suited to reason. It is the kind of world in which reason can arise and operate."[72]

Though "order" otherwise undescribed seems to be sub-personal and incompatible with God, an order that, if we (in our full being and not as "reason" alone) are to survive well in it, exacts (as Professor Sellars concedes) our very best, rewards satisfactory efforts with superior exactions, and sooner or later turns all else to ashes, is so consonant not with our comfort or average understanding but with our highest aspirations and thus so akin to and surpassing personality as we find it faintly in ourselves, that such an order rather suggests than denies what theism recognizes as a characteristic of deity.

But even though a theistic "order" may be the appropriate foundation and crown of humanism, Professor Sellars makes it plain that the "order" he refers to is a spatio-temporal, causally determined one. That at least is the part of his thought which justifies him in adopting the last half of the name "evolutionary naturalist." For some reason he seems to think that theistic religion requires a narrowly anthropomorphic cosmology as faithful to the "final" aspect of causation as he is to the "material," the "formal," and the "efficient" aspects. But, as he observes, "the old idea of a personal agent working in nature but not of it fades and the attention is focused upon actual events and things. For modern science and philosophy, nature seems self-sufficient and vast. . . . The modern mind has inherited two logics which are at war with each other: the logic of personal agency and the logic of causation. It is only of late that the solution of this conflict is seen and it consists in making personal agency a specific kind of natural causality.[73] But this solution obviously undermines the

[72] *ibid.*, p. 220.
[73] Throughout his works Plato was on guard against one form or another of "this most deceptive argument with its youthful looks."

whole superstructure which traditional religion erected upon the basis of a mystical exaltation of personal agency.[74]. . . Many of our riddles . . . arise from a crisscrossing of these two logics. . . . Thus evolution is thought of as a natural process and yet some divine agent is asserted to guide it. There is an attempt to *double* everything in a ghostly way. Personal agency is an added activity which somehow accompanies natural causality and robs it of its brutality. Plan and purpose can thus be discerned where science can find neither. The two logics are superposed upon each other."[75]

There is no need to examine at length the possibility that the common idea of causation may derive from an analogical extension to nature of certain volitional and habitual aspects of personal agency. The alleged "solution" afforded by "making personal agency a specific kind of natural causality" may be more verbal than real, since, especially for an emergent evolutionist like Professor Sellars,[76] it virtually denies the qualitative difference between the "levels" of the unconscious and the conscious, and, by stretching a concept strictly applicable (regardless of its origin) to the former level in order to include both levels, instead of discovering a genuinely new synthesis it merely deprives that concept of whatever meaning it had.[77] Professor Sellars's disparage-

[74] *Religion Coming of Age*, p. 160.

[75] *ibid.*, p. 161. Italics his.

[76] If acceptance of real novelty, new levels, and "emergents" characterizes emergent evolutionists, Professor Sellars may be called one. His view differs in several respects from that of S. Alexander and Lloyd Morgan, notably in the fact that he does "not apply the concept of evolution to the universe taken as a super-entity inclusive and containing all others, but only to physical systems within it." *The Philosophy of Physical Realism*, p. 3.

[77] Professor Sellars would probably claim that so far from "stretching" natural causality beyond its limits, he repudiates "a dead-level, mechanical causality" and advocates "levels of causality in accordance with levels of organization in nature." (*The Philosophy of Physical Realism*, p. 458.) The difficulty is that, on his own showing, human causality, or conscious purpose, belongs to a dimension so different from anything physical or amenable to science that it seems meaningless and misleading to call it "a specific kind of natural causality." True, "moral action is natural action for the kind of creature man is." (*ibid.*) But man as conscious is, according to Professor Sellars, not subject to "the categories which apply to physical things" (*ibid.* p. 414), which means, presumably, the rest of nature. The fact, if it is one, that consciousness, miracles, or anything super- or non-natural, have laws of their own may make them "natural" in their own

ment of an awkward view of the relation of the personal to the impersonal instead of undermining traditional religion reiterates criticisms made twenty years earlier by one of its best representatives against thinking of nature and supernature as *"alongside* of each other."[78] But there is no need to follow these cues for indications of the restricted range within which causality may be comparatively intelligible and valid, because Professor Sellars provides this material in his general conception of nature.

"In place of atomistic, or unsocial, mechanicalism," the evolutionary naturalist "grasps nature as a domain of pattern, activity and organization.[79]. . . Are not even atoms[80] social, that is, selective? Does not a chemical process reflect the properties of the chemical substances as well as the general conditions of temperature and pressure? This means that combination is not blind in the old sense but selective. At this level, selection does not mean purpose, though it is that out of which purpose may develop at higher levels of evolution.[81]. . . There are levels in nature, and each level has its own characteristics.[82]. . . The modern naturalist holds that order is intrinsic to nature however far down we go, that the units of nature are social and unite in ways expressive of their nature and the physical context. . . . Naturally the term, *organic*, must not be taken literally as a projection downward of biological conceptions. It stands for a *texture of nature* which is demanded by all the physical sciences.[83]. . . As a matter of fact, atoms combine to give molecules, and molecules combine to

spheres, just as a brigand abides by his own laws, but it makes them no more "natural" in the natural science or naturalistic sense than a brigand can be said to be "law-abiding" in the sense that has for a conventional citizen.

[78] F. von Hügel, *Selected Letters*, edited by B. Holland (London: Dent, 1928), p. 96. Italics his. cf. *ibid.*, pp. 94 and 95; *The Mystical Element of Religion* (London: Dent, second edition, 1923), Vol. II, pp. 367-86; and *Eternal Life* (Edinburgh: Clark, second edition, 1929), pp. 133-5.

[79] *Religion Coming of Age*, p. 226.

[80] Bertrand Russell warns against supposing that "atoms" banish mystery. "Atoms do not themselves exist, but are merely a compendious way of alluding to possible occurrences." *The Scientific Outlook*, p. 77.

[81] *Religion Coming of Age*, p. 218.

[82] *ibid.*, p. 183.

[83] *ibid.*, p. 218. Italics his.

give crystals and complex chemical substances and colloids, and these again combine in diverse ways. Under favoring conditions, this process of superorganization may be cumulative and, in that case, it seems quite logical[84] to believe that properties of the class we call vital appear.[85]. . . Life is not a peculiar kind of entity, or force, to be found in living things and which makes them living. It is only a term for certain ways of acting and behaving on the part of certain physical systems we call organisms.[86]. . . It is supposed, then, that, certain combinations having developed under favorable conditions, this vital stuff[87] possessed the power of maintaining itself and multiplying.[88]. . . Living things are thickened systems in space and time; they are packed with structure and interrelations. But it is only this extreme thickening or packing which differentiates them from inorganic things.[89]. . . This thickening or organization develops action-as-a-whole and the relative autonomy or spontaneity of life.[90]. . . Human purpose is a development of pattern in nature as this has attained the thickness and complications made possible by intelligence and memory. We are here at a very high level of evolutionary organization and we should expect the novel.[91]. . . A human being is his organism as conceived from every angle and thought of as lit up from within by his consciousness. Thinking and feeling are a kind of living as experienced on the inside of the organism.[92]. . . It is realized that the exact sciences can decipher only the pattern of the body as of other external things. They have no means of penetrating to the very content of the brain to tell us that consciousness is not there. It would seem, then, the most probable position, that, in his consciousness, the individual is on the inside of that physical

[84] Why? It seems natural only after we are used to it; otherwise it would be as inconceivable as the next level beyond Professor S. Alexander's deity.
[85] *Religion Coming of Age*, p. 175.
[86] *ibid.*, pp. 173-4.
[87] Which is not "a peculiar kind of entity."
[88] *Religion Coming of Age*, p. 175.
[89] *ibid.*, p. 223.
[90] *ibid.*, p. 226.
[91] *ibid.*, p. 224.
[92] *ibid.*, p. 196.

reality he calls his brain. Thus we have what I have long called a double knowledge of the organism. We know the brain from the outside, and we are also one with it and thus in a position to know it from the inside. Consciousness is intrinsic to the living organism, it is a complex of events[93] flowing with the response of the brain-mind to situations. Here we have integrative actions of a unique sort and a level of organic action which is reared upon the larger economy of life."[94]

If the reader now has some idea of Professor Sellars's position and has thus obtained a small but first-hand acquaintance with the more accomplished sort of humanistic cosmology, he may excuse those long quotations. They show at least three things. Firstly, humanists have found what they call the older naturalism or "atomistic, unsocial mechanicalism," to be inadequate. The strength of their claim to modernity for this discovery resides, however, almost entirely in the effectiveness of their publicity as compared with that of Plato, Christian theism, and the numerous schools of idealism. Secondly, most of their important representatives have adopted the luxuriant new universe of emergent evolution. Thus they can call themselves evolutionary naturalists or naturalistic humanists. And the fact that they cling to the word naturalism and merely modify it to some extent shows, thirdly, that, in spite of their boasted rejection of "the older naturalism," they still try to dress reality in its outmoded styles. They grant atoms "selection," provided it is neither "blind" nor "purposive." "Organic," of course, is not "organic" but "a texture of nature," not further defined, although "all the physical sciences" "demand" it. Only an "extreme thickening or packing" differentiates the living from the unliving. If a superorganized pattern of hyperthickness belongs to "intelligence and memory," if consciousness is "on the inside of the brain" and causes the organism to be "lit up," and if

[93] Later he wrote—which probably better expresses what he means—that science "is always dealing with the brain-mind and its states as physical events. Consciousness is not an independent event but a feature of a physical event. . . . Consciousness is a qualitative dimension of cerebral activity." *The Philosophy of Physical Realism*, p. 424.

[94] *Religion Coming of Age*, p. 195.

nobody can discover this remarkable thickness in the brain or elsewhere, one seems obliged to conclude that "thickness" obviously does not mean "thickness" but has some esoteric significance perhaps known only to Professor Sellars. Nobody resigned to metaphor in even the best knowledge and impressed by the courage a pioneer must have to disregard ordinary usage will begrudge Professor Sellars, his masters, colleagues, and disciples, their right to solve problems by "complications." But his entire cosmology tends to show that "le principe de causalité, dans sons usage scientifique, est loin d'offrir, comme on l'a cru longtemps, une signification univoque et simple, toujours valable sous la même forme grosse, à quelque niveau de pensée qu'on l'applique";[95] that, though their conceptions of science are fairly clear as far as they go, humanists quickly abandon it; and that in their "break" from the prison of science they fall into the moat of mythology, because (no matter how justly they protest against the charge in certain instances) in general they strive to explain the whole by the part, the higher by the lower, and the mysteries of thought by some of its least intelligible figments.

If this looks like too sweeping an indictment, let us pause to see what Professor Sellars means by saying that consciousness is "on the inside of" the brain. At about this point naturalism and materialism usually fail either to do justice to the uniqueness of thought or to remain self-consistent.

Professor Sellars's initial creed runs: "That which is physical is real, and that which is real is physical"[96]—a proposition fully deserving the title of naturalism. "I repeat that everything which exists is spatial and temporal and is either a physical system or is existentially inseparable from one"[97]—a point of view so far transcending naturalism that its right to the name may be questioned. Through the loophole of being "existentially inseparable" from a physical system he is free to smuggle in all sorts of things not physical and yet to call them real—to which nobody not a natural-

[95] É. Le Roy, op. cit., p. 339. cf. "Causality in Nature," Chap. II of The Philosophy of Physics, by Max Planck (New York: Norton, 1936).
[96] The Philosophy of Physical Realism, p. 13.
[97] ibid.

ist would object but which seems to contradict his first statement that only the physical is real. Rightly loath, however, to win a merely verbal victory, he undertakes "to show that mind and consciousness are in a very real sense physical."[98]

"It strikes me"—this is his conclusion—"that all the relevant facts force us to achieve a new category. . . . Consciousness is *in* the brain in accordance with the nature of consciousness. . . . Consciousness is the qualitative dimension of a brain-event. It is the patterned brain-event as sentient. It is because of its status that we, as conscious, participate in the being of brain-events. Here and here alone, are we, as conscious beings, on the inside of reality.[99] . . . The philosopher's task . . . is to think consciousness as a complex and changing event adjectival in some sense to the organism. It is evident that the categories which apply to physical things and their parts do not apply to it or to any of the factors in it. . . . The problem is obviously unique because one of the terms is unique. . . . If, then, consciousness is extended, it must be so after its own nature, which seems to be that of an *event*. It will be in the brain as an event can be said to be in a thing in which it occurs.[100] . . . The psychical can be extended ontologically in the same sense that an activity or an event can be. That is, it can permeate, and be integral to, a process which is as extended as the physical system which is its locus.[101] . . . The *inness* of consciousness is the participative inness of the qualitative dimension of brain-mind events.[102] . . . While I am inclined to hold that the psychical is a condition of the brain alone as a focus of stimuli and response, I quite agree that, in the large sense, thinking as a process involves the whole organism.[103] . . . It is

[98] *ibid.*

[99] *ibid.*, p. 414; order of one sentence changed without altering meaning.

[100] *ibid.*

[101] *ibid.*, p. 431.

[102] *ibid.*, p. 433.

[103] *ibid.*, p. 440. Can one stop there? Does not consciousness equally "involve" and "permeate" the environment of the organism? The nature of the organism expresses the nature of its environment, ultimately—but none the less actually at any point or moment—the whole universe. Consciousness, then, is not merely "under the hat"; it is a dimension of all reality.

my considered opinion that physical science, that is, science which deciphers nature in terms of the external revelatory capacity of sense-data, must ignore consciousness altogether. It should not deny it, of course, because it has no means of making either negative or positive assertions about the content of being. . . . Science cannot taste, or participate in, the veritable substance of physical systems; and, if our own experiencing suggests to us that the organism does have a sentient tang and a conscious dimension, there is nothing in science to contradict it."[104]

No one aware that never has the relation between body and mind been clearly elucidated will criticize Professor Sellars's ingenious efforts because they are not wholly successful. The fact that "the participative inness of the qualitative dimension of brain-events" no more explains what that "participative inness" is than "adjectival in some sense to the organism" reveals in what sense mind is "adjectival," may instead suggest a similarity between Professor Sellars and Plato, whose use of "participation" posed rather than solved a problem.

The unexpected thing, though, is that one who subscribed to the rejection of "the traditional dualism of mind and body" (third item of the Manifesto) should end by putting them not merely worlds but dimensions apart. If his new dimension and his new category are truly new, men, in so far as they are conscious, be-

[104] *ibid.*, p. 421. In several respects this view of consciousness resembles the position of Professor Oliver L. Reiser, an editor of *The New Humanist*, who, in his *Philosophy and the Concepts of Modern Science* (New York: Macmillan, 1935), refers to "consciousness as a new dimension which, like time, intersects the physical universe at right angles." (*op. cit.*, p. 182.) ". . . consciousness may lie outside the four-dimensional continuum of relativity theory. . . . We should not make the mistake of trying to force happenings which occur in many dimensions into a smaller number of dimensions." (*op. cit.*, p. 176.) ". . . while relativity theory requires only a fourfold continuum, quantum mechanics now requires more. In each case the lower dimension of any hyperspace may be regarded as expressing the *static* (or 'matter') aspect, with the orthogonal time-axis representing the *dynamic* (or 'consciousness') aspect, having associated with it the radiating field forces. From this point of view the most general formula for expressing the relation of consciousness to body is this:

$$\frac{\text{Consciousness}}{\text{Body}} = \frac{n + 1 - \text{dimensional space}}{n - \text{dimensional space}}"$$

long to a plane different from that of science and the rest of reality. That, however, disposes of any idea that only the physical is real, that science is "the only authority" for thinking men, that "humanism denies the existence of any realm outside the field of cause and effect"—in short, of any notion that humanism has peculiar claims on science or receives special support from it. In discovering for themselves (since they would not or could not learn from theism, idealism of various schools, and common sense) that man has a unique nature and dwelling "intersecting" but not interrupting other "dimensions" of reality, humanists have found the best basis for a specifically "humanistic" philosophy. The chief criticism that might be made is that they generally admit this new dimension only to ignore it. Does Professor Sellars— not as an individual but as a representative of humanism in its prevailingly naturalistic form—do justice to his new dimension? Does he treat the mind-body problem with equal or (as might be expected from an avowed humanist) more emphasis on the point of view of the conscious agent than on the point of view of an external observer? When he talks of introspection and consciousness, does he really speak from the mind outwards? On the contrary, he approaches mind from the outside. He is more intent on "locating" the mind in relation to something in the external world—on regarding it as "a condition of the brain"—than on considering the significance of the external world in our conscious lives. From the point of view of consciousness, the brain and its convolutions are, except for specialists or in moments of illness, insignificant compared with personal relations, ideals, and interests. Even when one of those interests is the study of the brain, somebody else's brain in a bottle generally occupies the student's attention more than his own brain does. The fact that science may have crudely to infer the inside (consciousness) from the outside (physical systems), or, if it discusses the former at all, to do so in terms of the latter, is no reason why humanism, having once broken away from the apron strings of science and immediately experienced a new dimension, should merely record the vision and then return unchanged whence it came.[105]

This chapter started with a brief exposition of some of the opinions about science and religion, which form the working philosophy of average humanists. It became evident that at bottom most of those opinions, notwithstanding avowed rejection or drastic reformation, continually reappear in subtler, less obvious forms in the views of more critical humanists. These may recognize that, so far from being a basis for humanism, science, taken not as a means of purification or as a useful instrument but as the last court of appeal or as the only authority for thinking men, is inimical to much that is best in humanity.[106] The logical, practical, and spiritual limitations of the sciences in regard to induction, abstraction, inference, the law of parsimony, the idea of the external world, and the relation of technical concepts to common sense notions and daily conditions, may be obvious to them.[107] Bertrand Russell, in one of his on-the-other-hand moments, may write: "The sphere of values lies outside science, except in so far as science consists in the pursuit of knowledge. Science as the pursuit of power must not obtrude upon the sphere of values, and scientific technique, if it is to enrich human life, must not outweigh the ends which it would serve."[108] Professor M. C. Otto[109] may assert: "There is no longer any reason why the principles or forms or categories under which the scientist finds it convenient to think, *must* be employed by *every* thinker, no matter what his field or his aim.[110] . . . This step—

[105] Because Professor Sellars is one of those rare people who can truthfully write, "I have long maintained that . . . ," and "It has long been my thesis that . . . ," it is not surprising to find him repeating, almost in the same words, the gist of what has just been quoted from his earlier writings, in an article called "An Analytic Approach to the Mind-Body Problem," *The Philosophical Review*, September 1938, pp. 461-87.

[106] Bertrand Russell, *The Scientific Outlook*, pp. 100, 128; E. S. Ames, *Religion*, p. 169.

[107] *The Scientific Outlook*, pp. 63, 64, 67, 68, 69, 73, 74, 81, 104, and 105; M. C. Otto, *Things and Ideals*, pp. 214, 216.

[108] *The Scientific Outlook*, p. 266.

[109] Professor of philosophy at the University of Wisconsin; co-author, with H. N. Wieman and D. C. Macintosh, of *Is There a God?* (1932).

[110] *Things and Ideals*, p. 218. Italics his.

the clean-cut recognition that facts determine method, not method facts, that science is for life, not life for science—is of the greatest significance."[111] And we may listen with special sympathy to Dr. E. S. Ames:[112] "When nature is itself humanized by the inclusion of man, personality and the social process become legitimate in defining the entire picture. The physical becomes the abstract, partial aspect of the world, and the personal is the more adequate characterization. It is when we allow ourselves to be imposed upon by the natural-science point of view as the more real, more actual, that the human sphere appears as subjective, illusory, or unreal."[113]

That imposition is, we believe, the crux of the difficulty for humanism. We have seen how Professor Huxley, Bertrand Russell, and Professor Sellars struggle out of the quagmire of "the natural-science point of view" only to lapse into it again. That will always be so, it was hinted, as long as the inspiration of philosophy comes more from science than from ethics and religion.

[111] *ibid.*, p. 219.
[112] 1918-1926 associate professor of philosophy at the University of Chicago; since 1900 pastor of the University Church of Disciples of Christ, Chicago.
[113] *op. cit.*, p. 170.

CHAPTER IV

SYNOPSIS OF CHAPTER IV

Of all sciences, psychology furnishes the most powerful ammunition for the humanistic attack on theism. And of all psychologies, that serves humanism best which interprets religion as a "deflection" of human emotions from their proper objects and a "projection" of them on reality. As humanists accept "deflection" and "projection" ready-made, we must go back to their original sources in order to examine them. Dr. Freud's theory of religion as an illusory projection of the father-idea is further developed in Dr. Jung's conceptions of libido-accumulation and symbolical replacement. Even on Dr. Jung's theory, theistic religion would seem to be more fundamental than humanism. But his opinion that God is merely "a psychological function of man" withstands analysis no better than the whole method of psychology presupposed by him, Dr. Freud, and humanists. Difference between phantasy and belief in God.

HUMANISM AND PSYCHOLOGY

> "Conjecturing a climate
> Of unsuspended suns
> Gives poignancy to Winter;
> The freezing fancy turns
> To a fictitious country
> To palliate a cold
> Not obviated of degree
> Nor eased of latitude."[1]

POPULAR theistic religion, according to Mr. Walter Lippmann, "rests on a theory which, if it is true, is an extension of physics and of history; the humanistic view rests on human psychology and an interpretation of human experience."[2] Though, as he would doubtless admit, compared with customs, institutions, needs, and emotions, theory, especially connected with abstruse matters like physics and history, forms a relatively small part of the foundation of popular religion, nevertheless his summary reveals striking differences between traditional theism and recent humanism. The former is predominantly cosmological and objective in outlook; for it an individual's feelings are less significant in themselves than in those features of reality to which they refer. In contrast with this widely prevailing and often naïve realism sophisticatedly expressed by sciences like physics and history (in so far as they seek objective facts of an external world), the boasted novelty of humanism in its restriction of religion to long-

---

[1] Emily Dickinson, *op. cit.*, p. 318.
[2] *A Preface to Morals* (New York: Macmillan, 1929), p. 143.

129

ings for objects held to be real only as echoes or reflections of the wishes for them suggests that humanism is less a permanent element of religion than the mood of a school and an age and that it rests, to a greater extent than theism, upon theory and psychological speculation.

According to that theory, theistic religion—belief in the kingdom of God—is "a grandiose fiction projected by human needs and desires."[3] "The world for early man . . . was full of mysterious forces which operated on his life. Is it any wonder that the tribe faced the world with apprehension and *projected* into it its fears and hopes? *Imagination* and *emotion* played over the world like a searchlight."[4] To "create" gods, primitive man "took the natural and easy way of personification and projection."[5] As the deity of monotheism emerged, imagination "magnified the powers of this divine agent and made him superlative, omniscient, and omnipotent; and on the other hand, it socialized and ethicized him. *In this fashion, man projected into the universe his own sense of personal agency.*"[6] "The values prized in those religions that have ideal elements are idealizations of things characteristic of natural association, which have then been projected into a supernatural realm for safe-keeping and sanction."[7] "What noble things might be accomplished if we recognized in our insistence upon cosmic companionship a deflection of the desire for fellowship with our kind, and in the craving for transcendental support of our ideals a distortion of our deep interest in human well-being and progress![8] Give up the quest for companionship with a being behind or within the fleeting aspect of nature; assume the universe to be indifferent towards the human venture that means everything to us; accept the stern condition of being psychically alone, adrift in infinite space on our little earth, the sole custodians of our ideals: and we may then, with new zest, enter the warm valley of earthly

[3] Walter Lippmann, *op. cit.,* p. 143.
[4] R. W. Sellars, *Religion Coming of Age,* p. 56. Italics are Professor Sellars's.
[5] *ibid.,* p. 68.
[6] *ibid.,* p. 159. Italics are Professor Sellars's.
[7] John Dewey, *A Common Faith,* p. 73.
[8] M. C. Otto, *Things and Ideals,* p. 279.

experience—warm with human impulse, aspiration, and affection, warm with the unconquerable thing called life—and so discover in a growing human solidarity, in a progressively ennobled humanity, in an increasing joy in living, the goal we have all along blindly sought, and build on earth the fair city we have looked for in a compensatory world beyond."[9]

Even for others equally avid to bare illusion, to assume proper responsibility for making ideals effective, and to enrich and enjoy life, doubts about this humanistic view of religion inevitably arise. If personification was natural, easy, and largely unconscious for primitive men, not only is it strange that, in so far as it "worked" for them, it was utterly false, but it is stranger still that, with the growth of civilization, it should deepen and develop instead of withering and dying—unless reality rightly evokes some sort of "personifying" response from us. False theories and false attitudes sometimes last as long as that, but they do not flourish in the same way. Whether we accept it or despise it, the idea of God is, according to its fullness, one of the most subtle, pervasive, and incredibly fruitful powers which affect our lives. "Atavism," "frustration," "deflection" may partially account for this miraculous state, but to do so entirely would be another miracle. Actual human fellowship, projected desires for companionship, and communion with God are distinguishable enough not to be confused. Deflections and mixtures of the first two may embellish or encrust the third, may be anthropomorphic features intrinsic to human experience, but so far from creating or exhausting divine communion they are recognized as woefully incommensurable with it. Though human solidarity and scientific invention may elbow it aside, neither one nor both of them can take its place.[10] Nor is there

[9] *ibid.*, pp. 289-90. Altered and condensed without changing the meaning.

[10] Nothing could testify more vividly to the unique worth of God and of communion with Him than the pathetic substitutes for Him which crop up continually in humanistic writings. An especially moving and sincere example appears in an address (entitled "What Has Happened to Humanism?") delivered in the Unitarian Church of Evanston, Ill. (which has "consciously followed Humanist lines and called avowedly Humanist ministers") on December 8, 1935, by its minister, Mr. R. Lester Mondale.

"In the last five years what you have seen develop here is only what has transpired in some degree and in one form or another everywhere in Humanism:

need of that; for nature and supernature, despite, perhaps because of, their tensions, complement rather than exclude one another. Our craving for ultimate worth is no "distortion" of "interest in human well-being and progress." It is a different matter altogether;

an increasing conviction that above the animal and the humanistic in man is a spirit, a transcending self; and that this self, this Emersonian Oversoul, once it obeys the laws of the spirit, laws such as we discover in the Sermon on the Mount or in some of the teachings of the Buddha, becomes not only a source of health and radiance, but seems somehow to bind us to all men and to the life of the universe. In fact we wonder at times if the essential self is not identical with that power in the universe which flames in the star, and which, with the tools of evolution, fashioned the human mind. My real self, a focal point of the creative power of the universe! How can this be Humanism? Don't forget that the Humanists used to talk about a creative power. The new development is simply that now, instead of talking vaguely about this power, we feel it, know it. I have recently found myself uplifted by many an old hymn that would have left me cold in the days of orthodox Humanism.

> " 'O Master, let me walk with thee
> In lowly paths of service free;
> Teach me thy secret; help me bear
> The strain of toil, the fret of care.'

> " 'O God, our help in ages past,
> Our hope for years to come,
> Be thou our guard while troubles last,
> And our eternal home.'

> " 'Life of all that lives below!
> Let thy spirit in us flow;
> Let us all thy life receive,
> From thee, in thee, ever live.'

"In my enjoyment of these verses, disallowing some leaps of poetic license, I do not for a minute feel that there is any blind leap of faith, but only the reality of common experience worked over by one whose mind is, I hope, as Humanistically realistic and critical as it ever was. . . .

"I believe we cling to the mental attitudes of science and scholarship as firmly as ever; and if we sing the hymn:

> " 'Life of all that lives below,
> Let thy spirit in us flow. . .'

and if we talk about an Oversoul, this development is not a mere retrogression to, a compromise with, Fundamentalism or Theism, but the natural unfolding of that long stretch of humanity in the religious traditions of Western Civilization."

We are willing to brush aside our personal conviction that theism fits this "reality of common experience" far better than humanism does, in the joy of finding, amid surface differences, a tacit agreement that religion involves (what theism has always but often, for some people, offensively maintained) "intimacy with the Ultimate."

or better—for there is continuity too—it is a stimulus, touchstone, and consummation for human activity. But it no more paralyzes the business of earth or detracts from mundane values than does a sunrise or a sunset or any other glory beyond our patronage and device. In short the command, "Down from the mountain tops; back to your burrows; eyes on the earth!" suggests, if not a fear of life, a fear of reality, an "escape mechanism" from a realm erroneously condemned as too large and alien for us. Hence a compensatory world here and a protesting-too-much rhetoric about how "progressively ennobled" we become by squeezing into a "warm valley" and ignoring everything else.

Such beliefs are held as consequences of the theory that religion is projection. Although some humanists may rightly protest that for them religion never was entirely a matter of projection, or that, if it once was, it is so no longer, a summary discussion of collective beliefs must occasionally slight the individual for the sake of his group. That humanism is typically subjective as regards religion and that its subjectivism rests chiefly on the idea of "projection" is an impression which most students of the movement cannot avoid. Hence in this chapter we shall examine briefly the hypothesis of projection, which humanists generally accept ready-made. We shall start with it where (at least in its current form) it started, in the works of Dr. Freud and Dr. Jung, and we shall follow it through some of its most important manifestations in humanism.

Before we were armed with the helmet of reason and the sword of science, we were—Dr. Freud assures us—helpless as children. And as a child rushes to his father for comfort, so we, when earthly parents failed, instinctively approached the sovereign forces of nature with the fearful love that we found effective in influencing our early environment.[11] "He shall cry unto me, Thou art my Father, my God, and the rock of my salvation."[12] "After this manner therefore pray ye: Our Father who art in heaven, hallowed be Thy name. Thy kingdom come. Thy will be done on

[11] S. Freud, *The Future of an Illusion*, translated by W. D. Robson-Scott (London: Hogarth Press, 1928), pp. 29, 30, 31, 38, 41; *Civilization and its Discontents*, translated by J. Riviere (London: Hogarth Press, 1930), p. 21.
[12] Ps. lxxxix. 26.

earth, as it is in heaven."[13] But the Bible is too full of traces of a "father-complex"[14] to exact quotation. Recourse to a divine father to correct the imperfections of society and to save from "the crushing supremacy of nature"[15] the "achievements and institutions" that "differentiate our lives from those of our animal forebears"[16] possesses, on Dr. Freud's showing, considerable "subjective" value (which naturally leads to some important "objective" effects) and testifies to a high level of civilization.[17]

But it is not the highest, because religious ideas instead of being "the residue of experience or the final result of reflection" are "illusions, fulfilments of the oldest, strongest, and most insistent wishes of mankind"—the longing for parental protection.[18] "An illusion is not the same as an error, it is indeed not necessarily an error.[19] . . . It is a characteristic of the illusion that it is derived from men's wishes;[20] in this respect it approaches the psychiatric delusion, but it is to be distinguished from this. . . . In the delusion we emphasize as essential the conflict with reality; the illusion need not necessarily be false, that is to say, unreliable or incompatible with reality. . . . According to one's personal attitude one will classify [a belief] as an illusion or as analogous to a delusion."[21] "It does not lie within the scope of this enquiry to estimate the value of religious doctrines as truth. It suffices that we have recognized them, psychologically considered, as illusions."[22]

Dr. Freud hesitates no more than anyone else to compare some religious doctrines to delusions—"taking adequately into account the psychological differences."[23] His desire to be scrupulously

[13] Matt. vi. 9-10.
[14] *The Future of an Illusion*, p. 53.
[15] *ibid.*, p. 37.
[16] *Civilization and its Discontents*, p. 49.
[17] *ibid.*, p. 58.
[18] *The Future of an Illusion*, p. 52.
[19] *ibid.*, p. 53.
[20] cf. "We call a belief an illusion when wish-fulfilment is a prominent factor in its motivation, while disregarding its relations to reality, just as the illusion itself does." *ibid.*, pp. 54-5.
[21] *ibid.*, p. 54.
[22] *ibid.*, p. 57.
[23] *ibid.*, p. 55.

accurate about differences and to keep within the scope of his enquiry does not deprive his work of references to religion as "the
universal obsessional neurosis of humanity," "incompatible with
reality," and "a state of blissful hallucinatory confusion."[24] But
such sallies, like dubbing religious dogmas "neurotic survivals,"
he relegates to a "so to speak" category[25] expressing less a rational
conclusion than a "personal attitude."

Though his attitude might oblige one to conjecture that his
atheism grew from unhappy incidents of childhood, isolation from
ordinary religious life, and the distorting effect of unusual exposure to abnormal situations and influences, those might be causes
or conditions of his belief rather than a reason for it. The nearest
approach to a reason seems to be his indelible idea that "scientific
work is our only way to the knowledge of external reality."[26] It
is vain for him partially to recognize that (since wishes and desires
animate them as well as religion) science, knowledge of the external world, society, civilization itself, can be (in all consistency,
must be) treated on his theory as illusions.[27] Such a theory would
seem to be either a pastime, like Adam's, or the "primal father's,"
naming things in the Garden of Eden, or an annihilation of the
facts—itself included—that it sets out to explain. It is vain for
him to admit that man has other needs, joys, and realities than
those of reason, least of all those of the narrowly restricted sphere
of scientific reason;[28] for, unconsciously retracting every wider
view, he concludes: "No, science is no illusion. But it would be an

---

[24] *ibid.*, p. 76. "Judgments of value made by mankind are immediately determined
by their desires for happiness: . . . those judgments are attempts to prop up
their illusions with arguments. . . . Each one of us behaves in some respect like
the paranoiac, substituting a wish-fulfilment for some aspect of the world which
is unbearable to him, and carrying this delusion through into reality. When a
large number of people make this attempt together and try to obtain assurance
of happiness and protection from suffering by a delusional transformation of
reality it acquires special significance. The religions of humanity, too, must be
classified as mass delusions of this kind. Needless to say, no one who shares a
delusion recognizes it as such." *Civilization and its Discontents*, pp. 143 and 36;
cf. p. 27.

[25] *The Future of an Illusion*, p. 77.

[26] *ibid.*, p. 55.

[27] *ibid.*, p. 59.

[28] *ibid.*, pp. 61-2.

illusion to suppose that we can get anywhere else what it cannot give us."[29]

When we try to discover why science supposedly undermines belief in God, the only reason that emerges from the jungle of conflicting assertions and psychological fancies is the occasional implication that sense-perception alone is the sufficient source and test of objective reality.[30] There is no need here to rehearse the limitations of "the senses"; to set forth the way in which other forms and functions of knowledge modify and supplement them; or to indicate that if he strained not merely God—who, as "dwelling in light unapproachable, whom no man hath seen, nor can see,"[31] is least likely to be found in such fashion—but supra-sensuous aspects of personal relations, esthetics, logic, mathematics (in short, of all science and experience), through the sieve of "verification by sense-perception,"[32] Dr. Freud would find little or nothing left. All this, which is obvious to most people, needs no exposition here, because—unless the preceding chapter erred—humanists themselves admit it as generally as they forget it.

Urging us to cultivate our "plots" like "honest crofters on this earth,"[33] Dr. Freud seems to be content with a socially efficient—though, to some, a small and tame—"warm valley." Where science and machinery fail—and they cannot begin to meet our wants—he tells us to resign ourselves. Resignation is inevitable. Does not the Christian come to the same end when he confesses the inscrutability of his God?[34] Needless to say, the Christian can be as honest a crofter, as good a mechanic, as any other. But as the inscrutability of his God is not that of meaningless Ananke,[35] his is no blank resignation but joyful trust in One whose love and wisdom

[29] *ibid.*, p. 98.
[30] Dr. C. C. J. Webb reaches the same conclusion in Chap. IV of his *Religion and Theism.*
[31] I Tim. vi. 16.
[32] C. C. J. Webb, *Religion and Theism* (London: Allen and Unwin, 1934), p. 129.
[33] *The Future of an Illusion*, pp. 85 *ff.* "Plots" and "crofters" are in the singular in the original text.
[34] *Civilization and its Discontents*, p. 42.
[35] cf. *ibid.*, p. 136.

exceeds all that he can desire. "I bow," Dr. Freud remarks, perhaps with sadness as well as amusement, "to their reproach that I have no consolation to offer them; for at bottom this is what they all demand—the frenzied revolutionary as passionately as the most pious believer."[36]

As the foundation of his philosophy of religion, Dr. Jung develops Dr. Freud's concept of libido. A notion so subtle that it eludes many critics and so hospitable to countless unknown manifestations of non-rational elements of our nature that it appears to others as an explanation needing explanation,[37] merits definition by its principal employer. "Originally taken from the sexual sphere, this word [libido] has become the most frequent technical expression of psychoanalysis, for the simple reason that its significance is wide enough to cover all the unknown and countless manifestations of the Will in the sense of Schopenhauer."[38] It "has functionally the same significance in the biological territory as had the conception of energy since the time of Robert Mayer in the physical realm."[39] Libido, "in my view," Dr. Jung continues, "is synonymous with *psychic energy*. Psychic energy is the intensity of psychic process—its psychological value. By this I do not imply any imparted value, whether moral, esthetic, or intellectual; the psychological value is simply conditioned by its *determining* power, which is manifested in definite psychic operations ('effects'). Neither do I understand libido as a psychic *force*, a misunderstanding that has led many critics astray. I do not hypostasize the concept of energy, but employ it as a concept denoting intensity or value. The question as to whether or no a specific psychic force exists has nothing to do with the concept of libido."[40]

[36] *ibid.*, p. 143.
[37] cf. A. R. Uren, *Recent Religious Psychology*, pp. 272 and 275.
[38] C. G. Jung, *Psychology of the Unconscious*, translated by B. M. Hinkle (London: Kegan Paul, Trench, Trubner, 1921), p. 75.
[39] *ibid.*, p. 76.
[40] C. G. Jung, *Psychological Types*, translated by H. G. Baynes (London: Kegan Paul, Trench, Trubner, 1923), p. 571, as there italicized. cf. p. 138 of Dr. Jung's *Modern Man in Search of a Soul* (London: Kegan Paul, Trench, Trubner, 1933).
"It will have become fairly clear that while we set out without defining too precisely what we mean by 'sex,' or what Freud calls 'libido,' the term grows

137

God, for Dr. Jung, is "the representative of a certain sum of energy (libido)," which is "projected (metaphysically)" in accordance with its way of working "from the unconscious outwards."[41] The "strong feeling" identified with the "sum of libido" "is what gives character and reality to" the representation-complex. *The attributes and symbols of the divinity must belong in a consistent manner to the feeling (longing, love, libido, and so on).* If one honors God, the sun or the fire, then one honors one's own vital force, the libido. . . . God is our own longing to which we pay divine honors."[42] The strength of libido gives it "the character of absolute superiority to the conscious will of the subject; hence it can enforce or bring about a standard of accomplishment that would be unattainable to conscious effort. This overwhelming impulse—in so far as the divine function is manifested in action— or this inspiration that transcends all conscious understanding, proceeds from a heaping-up of energy in the unconscious. This libido-accumulation animates images which the collective unconscious contains as latent possibilities. Here is the source of the God-*imago*, that imprint which from the beginning of time has been the collective expression of the most powerful and absolute operation of unconscious libido-concentration upon conscious-

wider as we examine it. Freud himself has been led to an ever wider conception of 'libido,' and some of those psychoanalysts who were at first his disciples even go to the extreme in minimizing what is ordinarily understood as the impulse of sex. . . . This enlargement of libido is . . . in accordance with the general tendency of psychology, which now seems to regard innate tendencies we inherit from our animal ancestors as merely specific differentiations of a single life-impulse. . . .

"It is, indeed, interesting to note that Jung in his much criticized enlargement of the connotation of 'libido,' beyond the earlier Freudian exclusively sexual sense, was really returning to the original classical sense of 'passion or desire in general.' It thus comes into line with Schopenhauer's 'Will' and Bergson's 'élan vital,' and Burt is able to define it as general conative energy proceeding from all the instincts." Havelock Ellis, *Psychology of Sex* (New York: Emerson, 1935), pp. 357-8.

Schopenhauer and Bergson use Will and *élan vital* as cosmic or ontological concepts, whereas Jung keeps libido almost exclusively within the bounds of psychology and biology.

[41] *Psychology of the Unconscious*, p. 38.

[42] *ibid.*, p. 52, as there italicized.

ness."[43] "Psychologically, God always signifies the greatest value, hence the greatest sum of libido, the greatest intensity of life, the *optimum* of psychological activity."[44]

The expression of "unconscious contents" or "libido-accumulation" identified by Dr. Jung with God has, he claims, been historically thought of in almost any combination and transition of dynamic images, animal attributes, and human personification, male or female, adult or infantile.[45] Increasing civilization, or insulation from the elemental forces of nature, has apparently tended to supplant inanimate and animal attributes with symbols derived from the parent-complex. Dr. Jung elaborates Dr. Freud's position that a child's reminiscences and impressions of his parents, or of those who stand to him *in loco parentis*, together with the influence of racial phantasies and sentiments connected with the relations between parents and children, direct and color his religious (and much of his other) experience.[46] Though Dr. Jung agrees with Dr. Freud that "resistance to incest"[47] represses the parent *imago,* so that we rarely if ever think of God in the forms of our actual parents, he does not believe that explanation to be exhaustive, "since it overlooks the extraordinary significance of this symbolical replacement."[48]

He criticizes Dr. Freud and Dr. Alfred Adler because their methods are "reductive." They treat the idea of God, he argues, as a sign, "as merely a semiotic expression," of either "reminiscences of actual events" or of infantile, or primitive, elementary processes "of wishing or striving." Hence the unconsciously produced "father-complex," or idea of God, becomes figurative and

[43] *Psychological Types*, pp. 300-1.

[44] *ibid.*, p. 222; cf. *ibid.*, p. 307.

[45] *ibid.*, p. 306; *Psychology of the Unconscious*, p. 38.

[46] *Psychology of the Unconscious*, p. 53; *Psychological Types*, p. 156. cf.: "The best proof of the immortality of the soul, or of God's existence, etc., is the impression of it one gets in childhood—that is to say the proof which (in contrast to the many learned and grandiloquent proofs) might be expressed thus: It is perfectly certain, for my father told me so." (Kierkegaard, quoted by Dr. Lowrie, *op. cit.*, p. 311.)

[47] cf. *Psychology of the Unconscious*, pp. 256-7.

[48] *Psychological Types*, p. 157, as there italicized; cf. *Psychology of the Unconscious*, pp. 38, 54.

unreal. Its intrinsic significance is robbed, either by being traced back to its historical antecedents instead of being considered on its own merits, or by being "once again reintegrated into the same elementary process from which it arose"—a reintegration almost equivalent to saying that the seed and the flower are identical.[49] In either case their method of explanation tends to dissolve the fact to be explained and to equate it, historically or actually, with something simpler, poorer, and other than itself.[50]

Attempting to avoid this pitfall, Dr. Jung distinguishes between sign and symbol, eschews the former, and cleaves to the latter. "Every view which interprets the symbolic expression as an analogous or abbreviated expression of a known thing is *semiotic*. A conception which interprets the symbolic expression as the best possible formulation of a relatively unknown thing which cannot conceivably, therefore, be more clearly or characteristically represented is symbolic."[51] Religious devotion "is a regressive movement of the libido towards the primordial, a diving down into the source of first beginnings."[52] In those primeval depths it finds vague but vivid impressions of its own and its race's infancy. Did it remain content with concrete or sensuous reminiscences of parental care, it would indeed have merely "regressed." But (if others may mix metaphors as freely as Dr. Jung) a "sign" of actual parents does not hang like a millstone to the neck of true devotion, anchoring it in the unconscious. Rather devotion creates, or discovers, or somehow becomes assimilated to, and "emerges" with, a symbol (God) representing "a comprehensive resultant of all the unconscious factors." Thus it stoops ("regresses" into the unconscious) to conquer (to "progress" into the conscious).[53]

The God-*imago* possesses strength and universality because it formulates "an essential unconscious factor." "Since, on the one hand, the symbol is the best possible expression of what is still un-

---

[49] cf. R. H. Thouless, *An Introduction to the Psychology of Religion* (Cambridge University Press, 1924), p. 138.
[50] *Psychological Types*, pp. 584-5.
[51] *ibid.*, p. 601. Italics his.
[52] *ibid.*, p. 157; cf. pp. 309-11.
[53] *ibid.*, pp. 157-8.

known—an expression, moreover, which cannot be surpassed for the given epoch—it must proceed from the most complex and differentiated contemporary mental atmosphere. But since, on the other hand, the living symbol must embrace and contain that which relates a considerable group of men for such an effect to be within its power, it must contain that which may be common to a large group of men. Hence, this can never be the most highly differentiated or the highest attainable, since only the very few could attain to, or understand it; but it must be something that is still so primitive that its omnipresence stands beyond all doubt.[54] Only when the symbol comprises this something, and brings it to the highest possible expression, has it any general efficacy.[55] Therein consists the potent and, at the same time, redeeming effect of a living, social symbol."[56] The "redeeming effect" is not "rational" (though it may accord with reason), because ordinary reason—Dr. Jung might better have said "rationalism"—cannot "turn" the symbol "to account in the objective world." Nevertheless the God-*imago* and religious devotion create and assure "subjective happiness and well-being, irrespective of the changing aspects of outer conditions."[57] They do so (though Dr. Jung does not make this too evident) when men want not merely the crumbs called truth and science but the entire loaf of reality.

And they do so (as he frequently observes) when men believe that God is not a by-product of something else but has an inde-

---

[54] That which is common to a large group of men and not highly differentiated by them need not be "primitive" in the sense of rude or debased. Man's moral and religious nature is a primitive (i.e. ancient, fundamental) element of his constitution, which as much as—often more than—anything else binds him to his fellows. It may be "beneath" him in blind power and yet "above" him in potentialities exceeding his grasp but not his reach. This is recognized by humanists who (like those in The Fellowship of Liberal Religion, Ann Arbor, Mich.) sing as a hymn the following lines by A. S. Isaacs:

"A noble life, a simple faith,
An open heart and hand—
These are the lovely litanies
Which all men understand."

[55] Such a test would seem to favor popular theistic religions as against the speculations of humanists and their like.

[56] *Psychological Types*, p. 605.

[57] *ibid.*, pp. 311-12.

pendent reality of His own, superior to all others, and one that must be reckoned with. The effectiveness of religion and the health of civilization—for Dr. Jung, like Dr. Freud, recognizes that religion is, or at least until now has been, essential to society—depend on the strength and purity of that belief and the character of its object. Yet according to Dr. Jung the belief is a delusion, because religious devotion, which claims to refer to what is the most intimate and ultimate[58] in all reality, truly refers to what is most intimate and ultimate in ourselves, namely, libido. It is beside the point to note that, in his occasional caricatures of theism, Dr. Jung seems to ignore the distinction between relativity in our knowledge of God and the absoluteness of His being; to overemphasize His transcendence; and so far to underrate His immanence as to imply that, for theism, He is completely severed from the unconscious.[59] Such an involuntary misrepresentation results from psychology's attempt to become a natural science by the common but suicidal method of treating abstract mental states as alone real and by assuming that philosophy and theology are unaware of psychological functions and relativities and deal only with the illusive or delusive ontological objects to which they refer. Applied to psychology itself this method would find there, as wherever it looks, a welter of relativism, wish-fulfilment, and subjectivism.[60] Even had Dr. Jung given theism credit for recognizing relative and psychological aspects of our apprehension of God, that would not have perceptibly lessened the gulf between the older opinions and his own; because for him "God is not even relative, but a function of the unconscious, namely the manifestation of a split-off sum of libido, which has activated the God-*imago*."[61]

We end, as we started, with libido. But how did Dr. Jung ever come to think of God as merely "a psychological function of man"?[62] He followed a course of abstraction similar to that by

[58] The adjectives are Dr. C. C. J. Webb's but they are not inappropriate here.
[59] *Psychological Types*, p. 301.
[60] cf. C. C. J. Webb, *Religion and Theism* (London: Allen and Unwin, 1934), pp. 94 *ff*.
[61] *Psychological Types*, p. 301.
[62] *ibid.*, p. 300.

which people pretend to be persuaded, for instance, that tables and chairs are "really" nothing more than light waves or some other sort of "pointer readings." As a problem in physics may begin, "An elephant slides down a grassy hillside," which is inserted simply "to give an impression of realism,"[63] so Dr. Jung asks us to start with belief in God in all its concrete fullness. Now, if you do not object, use a little "more than ordinary attention" and have your "unconscious contents" "withdrawn from their projections into objects."[64] To do this, switch from the personal point of view of one practising religion to the impersonal point of view of one observing it from the outside. Now quietly alter what you are observing; that is, drop out God while at the same time continuing a phase of consciousness (religious devotion) that has no value, significance, or existence, apart from its reference to Him, or—if the word "God" is not used—at least to what is held by the believer in the moment of worship or supplication to be, for all practical purposes, reality in its fullest, most intimate, and ultimate form. If you find it difficult directly to discern that "unconscious process" (religious devotion minus religion), you may discern it "at least by inference."[65] How now does communion with God appear? If you will ignore the fact that for that communion you have substituted an amorphous indescribable psychological state abstracted as far as can be conceived—indeed considerably farther —from any sort of object or reference other than itself, you must answer with Dr. Jung, "as belonging to and conditioned by the subject."[66] Let us be a little more precise. Without speculating as to what the subject is, let us content ourselves with considering belief in God—now recognized not merely as conditioned by the subject but (apart from its racial connections) as cut off absolutely from anything but the subject—as an intensity of psychic

[63] Sir Arthur Eddington, *The Nature of the Physical World* (New York: Macmillan, 1929), p. 251.
[64] *Psychological Types*, p. 301.
[65] *ibid*.
[66] *ibid*.

process, as an abstraction of an abstraction, as, to repeat, a "man-ifestation of a split-off sum of libido."[67]

Thus with a clarity at which one might think he would be dis-mayed Dr. Jung outlines an "explanation" of theistic religion as "reductive" (though in a different way) as those he criticized in Dr. Freud and Dr. Adler. With them he concludes, "*I think belief should be replaced by understanding*"[68]—a proposition which many accept (differently) but which for him implies a view of reality roughly similar to that of the pessimistic humanists. As re-ligion is an adaptation (in Dr. Jung's eyes a faulty one) to the demands of life, so reason, or understanding, is a firmly estab-lished complex "handed down to us through the ages, to the or-ganization of which countless generations have laboured with the same necessity with which the nature of the living organism, in general, reacts to the average and constantly recurring conditions of the environment."[69] But a blended psychological, evolutionary, and pragmatic account of reason being accepted as at any rate partially true, has not the experience of the race found it richer and more fruitful—without minimizing the stimulus and the light one discipline affords another—to appreciate or to criticize religion through religion, science through science—each sphere of life through its own practice or enjoyment—rather than, as Dr. Jung and Dr. Freud actually if not intentionally prefer, religion through science and science through something less than itself?

The overawing psychological genius of Dr. Freud and the im-pressive contributions of his disciples probably are sufficient to account for the uncritical manner in which humanists accept as a palpable fact what others have long dismissed as a vagary, namely, the notion that belief in God is merely "projection." In one form or another that mixture of subjectivism and relativism can be traced over two thousand years to the sophists. Although earlier but less well known names possibly deserve the distinction, Leibnitz is usually given the honor of having first adumbrated the closely

[67] *ibid.*
[68] *Psychology of the Unconscious*, p. 145, as there italicized.
[69] *Psychological Types*, p. 583.

related ideas of the subconscious and the unconscious, which play an important part in "projection." Psychoanalysts like Dr. Freud and Dr. Jung have revived rather than created, and exaggerated rather than normally developed, these historic tendencies. About the beginning of the twentieth century Baron Friedrich von Hügel showed the limitations of many ideas and fallacies discussed so far in this chapter, which were then rampant in psychology of religion, though they have only recently been promulgated by humanists. His knowledge was common property; for his philosophical gift—less striking than his religious insight—lay in sifting and synthesizing the best thought of his time. None of this, however, seems to have made any impression on humanists. Unless memory fails, Dr. Inge somewhere remarks that he has reached the happy stage of being able not to read books: those with which he agrees, because he knows what they will say; those with which he disagrees, because he does not care what they will say. But that which Dr. Inge prizes as a luxury of old age, humanists appear to exercise as a birthright.

Owing to its many kinds and degrees, religion has acquired in popular usage a vagueness to which the rise and fall of new sects daily testify. These pages perhaps follow Mr. Thwackum too closely in thinking of religion primarily in its higher theistic forms.[70] They differ from him not in preferring a definite type of Christianity to "religion-in-general," but in confining themselves to reasons for supposing a theistic conception of God to be essential to religion at its best, or, at any rate, to be preferable to any substitute now available. The apprehension of a God worthy of human worship, which they thus presuppose as a condition of mature, rather than of any, religion, has, like most kinds of human experience, objective and subjective aspects. The worshipper is aware of his own gropings and of something incomparably other and superior to himself, towards communion with which he is

[70] "When I mention religion I mean the Christian religion; and not only the Christian religion, but the Protestant religion; and not only the Protestant religion, but the Church of England." *The History of Tom Jones*, by Henry Fielding, Book II, Chap. III.

145

drawn. As a later chapter will indicate, this state differs from any other form of subject-object and subject-subject relationship. Nevertheless a psychology apt to throw light upon it must be capable of dealing successfully with those simpler experiences.

But the method of the psychology presupposed by humanists prevents it from doing this. As Dr. Webb has shown in his *Religion and Theism*, unlike the natural sciences, which deal with objects of consciousness, psychology—at least the kind used by humanists, which, in spite of its being one school among many, will in this discussion be referred to, for convenience, as psychology—attempts to deal with consciousness itself. Yet consciousness, certainly in its clearest form of knowledge and perception, is always consciousness of something distinguishable from itself. This psychologists realistically presume in regard to their own knowledge. But when they deal with anything other than psychology and try to be "scientific" about it, they usually begin by describing knowledge, tacitly or explicitly, as a "correspondence between our thoughts and feelings on the one side and sensible experience on the other,"[71] sensible experience being the source and the criterion of knowledge. To this as a frankly admitted, clearly understood, experimental, and descriptive expedient there could be no objection so long as a better procedure was lacking. But when psychologists, dulled by custom, use this abstractive device not merely as a method of classification but as an ultimate means of discriminating between truth and error, reality and delusion, they wreck themselves. As has already been remarked, a materialism, naturalism, or sensationalism of that sort is, when they are aware of it, rejected by humanists as heartily if not so effectively as by Messrs. C. C. J. Webb, R. H. Thouless, J. H. Leighton, F. R. Barry, S. Wilde, and J. B. Pratt, to mention but a few names well known in the field.

What is more, psychologists themselves, apparently struck by the arbitrariness of their distinction between sensation (as the only source of reality) and other forms of consciousness (as misleading or ontologically irrelevant), soon move on to the more

[71] *Religion and Theism* (London: Allen and Unwin, 1934), p. 96.

consistent but remote stage of confining themselves entirely to consciousness and of abandoning, to other disciplines and ultimately to the "scrutiny of the critical intellect," the discussion of the reality or the falsity of objects to which consciousness, even as sensation, refers.[72] But the barrenness of conscious states apart from their objective references (above all in religion) and the human proclivity to take upon ourselves the duties of judges and oracles soon lead these psychologists to retrace their steps to the point of asserting that religion can be explained entirely by "natural causes."

If this involves no return to crude sensationalism and no denial of the countless levels of reality, it is an obsure, encouraging, over-optimistic statement. Over-optimistic, because no science (nor all of them together) is yet rash enough to pretend—or of such a nature as ever to be able justly to pretend—that it has correctly discovered, analyzed, and interpreted all the causes of a given effect. That of itself need not imply breaks in the causal order but only our inability to deal with it adequately. The progress of psychology or of any other science in extending the sway of the concept of causality should be encouraging as an intimation of harmony between "external reality" and one of the most fundamental exigencies of our minds. But the notion of explaining religion (or anything else) entirely by natural causes and of expecting complete satisfaction from such a course is intrinsically obscure. In ordinary scientific procedure, a cause describes "how" but not "why" anything is or happens, nor how it should be valued by us. Projection, suggestion, wish-fulfilment, in one form or another, are the "causes" upon which humanists rely when others fail. A strange intellectual asceticism compels them to treat "effective grounds," or "practical motivation," of beliefs and actions with which they cannot sympathize, as false, irrational, and un-

[72] This degree of abstraction and of almost heraldic ineffectualness is well summed up by A. R. Uren, *op. cit.*, p. 196: "It is the prerogative of psychology to make authoritative reports concerning human consciousness and its experiences; but the pronouncements of such a science, affirmative or negative, as to the real existence of the ultimate causes, and realities corresponding to subjective experiences, are as gratuitous as they are valueless."

real.[73] They take care, however, to use their *argumentum ad hominem* in situations where it is unlikely to be turned against themselves. But even supposing that—as everybody believes and desires—natural causes can be found for religion and can be utilized to enlighten and enrich it and the lives of which it is a part, humanists will scarcely help to bring this about so long as they argue in the manner that Professor Thouless, for example, exposed some time ago in his *Introduction to the Psychology of Religion*. Simply to outline the argument is the best way to refute it. Where nature and natural causes are—thus they start—supernature or God cannot be also. God, therefore, if He exists at all, must appear in the gaps of natural causation as psychology (which turns out to be the psychologist of the moment) understands it. But there are no gaps; so religion cannot be proved by psychology. Then comes the final jump: if it cannot be proved by psychology, God's existence (or anything else?) is not real.[74]

This chapter has emphasized "projection" and the "father surrogate" view of God not because it is the only or the major feature and foundation of religion but because it best exemplifies that "deflection" of human love upon which, in one form or another, humanists usually base their theory of religion. The "fatherhood of God," which for humanists suggests an unfortunate complex, libido accumulation, projection, and delusion, is for theists an inadequate metaphor struggling to express one of the personal relations between ultimate reality and human beings. The humanistic attack loses much of its force once it is recognized, as by Dr. Jung, that the divine "fatherhood" is not a finished, literal "sign" but a living "symbol"; that the childlike attitude prized in the Gospels is not the spoilt child's; and that disinterestedness, praised, for example, by Mr. Walter Lippmann, is, if accompanied by appro-

[73] cf. Thouless, *Introduction to the Psychology of Religion*, pp. 84, 85, 264, 265; Uren, *op. cit.,* pp. 227, 265, 274; and D. C. Macintosh, *Humanism, Another Battle Line*, p. 60.

Yet the unexpected will happen: Mr. Mondale (*op. cit.,* p. 11), for all his "clear-cut agnosticism," calls, more like a Catholic than a Unitarian, for "warmth, ruddiness, and reality of emotion in religion."

[74] cf. Thouless, *op. cit.,* pp. 261, 263.

priate warmth, imagination, and action, not alien to theistic religion, but, as long as so-called "impersonal" elements like truth, beauty, and goodness remain the essence of personality, the highest, most natural quality of personal relations between man and God.

That genuine walking with God is "redeeming," "the optimum of psychological activity," "uplifting," "creative," in short, at its best, the most indomitable force for good of which we are aware, is generally admitted by any student of religion, regardless of his explanation of it. The humanistic explanation, in so far as we could understand it, proved to be fallacious in itself, incompatible with belief in God (for which it realizes that it must, but not that it cannot, find an equivalent), and inconsistent with the commonly accepted postulates of science and civilization. That indicates not necessarily that humanism is false but that its argument is. If its argument reflects its nature, however, humanism would seem to err. Though it has gloated over past and present weaknesses of theism, nothing it has said so far logically precludes seeking God along fundamentally theistic lines. Whether such a search is normal or diseased, conducive to reality or to delusion, was the central question of this chapter. The result of the interminable discussions of this point, at least according to competent opinion then and now, was perhaps most simply, wisely, and inadvertently summarized in the following quotation from Professor Thouless.

"It has been said that religion is only a form of neurosis which, for some reason, is not regarded as pathological. There is, however, a good reason why the religious redirection of the libido is not considered to be pathological, for, unlike the neurotic symptom, it provides a permanent and satisfactory solution of the erotic conflict. . . . This would seem to suggest very strongly that the religious solution of the erotic conflict is different in kind from the neurotic solution, and that when the soul which has found no earthly satisfaction for its love[75] directs that love to God, it is doing something very different from the creation of a phantasy love-

[75] Or, as not infrequently happens, the happy soul which has found earthly satisfaction but is capable of more.

149

object in place of a real one. It has found a satisfactory resting-place for its love instead of finding an unsatisfactory solution of the conflict between desire and reality in the neurotic symptom or in the phantasy.[76] Now, many of the theories about religion which have been suggested by psychology of this type do, in fact, suppose that the objects of religion are merely phantasies woven by man to satisfy his emotional needs. But that there is this difference between the effectiveness of these two ways of dealing with his desires, seems to suggest that such different effects do not proceed from the same cause. . . . It seems reasonable to suppose that the genuine satisfactoriness of the religious solution of the erotic conflict is the result of the fact that its object is a real one—that God is not merely a phantasy creation of the worshipping mind."[77]

[76]
"It was too late for man,
But early yet for God;
Creation impotent to help,
But prayer remained our side.

"How excellent the heaven,
When earth cannot be had;
How hospitable, then, the face
Of our old neighbor, God!"
—Emily Dickinson, *op. cit.,* p. 171.

[77] *op. cit.,* pp. 277-8.

CHAPTER V

SYNOPSIS OF CHAPTER V

The opposition of humanistic liberalism to theism.
The "problem of evil." Humanistic caricature of
Christian morality. Relation between religion and
ethics. The place of emotion in morality. "The supremacy of personality." Humanistic principles and
proposals regarding the family and social, economic,
and international relations. The man-on-the-street's
response to these. A comparison of the humanistic
program with Comte's. The humanistic idea of democracy. The possibilities of humanistic education.

HUMANISM AND PRACTICAL ETHICS

H UMANISTS like to think of themselves as "liberals" in theology, ethics, sociology, and politics. Theoretically "liberalism" means to them, as to others, an independence, openness, and impartiality of mind, which welcomes truth regardless of source and consequence. Thus defined, liberalism, like science, is more an attitude than a body of doctrines. Difference of opinion about fact may lead liberals to positions virtually indistinguishable from those of radicals or reactionaries. But in practice liberalism for humanists is almost synonymous with democracy. They are not alone in prizing democracy for its recognition of every normal human being as an end in himself. Their belief in the supreme value of personality—a vestige of Christian regard for the worth of the immortal soul—naturally favors political, economic, and social conditions conducive to the best personal development possible for the greatest number.

From the beginning humanism applied its notion of democracy to religion. In 1917 or earlier Dr. Curtis W. Reese thus addressed his congregation from the pulpit of the First Unitarian Church, of Des Moines, Iowa: "The theocratic view of the world is autocratic. The humanistic view is democratic. . . . The humanistic or democratic view of the world order holds that this is man's world and that it largely depends on man what the world order shall be like. . . . This revolution in religion, from theocracy to humanism, from autocracy to democracy, has been brewing a long time. . . . Democratic religion takes the form of 'this-worldliness.' . . . The chief end of man, according to democratic religion, is to promote man's welfare here and now."[1]

For twenty years Dr. Reese's fellow humanists have echoed him. God's law, they have stoutly affirmed, is not our law. To obey Him is to deny ourselves, to become means to an end not ours.[2] How can The Other, possessing qualities beyond compare, help us to lead what He has never experienced—a moral human life?[3] Does not the distinction between God's law and our ethical practices and standards "distract energy, through dividing the objects to which it is directed"?[4] Are not the churches kept from promoting "social ends on a natural and equal human basis" by their peculiar, exclusive, and authoritative relation to supreme values?[5] A result of such "diverted aspiration is that the conditions of life are fixed by those who have no concern for human destiny, either in this world or any other."[6] Let us renounce, therefore, the "escape mechanism" of a kingdom of heaven and establish a rule of justice and goodness on earth. Though "Utopias are outmoded,"[7] let us meet natural evil (death, earthquake, storm, disease) with science, and social and individual evil with "intelligent adjustment of personal relations."[8]

That twenty years of such preaching (much of which sounds trite to everybody) should not have galvanized Christians dozing in their pews suggests that though humanists have found indubitable faults in the popular exposition and the practice of certain forms of organized religion they have no inkling of how real the immanence of God, and of how immaterial clumsy formulations of that fact, can be for believers. The Incarnation, the Atonement,

[1] Quoted by Mr. Edwin H. Wilson in "The Humanist Controversy in History."
[2] J. A. C. F. Auer, *op. cit.*, p. 65.
[3] *ibid.*, p. 72.
[4] J. Dewey, *A Common Faith*, p. 73.
[5] *ibid.*, p. 82. Wasn't this question answered by "the Episcopal clergyman who at an interdenominational meeting said, with benign tolerance, 'There may well be other ways of salvation, but of course no gentleman would take advantage of them'"? (*Amherst Alumni Council News*, Vol. XII, no. 4, March 1939, p. 163.)
[6] M. C. Otto, *Things and Ideals*, p. 288.
[7] A. E. Haydon, *The Quest of the Ages*, p. 148.
[8] *ibid.*, p. 147; cf. *ibid.*, pp. 141 *ff.*

and other contents of "the vocabulary of Christian dogma" are admittedly "old shibboleths" to humanists.[9] Perhaps it would not be polite to mention the provincial Protestant theology on which many humanist leaders were brought up and which, after they have abandoned it, they still unnecessarily confound with Christianity. It may be that humanism fails to impress Christians less because they are "unenlightened" than because their experience and constitution lead them to judge the same—and sometimes wider—evidence differently. The predominance of the tendency to absorption, synthesis, concreteness, continuity, and conservation, which roughly characterizes the "orthodox" in any field of thought or activity, will, under as nearly the same circumstances as possible, obviously lead to results differing from those of the proclivity to discrimination, analysis, abstraction, novelty, and change. The latter tendency in most people exercises its influence within the former. For them doubts and difficulties do not devastate; adjustments and compromises enrich more frequently than betray; gradual growth they prefer to haste, tension to simplification, fullness of life to "reason." Theists of that constitution regret God's absence more than His interference. If they are Christians, they become aware of Him, though imperfectly and subject to general Christian judgment, through intimations of sense, conscience, beauty, love, and truth. Duly authorized tradition (in human affairs, as Paul Bourget remarked, the nearest equivalent to experiment in natural science) is accepted, however, as a touchstone, norm, or rule of taste, only in so far as it proves itself to be the most fruitful guide available. As open and free as the scientific spirit, but in religious matters more sensitive, it preserves perennial youth through constant assimilation of the new.[10]

[9] cf. *The Humanist Bulletin,* March 1939, pp. 6, 7.

[10] "The Church must be forever building, for it is forever decaying within and attacked without." T. S. Eliot, *Collected Poems 1909-1935,* p. 187. Humanists sometimes pretend that if the Christianity of today is not exactly the same as that of yesterday or of tomorrow, it is not Christianity. Such a notion, perhaps partially applicable to inanimate objects, is certainly irrelevant to life, thought, and spirit. The gradual growth of Christianity, which humanists tax as a repudiation of the past, is as normal and enriching as that of the sciences.— "Every single generalization respecting mathematical physics, which I was

Ready as humanists to admit and combat the abuse of religion, theists seek that end not in reducing religion to something else but in making the most of it—in cultivating, through the proper use of natural means, better relations with God, which when true and sure improve (as when timid and false they warp) thought, feeling, and action.

Remembering these fundamental differences of outlook, in this chapter we shall touch briefly on some of the commoner concerns of humanistic ethics—the ancient "problem of evil," the nature of morality, and its relation to religion and emotion. In seeking the improvement of personality humanists and Christians agree as much as they disagree on what best constitutes that ideal and the means to it. We shall find that, on the level of thought on which this chapter moves, humanists, who usually confine themselves willingly to that level, accept the supreme worth of personality on faith, without scientific criticism or speculative justification. They do this in the name of practicality. In that name, therefore, we must examine their working principles and their program (in so far as they can be said to have one) for social relations, the family, economics, and world politics. On these points (which recall some of Comte's objectives) they speak neither at length nor as experts. But running through them all and determining the humanist attitude towards them are certain beliefs, which should not be ignored, about democracy and education and the conditions and the training that abet or retard them.

In view of their virtual immunity to one another's persuasion, it is not surprising that the occasional accords of humanists and theists rest on divergent grounds. Concerning evil, for example, a leading humanist writes: "Instead of escape and compensation, there is now courageous and confident acceptance of human responsibility."[11] Though it is difficult to know to whom we are responsible at the stage in humanistic ethical theory in which God

taught at the University of Cambridge during my student period from the year 1880 to 1885, has now been abandoned in the sense in which it was then held. The words are retained but with different meanings." A. N. Whitehead, *loc. cit.*, p. 262.

[11] A. E. Haydon, *The Quest of the Ages*, p. 148.

and a moral order of any sort are ruled out, the quotation at least implies the obvious fact that the mitigation of evil profits us. Putting aside questions of blame and desert and treating evil as impersonally as the weather, we can consider it—humanists suggest—entirely from the point of view of social utilitarianism. Instead of being related to a categorical imperative, or to a divine duty, or to one's sense of honor, responsibility, rescued from a morass of subjectivity and sentiment, takes on the color of a civic regulation, like that of keeping one's sidewalk clear of snow.

Welcoming this as an illustration of mundane, good-citizen morality, which (while denying that it is exhaustive) they would foster too, theists rejoice at the alleged ability of humanists to meet evils calmly and to accept full responsibility for those of their own production.[12] Suspecting the truth of a sheer antinomy between omnipotent righteousness and real evil, believers in God —when they lapse into an "explanation" of what they admit is, as commonly stated, inexplicable—tend to view evil as necessary to the evolution of finite creatures. If those claim exemption from evil least who, like the saints, best know how far they are from what they could and should be; if, as Hobbes says, only a present uneasiness makes us shift from one foot to another and, as history

[12] "Humanism accepts the responsibility for the conditions of human life and relies for their improvement entirely upon human effort, exerted in cooperation with cosmic forces. [Note the personal flavor of "cooperation," which suggests "response" from cosmic forces rather than mere "reaction."]

"The Humanist makes no attempt to shove the responsibility for the present miserable conditions of human life on to some God or some cosmic order.

"He fully realizes that the situation is in our own hands, and that practically all the evils of the world have been brought upon men by themselves.

"He frankly assumes the responsibility for the injustices inherent in our present social and economic order, and knows that if ever these are to be eliminated, it must be done by man himself.

"He assumes the responsibility for the feelings of envy and hatred and cruelty and murder which make these things possible, and knows that if ever we are to approach a state of brotherhood, in which justice and good are to prevail, man himself must eradicate the one attitude and foster the other.

"Humanism finds no other place of responsibility than human shoulders and no other hope of improvement than human effort." [How about the "cooperating" cosmic forces?]

From *The Liberal*, March 9, 1933, published weekly by The Liberal Center of Kansas City (Unitarian).

shows, only the worst suffering of the least guilty is likely to stir a qualm within us when our immediate interests are not affected: evil, though bad in itself, may, under certain conditions, develop our souls as Mephistopheles did Faust's. To turn to a bravely suffering finite godling in no wise mends matters; for, without solving the problem of evil—indeed aggravating it by subjecting God Himself to evil—it denies one of the deepest intuitions of religious faith, namely that in the Father of lights there is no variableness, nor shadow of turning.[13] He is the reality presupposed by our apprehension (in every aspect of consciousness) of the absolute, the perfect, and the infinite, on which depends a just appreciation of the relative, the imperfect, and the finite. Nor can it be said that humanists face evil calmly because they have no god to blame it on. Like their colleagues of the pessimistic school, they could "defy" an evil-tainted universe or chaos, instead, like theists, of meeting evil without disparaging the reality it haunts. Only when their confidence in "progress" as an elimination rather than a refinement of evil[14] becomes qualified by scrutiny do humanists cast about for "a power, not ourselves, that makes for righteousness,"[15] and, in diverse degrees of "moral order," face again—no more successfully—the same difficulties—slightly disguised—about evil in a good world, which first undermined their belief in God.

[13] Jas. i. 17. cf. "The Lord is King, be the people never so impatient; he sitteth between the cherubim, be the earth never so unquiet." Ps. xcix. 1.

[14] "La chrétienté passe actuellement par de trop effroyables catastrophes pour défendre plus longtemps un évolutionisme optimiste. Elle voit trop clairement que les plus grands efforts de l'homme pour créer de ses propres forces un monde meilleur, un royaume de justice, n'aboutissent pas. Si certains chrétiens identifiaient la Société des Nations avec le royaume de Dieu, c'était une erreur." Dr. Adolf Keller, "L'influence des révolutions continentales sur le protestantisme," Œcumenica, July 1935, p. 167. How poorly past disappointments prepare us for future ones! That an improved "standard of living" will inevitably sow new wants and defects does not justify the status quo. But humanists seem unable to recognize that no earthly success can bring full satisfaction, which is to be found —though some of them question whether it can be found at all—"where neither moth nor rust doth corrupt, and where thieves do not break through nor steal." Far from conflicting with or excluding one another, the two types of satisfaction (material and spiritual) should be complementary.

[15] Matthew Arnold, *Literature and Dogma*, Chap. X, section 4.

If the Church today impedes the spiritual and the material progress of individuals and society, if its theology disgusts and corrupts the mind, humanists prove their honesty by defending an
ethic uncontaminated by religion—as long as religion means communion with God. Morality, they maintain, as independent of belief in Him, suffers from contact with theism. To identify right
conduct with obedience to "a set of absolute moral rules of supramundane origin" in a deity of questionable existence[16] is, as
humanists claim, absurd. But who makes the identification? Presumably we are to suppose that Christians do, although few if any
of their thinkers today would dream of envisaging morality in
that manner. Indeed were it not for certain Protestant revivals of
Old Testament "legalism" and for a misunderstanding of Catholic
casuistry and codes of conduct devised more for disciplinary convenience than as epitomes of morality—were it not for mistaking
side roads for the highway of Christianity, it is difficult to see how
such a notion could become associated with a religion that from
the first has preferred the spirit to the letter of the law. But there
are as many types of that great living tradition, or of any other,
as there are times, places, people, and purposes. Not with the God
of St. John, or St. Paul, or St. Thomas Aquinas, not with the
God of artists, or scientists, or missionaries, or children, not with
the God of triumph or of despair, but only with the God of contemporary theists in their philosophical moods are we at this
particular instant concerned. However else they may have come to
think of Him, He is at least—as an abstract minimum—that which
makes things what they are. A "principle of concretion," an Absolute, the Idea of the Good, these and their numberless counterparts attempt not to describe fully (as those who easily ridicule
them pretend) but at least to point towards an ultimate reality
that must exist if we live in a world where diversity flourishes in
unity. Though Bertrand Russell argues that we may not live in
such a universe, it probably could be shown that the full flowering
of logic, science, art, morality, religion, and practical personal life,
on their deepest levels and in closest interrelation, presupposes the

16 J. A. C. F. Auer, *op. cit.*, p. 74.

159

contrary. That at least seems to be the verdict of the central or idealistic stream of human thought, which minor schools of philosophy and science divert and retard only to free again with accumulated force. Dostoevski asserts that some people think and feel with their stomachs, others with their heads. Life and thought for believers in God are less an observation of a set of rules than a tropism—than an obscure but fruitful awareness of and response to a reality essentially unlike us yet satisfying our most exacting demands in proportion to the fullness and justness of our devotion to it. This awareness of the uncomprehended but not unapprehended God is, to use Baron von Hügel's terms, the raw material out of which historic religions have been fashioned. The styles and the uses suit the material variously. The ultimate test is that of the material. If one can be a Catholic without being a Christian, so one can be a Christian without being religious. Christ is accepted only in so far as He *is* the way, the truth, and the life. In so far as He or any part of the religion bearing His name proves false to the underlying religious "tropism," modification of Christianity rightly ensues.

Hence to insinuate, as humanists virtually do, that Christian ethics is a set of absolute moral rules of supramundane origin in a deity of questionable existence[17] is about as accurate as to identify modern French art with the maxims of a contemporary Parisian studio. The supposition that we must live either by such a set of rules or "by a set of moral rules relative in their nature and of a this-worldly origin"[18]—which is only another way of saying that if we ascertain what is good or bad, false or true, God is thereby excluded[19]—strikes Christians as being (despite its merit as a protest against unbalanced absolutism, mere transcendence, and "static" authoritarianism) a false simplification. The disproof of an exclusively transcendental hypothesis instead of establishing a

[17] For philosophy and science God's existence is questionable. "The primary assurances of Religion are the ultimate questions of Philosophy." (W. Temple, *Nature, Man and God*, p. 35.) But the fact that philosophy does not reach God with the certainty of religion is no refutation of His reality.

[18] J. A. C. F. Auer, *op. cit.*, p. 74.

[19] cf. *ibid.*, pp. 75-6.

purely immanental one seems to call for the theistic midway position in order to give any meaning to the extremes. What philosophers have shown to be probable it would be vain to attempt to substantiate here, namely, that our herculean but indispensable task is not to seek either the infinite or the finite, the absolute or the relative, the this-worldly or the other-worldly, the individual or the group, the universal or the particular—examples of abstractions apparently denying yet really presupposing and supplementing one another could be multiplied indefinitely—but, in different degrees according to individual requirements, to appreciate and utilize them all. On this issue humanists and theists differ. The former have a way of swinging from one extreme to another without suspecting that truth and fact rather than—and as well as—compromise and confusion may lie between. The either-or complex, in one form or another, dominates humanism.[20] Hence, in its earlier stages at least, it cannot admit that every activity of our life is a reflection of the universe as well as of ourselves, who are nothing apart from it; that human happiness depends upon obedience not merely to our conventions but to what they faintly express (a structure of reality which, other things being equal, obliges us —upon pain of slow or swift, spiritual or physical, death—to prefer the good to the bad, the true to the false, the beautiful to the ugly) ; and that a reality thus guaranteeing our happiness only in the pursuit of what we sooner or later recognize as if not the best at least the better in any situation, is alone worthy of being called God or divine. Our delight and duty thus become, as any catechumen knows, to apprehend Him more clearly, to love Him more dearly, to follow Him more nearly. From time to time transitory

[20] Humanists sometimes resent this charge. Dr. L. M. Birkhead—referred to here not from any desire to indulge in personalities but simply as an illustration —asserts of himself, "I suspect every 'either-or.'" (*The Liberal,* January 21, 1934.) Yet his Little Blue Book, no. 1440, *Can Man Know God?* (Haldeman-Julius Publications, Girard, Kan., 1929), colored with much the same type of reasoning as disfigures Professor Leuba's *God or Man,* impresses at least one of its readers as being a hodgepodge of either-or's, e.g.: either God is merely a reflection of man or He is nothing at all; either religion must be perfectly heavenly or it is utterly hellish; either science must give knowledge or there is no wholesome intellectual sustenance whatsoever.

means are formulated to that end, but the stability of the goal should not preclude fluidity of expedients. While properly rejecting a wooden parody of life with God, humanists transgress the limits of their evidence in repudiating Him also.

Their insistence that morality must be segregated from religion emphasizes the fact (which they later obscure) that morality and religion are different elements of our constitution. Considerable juggling of concepts enters humanistic writings on this score. First comes the assertion that morality is independent of religion. Then our everyday conduct is sadly recognized as tangled in the webs of Christianity. Finally usurping, with science, the ancient throne of the churches, humanistic morality proclaims itself the new religion.

The first assertion generally seeks support from the unquestioned fact that moral growth has purified the idea of God. Then, overlooking the difference in kind between religion and ethics and their relative autonomy (illustrated by the different degrees in which the two are often developed in the same races and individuals[21]), humanists frequently imply that religion is a perversion, or a by-product, of ethics. One has only to turn to the New Testament, to the Stoics, to Spinoza, or to Kant, to observe how religion, in its turn, has deepened, freshened, and reanimated deontology. Nor should we overlook other parts of man's endowment: his art, his social and economic activities, his physical feelings and perceptions, his scientific technique. Though these different elements can be distinguished, human health depends upon their coordination as well as upon the free cultivation of each;[22] for a denial or a distortion of any one to some extent impairs the others.[23]

[21] Note the strong religious sense and less developed moral fineness in parts of the Old Testament and in Benevenuto Cellini.

[22] cf. "Science (the search for order realized in nature), Hellenism (the search for value realized in human nature), Religion (the search for value basic for all things), express three factors belonging to the perfection of human nature. They can be studied apart. But they must be lived together in the one life of the individual." A. N. Whitehead, loc. cit., p. 269.

[23] An illustration of this—which for most men is a platitude—humanism provides in its effort to compensate its lack of religion (as commonly understood) by straining science and morality beyond their limits.

The relative autonomy of morality and religion is sometimes taken by humanists as indicating that morality can be completely independent of religion and that such a severance is desirable. (But as long as religion exists, its debt to morality can never, they affirm—theists concurring—be cancelled.) Except in cultures where one or the other is primitive, it would, however, be difficult to find instances of an ethic uncolored by religion. Humanistic ethics, for all its vaunted "modernity," is—like Ethical Culture and most current Anglo-Saxon "liberalism"—an uncertain mixture of Protestant, Humanitarian, and Romantic dilutions of Christianity, adulterated by popular science. Though we should be poorer without those strains, we are now discussing not their merits but the failure of humanists to recognize the dependence of humanistic morality on its Christian origin and environment.[24] The fact that some people can pursue an admirable moral career without belief in God proves no more than that others can sculpture well without being carpenters—that is, one can leave talents dormant if the rest of mankind makes up for them. But, as we shall see in the theories of Professor Nicolai Hartmann, and as seems to have been true of the late Dr. Felix Adler,[25] when people embrace ethics with an enthusiasm greater than that of the scribes and the pharisees they usually show a devoted reverence for and communion with the right, or the good, or whatever they take to be the most fundamental reality in human life, which appears to theists as tantamount to an unconscious longing for and (in one aspect or another) appreciation of that which is at once the ultimate and the most intimate—God. In other words, morality, like any worthy human endeavor at its deepest level, seeks not necessarily its daily functioning but its fullest life, justification, and consummation, in God.

[24] This should not be misinterpreted as an assumption that Christianity is the only source of ethics, or "that historical Christianity has done equal justice to all the ethical principles which it has acknowledged," or that "Christianity has nothing to learn in this or other fields from other religions." (C. C. J. Webb, *The Contribution of Christianity to Ethics*, p. 4.)

[25] In New York, N.Y., in 1876, Dr. Adler founded the first Ethical Culture society.

A protest, like Dr. Freud's,[26] against basing ethics on religion in such a way that if the masses doubt the existence of God they will destroy civilization is itself tacit testimony to the interdependence of morality and religion. "We do not," he writes, ". . . tell others of [the] rational basis for the murder prohibition; we declare, on the contrary, that God is its author."[27] A remark like that could apply only to what humanists would probably call "the unemancipated." Certainly in Russia and elsewhere countless people professing atheism do not recognize any need to combine morality with religion.[28] Though one may argue that they lose much thereby and that in ignorance they are simply rehearsing an experiment already often proved futile, for the moment they get along. Fortunately, unrecognized by them, the religions of the past and of the present indirectly temper their characters and supply many of their spiritual wants. But they can hardly be said by humanists to have turned from superstition to reason. An "irresistible emotional reaction" is in most people more significant in conduct than any supposedly "rational basis." Without in any way minimizing the importance of intelligence in morality—in fact, even while maintaining with Dr. Warner Fite[29] that the morality or the immorality of an act, from an individual point of view, depends upon the richness or the poverty of the agent's consciousness[30]—one must, with Dr. Freud, admit that the motive force of most important moral acts is largely emotional. Reason finds a way to justify its crimes, but remorse never forgives itself. In one of his famous "Just-So Stories," which, however, he "strongly inclines to believe historical,"[31] Dr. Freud traces the strength of the prohibition against murder to repulsion at "the

[26] cf. *The Future of an Illusion*, pp. 65 *ff*.

[27] *ibid.*, p. 71.

[28] At least with theistic religion. In Russia and Germany certain theories about the state, and life in accord with them, tend to take the place of previous religions and moralities.

[29] Formerly Stuart professor of ethics at Princeton University. cf. his *Moral Philosophy, The Critical View of Life* (New York: MacVeagh, 1925).

[30] That is, his ability or inability to appreciate properly everything relevant to the act.

[31] C. C. J. Webb, *Religion and Theism* (London: Allen and Unwin, 1934), p. 122.

slaughter of the primal father."[32] The moral judgment of the Cain (or the Abel), projected or rediscovered by psychoanalysis, was —Dr. Freud guarantees it—largely emotional, a feeling of horror, naturally not much contaminated by a conscience born of ancient religious taboos and social prejudices. Dr. Freud and we who share with him and our common ancestors that horror experience it even now, on his theory, less as a result of culture or reason than as an emotional atavism. But the theory that such emotional reactions are illusory and delusory—the theory held, as Dr. Webb shows,[33] by Dr. Freud and most humanists—vitiates moral judgments derived from them. If the feeling "I ought to have done that," or "I ought not to do this"—a feeling of unconditional, moral obligation, as distinguished from its utilitarian and prudential affiliates—is not merely imperfect and open to revision but *ex hypothesi* essentially false, men are left in a sorry state. Instead of becoming, as humanists desire, more friendly towards law and society on account of their presumably "purely human origin,"[34] they are likely to view themselves, their civilization, and similar idiosyncrasies, with the hopeless pity, if not contempt, of Mr. Krutch and the pessimistic school. Misled by the notion that

[32] *The Future of an Illusion,* p. 74. He reaffirms this hypothesis in *Moses and Monotheism.*

[33] *Religion and Theism,* Chap. IV. One of the signers of the Manifesto, Professor O. L. Reiser, asserts: "Humanism represents the belief that reason is the only method and tool for obtaining knowledge and finding solutions to our problems. Humanism is therefore opposed to . . . the belief in intuition, revelation, or any other non-rational source of knowledge." (*The New Humanist,* December 1934, p. 23.) Though agreeing that the sources of knowledge are no more knowledge than unmined silver ore is a teakettle, one may feel that many humanistic errors arise from exalting knowledge at the expense of the luxuriant experience of which it is a highly differentiated product and but a partially adequate expression. In Dr. A. N. Whitehead's terminology, "our experience is dominated by composite wholes, more or less clear in focus, and more or less vague in penumbra, and with the whole shading off into umbral darkness, which is ignorance." (*loc. cit.,* p. 264.) Compare this with what Abbé Huvelin said of Baron von Hügel: "La vérité est, pour vous, un point lumineux qui se perd, peu à peu, dans l'obscurité." (*Selected Letters,* p. 58.) cf. Baron F. von Hügel, *Essays and Addresses on the Philosophy of Religion, Second Series* (London: Dent, 1930), p. 21. The *obscurité* and the dominating wholes must be reckoned with in order to understand the *point lumineux.*

[34] *The Future of an Illusion,* p. 73.

anything not completely within our grasp must be "outside of life,"[35] humanists continually err in supposing us to prize the small area of familiar focus more than its shadowy but dawning horizons. They seem to suppose that we resent "appeal to an outward agency,"[36] whereas one of our chief joys is to explore paths leading away from our "warm valley" and to commune with the realities and visions that surround and mould us. God and religion are no more cut off from or strange to men than are music and its more-than-human leads and laws. By assuming that the prompting of conscience is, according to proverbial phrase, the voice of God and by insisting that such alleged communications be analyzed and interpreted in every properly available fashion before being accepted as authentic as conditions allow, theism provides morality with an ultimacy, an intimacy, a vitality, and a criticism, without which it is fitful and extreme. More thoughtful humanists tacitly recognize this, when they write: "What is best in the old religions, Catholic or liberal, is the desire to link up man's life with an infinite and a perfect life. We have yet to learn how to call out more effectively this deepest urge in people's lives, the inner propulsion towards perfection."[37] Not any fault in religion at its best but a misunderstanding of it and of science seems to prevent humanists from finding that power where, as they admit in disinterested moments, it exists most fully.

If humanists want the joy of what for Christians is the first and great commandment, they approximate, as "an elemental item in the creed of humanistic liberalism,"[38] the one like unto it: thou shalt love thy neighbor as thyself. In spite of their science, they are anthropocentric enough to maintain "the supremacy of human personality above all other considerations."[39] In "the supreme

[35] J. A. C. F. Auer, *Humanism States Its Case*, p. 78.
[36] *ibid.*, p. 77.
[37] H. Neumann, *The Standard*, March 1935, p. 149. The article from which the passage is quoted is humanistic. *The Standard* is an Ethical Culture publication.
[38] *The Liberal*, January 7, 1934.
[39] *ibid.*

worth of human life,"[40] in "the twin visions of an ideal developed personality and an ideal commonwealth made up of such persons,"[41] lies the principal strength of humanism. "Humanism favors any movement which tends to improve human personality and opposes any which degrades it."[42] The same could be said of Christianity. Almost all the reforms approved by Dr. C. F. Potter[43] have been supported by Christian (especially Protestant) churches.

But whereas a certain combination of virtues[44]—love, joy, peace, long-suffering, goodness, faith, hope, meekness, temperance —distinguish the Christian ideal life of the spirit from the ways of the world, the flesh, and the devil, it is almost impossible to ascertain what an "ideal developed personality" is for humanists. Jesus, one of their influential writers reports, is "historically doubtful and not religiously helpful."[45] From the way in which

[40] J. H. Dietrich, "The Advance of Humanism," address delivered in 1927, published by The First Unitarian Society, Minneapolis, Minn., p. 45.

[41] C. F. Potter, *Humanism, A New Religion*, p. 115.

[42] *ibid.* cf. Dr. Dietrich's address just referred to and *Humanism—A Religion for Today*, a pamphlet published (no date) by the First Unitarian Society, Minneapolis, Minn.

[43] In *Humanism, A New Religion*, pp. 124-5.

[44] cf. Matt. v, vi, vii, and 1 Cor. xiii.

[45] C. W. Reese, *Humanist Religion* (New York: Macmillan, 1931), p. 50. In regard to the merits of Christ as a partially fictitious, partially adequate, expression of the experience of the Church, humanists seem to reach a swifter, simpler agreement than almost any other group of responsible persons. After noting the admitted fact that, without the Church, Christ would probably not be so well known today as He is and after ignoring—as a patent absurdity—the possibility that He is known by the Church better than by the indifferent and the hostile, Mr. E. Haldeman-Julius (here quoted simply as reflecting humanistic sentiment) comments on Dr. L. M. Birkhead's essay called "Can We Follow Jesus Today? No!" thus: ". . . we want living leaders. And, even more, we want to follow ideas rather than men. . . . If it is a question of following men, then how much more sensible to turn from the remote and disputed figure of Jesus and, let us say, follow Bertrand Russell in social idealism, Clarence Darrow in toleration and personal liberty, Havelock Ellis [died in July 1939] in sex and marriage, Joseph McCabe in rationalism and scientific culture, Ramsay Macdonald [does death make him out of date?] in world peace and coop eration. . . ." (*Can We Follow Jesus Today?*, Little Blue Book no. 1531, Haldeman-Julius Publications, Girard, Kan.) Mr. Haldeman-Julius does not ask whether the spirit of Christ excludes anything that is good and true in those whom he mentions; or whether they are to any extent directly or indirectly indebted to that "remote and disputed" figure; or whether, with all due respect to

167

they ignore some of the virtures just referred to (often called "soft" or "feminine" traits, but in a world like this better termed Amazonian), one may suspect that they confuse Christian "inwardness" with "the shrinking violet type,"[46] which some of them "have never taken seriously."[47] To whom then do they turn? "There are few things more thrilling than committee meetings, especially if the committees are large ones."[48] It would be unjust to isolate, as typical of a group's belief, a single sentence from a single author, did not humanists in general seem to find "serving on the boards of various community organizations" their principal goal.[49] If science must be "humanized," if religion, morality, philosophy, and art have no ontological significance, social enterprise of an essentially practical and political nature remains as the highest type of life to which one may aspire. Critics have described humanism as a sentimental sublimation, projection, or expression, of "civic-minded" American (particularly Middle Western) businessmen, whose "sound intellectualism" sheepishly consorts with "a valid emotionalism" of possibly "aesthetic worth."[50] By failing to note that the imperfections associated with such a conveniently vague type are more widespread than its peculiar good qualities, these critics give the impression of disparaging rather

them, they are or will remain as "alive" as the "long-dead Jesus." (*ibid.*, p. 63.) Hence he can say, "As a god, Jesus is incredible; as a man he is not very real or important." (*ibid.*)

[46]
       "How dreary to be somebody!
       How public, like a frog
       To tell your name the livelong day
       To an admiring bog!"
                —Emily Dickinson, *op. cit.*, p. 15.

[47] C. W. Reese, *op. cit.*, p. 65.

[48] *ibid.*, p. 67.

[49]
       "The first thing to do is to form the committees;
       The consultative councils, the standing committees,
          select committees and sub-committees."
               —T. S. Eliot, *Collected Poems 1909-1935*, p. 160.

[50] "Finding that the liberal-minded need a valid emotionalism in their lives, along with a sound intellectualism, a Twilight Service of beauty and aesthetic worth, supplants the traditional morning worship during the winter months." From a leaflet of The Fellowship of Liberal Religion (Unitarian), "where [despite a dangling participle] the Best of the University Tradition Prevails," Ann Arbor, Mich.

than of complimenting humanism. But, the idol's merits and defects being left to the reader's judgment, it is hard to see, in view of the exigencies of their theory and the region and the manner in which the majority of them live,[51] how most humanists could conceive of an "ideal developed personality" with any warmth and concreteness except in some such fashion.

Unlike Oliver Alden, who "could find no peace unless he justified his natural sympathies theoretically,"[52] "the humanist stoutly affirms that no particular metaphysical system is needed to convince him of the supreme worth and the great potentialities of human personality."[53] "Humanism declares that the good life is not dependent on beliefs as to the ultimate nature of things."[54] Though the conviction that "human personality at its best, imperfect as it is, is yet sufficiently worthy and admirable to justify the universe"[55] reeks with metaphysics; and though the Manifesto and the writings of humanists prove their inevitable interest in "the ultimate nature of things," one can regard favorably their desire to make human personality appear as so obviously of supreme value that no sane person would dream of questioning it. Respect for personality is a matter of course in the heart of Judaeo-Christian civilization and in the aureole of liberalism formed by its rays. But, were it not for their religion, Christians might find the barriers of race, nationality, taste, and occupation, which divide humanity into different and often antagonistic groups, still more impervious to the influence of long-suffering good will than they do. Even with their religion, especially now in a temporarily debilitated phase, it is absurd to say of Christians what used to be

[51] "Divorced from the feudal and theological heritage, American life has been in the main hard, economic, and realistic—a conquest of material things, and American thought has been essentially empirical, not metaphysical and theological. . . . The outstanding positive characteristic of American civilization is preoccupation with economy in practice and empiricism and humanism in thought." Charles Beard, quoted in "Personal and Otherwise," *Harper's Magazine*, October 1936.

[52] George Santayana, *The Last Puritan* (New York: Scribner, 1936), p. 318.

[53] *Humanism—A Religion for Today.*

[54] L. M. Birkhead, *The Liberal*, May 28, 1933.

[55] C. F. Potter, *Humanism, A New Religion*, p. 16.

observed of them centuries ago: "How much they love one another!" Nothing so exasperates the capable and exacting man or woman of the world as the excuse of the less successful that after all they too are human beings and must be treated as such—that is, indulged and endured. "Il n'y a guère que Dieu qui empêche de mépriser les hommes"[56]—même soi. But the teaching, the example, the life, and the person of their Saviour; the belief that everybody (regardless of earthly distinctions) is dear to God and, by His grace, capable of loving Him; and the conviction that those, quick and dead, seeking Him and His righteousness form a communion of saints, compared with which mundane manifestations of affection and sociality are adumbrations: these elements of their religion reinforce Christians against the common failing of rating themselves more, and others less, highly than they deserve.[57] That weakening of that faith leads to a corresponding contempt for individuals, humanists, by reference to the inquisitorial delirium following the Reformation, recognize in the domestic annals of the Church. But when the Church champions individual conscience against the inordinate claims of the state, humanists, for all their liberalism, usually remain silent. Once God or His equivalent goes, reason begins to parley with the old Adam. We know this too well in ourselves, we have observed it too often in others and in history, to feel that it needs proof. Not it but its denial is a fiction of special pleading.[58] As individuals become, or are thought to be, of

[56] René Bazin, "Notes Intimes," *Revue des Deux Mondes*, February 15, 1936, p. 788.
[57] "Les pauvres n'ont jamais été aimés pour eux-mêmes que par l'Église et par les saints de l'Église. L'humanité simplement humaine les a constamment rejetés ou exploités. Et tout affaiblissement du Christianisme leur a été nuisable, rapidement et sans compensation." *ibid.*, p. 772.
[58] "The real issue is between humanistic works without the support of theistic faith, and theistic faith at its moral and intellectual best, a rational theistic faith made instrumental to humanistic works." (D. C. Macintosh, *Humanism, Another Battle Line*, edited by W. P. King, Nashville, Tenn., Cokesbury Press, 1931, p. 64.) "Let us consider . . . the . . . opinion of Benjamin Kidd, who affirms that the function of religious beliefs in human evolution is to 'provide a super-rational sanction for that large class of conduct in the individual, necessary to the maintenance of the development which is proceeding, and for which there can never be, in the nature of things, any rational sanction.'. . . Leuba's confident opinion that the withdrawal of religious sanctions from the

less worth, the state must be proportionally aggrandized, so that, lest its citizens devour one another like wolves, it may reserve that right to itself in the company of nations.

> "Men have left God not for other gods, they say,
>   but for no god; and this has never happened
>   before
> That men both deny gods and worship gods,
>   professing first Reason,
> And then Money, and Power, and what they call
>   Life, or Race, or Dialectic."[59]

In other civilizations, in other parts of the globe, and today even in regions nominally Christian, respect for individual personality is in theory and practice condemned as illusory, wicked, or deleterious to the welfare of the race, the state, or the system. To mankind at large there never was and is not now anything obvious about the supreme, or even the great, value of human personality.

Retreating to our "cool sequestered vale"[60] and making the most of health and useful enterprise cannot insulate us from the disagreements of the world without or preserve us from difficulties that spur the mind to thought.

ethical life of modern society would make no difference to the body politic is not shared by social psychology." Among eminent social psychologists, Professor McDougall, for example, "holds that in connection with this question of religion and morality 'we must recognize that a firm and harmonious relation between them has been in every age a main condition of the stability of societies.' . . . Professor Pratt . . . records the significant fact that in answer to his question, 'If you became thoroughly convinced that there was no God, would it make any great difference in your life, either in happiness, morality, or in other respects?' the majority of his respondents affirmed that it would certainly weaken their morality. Pratt, commenting on this result, says the thought of a Divine Friend who cares does support the feeble virtue of most of us, and the categorical imperative of Kant would not have the same helpful power. We believe that a dissolution of the vital union which obtains between morality and religion will be fraught with disaster to both. . . . History teaches that decay of religion and moral decadence are bound up with each other in a singularly sympathetic and vital manner." A. R. Uren, *op. cit.*, pp. 189-90.

[59] T. S. Eliot, *Collected Poems 1909-1935*, p. 200.
[60] Thomas Gray.

"They sleep and rise, they toil and buy and sell;
No quest, but trivial certainties are theirs;
No cry to know what it is all about,
No winged wonder—and no haunting doubt."[61]

Does admiration of the insight of the simple and the humble, compared with the restless candle of "the rational and enlightened mind,"[62] and appreciation of the elemental beauty of lives expressing, like trees and flowers, the power of nature more than their own premeditated art, lead humanists to glorify a *foi du charbonnier* in at least one dogma—that of the supremacy of human personality? Is that attitude compatible with the dictum of a great humanist: "the unexamined life is not fit for human living"?[63] It is hard to see how an attitude possible for the "unscientific" Socrates (whose moral faith was not dissolved by intellectual scepticism) can survive in those humanists whose "scientific" aspiration is unreservedly to hold "doctrines as hypothetical and ideals as tentative."[64] There is, we believe with Socrates, in every normal person a kernel or spring of morality, which, though it manifests itself in a baffling multiplicity of ways, can no more be actually (though it can be verbally) denied by its possessor than can his own existence. If humanists direct their "science" only to the emanations or shadows of this element, as they appear in doctrines and ideals, they thereby constrict the scope of science more than they do in the cases of religion and the observation of the external world. In the supposed interest of science, they were willing to explain away, as far as they could, mankind's religious endowment. If they were as consistently "scientific" as they would apparently persuade one that they are, they would query such seeming moral facts as that truth is better than falsehood, courage than cowardice, consideration than cruelty. They would use every re-

[61] H. R. Orr, *The Liberal*, Vol. V, no. 15.
[62] T. S. Eliot.
[63] Socrates, *The Apology*.
[64] C. W. Reese, *Humanist Religion*, p. 5. cf. W. Pauck, *The New Humanist*, March-April 1931, p. 26.

lentless ingenuity of science to aid them in ascertaining experimentally whether personality might not be worthless, evil good, and right wrong. We might then admit that, according to their lights, they were scientific, but we should find little reason for thinking of them as humanists. Needless to say, when pushed to this point they all agree, in fact if not in theory, that the supreme value of human personality is a matter of faith and not, in spite of of their vaunted reliance on reason alone, a scientific demonstrate.[65] If Christianity, which for centuries presented a fairly coherent ideal of personality and strengthened respect for it, must go, or—as some humanists state—has already gone, those who look to humanism to take its place will find an ideal of personality which, whether too narrow or too vague, rides like a ring of tobacco smoke only on the breath of those who stoutly affirm it. Faith in God is notoriously difficult, but faith in man's "supremacy," especially when "defended" by a supposedly "moral" disregard, or an unnecessarily "daring challenge," of facts, rather than by their observation, is harder still.

But if the humanistic "ideal developed personality" is essentially practical, speculative thinness would, from that point of view, be a venial offense, provided that practice made up for deficiencies of theory. An understanding of humanistic ethics, requires some acquaintance with its practical program. Instead of formulating this in detail, humanists—possibly not wishing to infringe the rights of legislators—usually content themselves with generalizations about principles supposedly comprehensible to everybody. And, for all their emphasis on individual worth, they follow a contemporary trend to concentrate on the social in preference to the individual aspects of morality. Their commonest ethical principles may be schematized as follows:[66]

[65] ". . . faith in man is the central doctrine of humanism. It is a challenge to all men to dare to believe that human personality is of supreme value." C. F. Potter, *Humanism, A New Religion,* p. 16.

[66] cf. C. W. Reese, *Humanist Religion,* pp. 35, 56-9, 60 *ff.,* 71 *ff.,* 91 *f.*: L. M. Birkhead, *The Liberal,* January 21, 1934; *ibid.,* March 27, 1935: O. L. Reiser, "The Social Objectives of Humanism," *The New Humanist,* December 1934.

Humanists Favor	Humanists Oppose
Human control	Laissez-faire
Science and intelligence	Anti-intellectualism
Democracy	Aristocracy
	Personal dictatorship
	Proletarian dictatorship
Liberty	Compulsion, tyranny
Tolerance, free discussion	Fanaticism, regimentation
Orderly, gradual change	Revolution, class conflict, violence, terror, hate
Peace	War, militarism
Industrial democracy	Domination of profit motive and
Economic security	subsequent exploitation
Public education	Unethical propaganda
A state existing for the welfare of its citizens	A totalitarian state

Probably Professor O. L. Reiser's is as pithy a list as any of the more detailed (though still general) humanistic applications of the above principles. What he takes to be "the social objectives of humanism" are these:[67]

"I. *Social Relations:*

1. Equality of opportunity according to capacity.
2. Abolition of institutional authority in fixing beliefs.
3. Modernization of courts and legal procedure.
4. Minimizing of crime and political dishonesty.
5. Equal rights for women.
6. Social equality for all races.
7. Sterilization of defectives unfit to be parents.
8. Abolition of capital punishment.
9. Socialized medical care.

[67] "The Social Objectives of Humanism," *The New Humanist*, December 1934.

II. *The Family:*

1. Eugenics.
2. Birth control.
3. Abolition of child labor.
4. Divorce by mutual consent.
5. Removal of illegitimacy stigma.
6. Old-age pensions.

III. *Education:*

1. Abolition of illiteracy.
2. Education for rational use of leisure.
3. Elevation of standards in the radio, movies, literature, etc.
4. Mental hygiene facilities (clinics) for all.
5. Minimal intelligence tests for voters.
6. Information tests for public officials, legislators, etc.
7. Development of respect for civil liberties.

IV. *Economic Relations:*

1. Unemployment insurance.
2. Government ownership of public utilities.
3. Unionization of labor and collective bargaining.
4. Cooperative movement.
5. Capital tax and tax on unearned wealth.

V. *International Relations:*

1. Cancellation of War Debts.
2. World disarmament.
3. Abolition of 'nationalism' and economic imperialism.
4. Cooperation with League of Nations and World Court."

As a definition of humanism compatible with these objectives Professor Reiser offers: "Humanism is the doctrine that men, through the use of intelligence, directing the institutions of democratic government, can create for themselves, without aid from 'supernatural powers,' a rational civilization in which each person enjoys economic security and finds cultural outlets for whatever normal human capacities and creative energies he possesses."[68]

Even without knowing who advocated the above principles and proposals, one might recognize them as typical of middle-class, Anglo-Saxon, rationalistic liberals, probably residing in the United States. Middle-class, because of their distrust of the powerful few in some sense above them[69] and of the even more powerful many in some sense below them[70] and because of their possibly unconscious, "rationalized" defense of their material welfare by means of a guardedly democratic capitalism, or of a somewhat academic socialism, capable of diffusing sufficient general comfort to prevent an outbreak of class warfare.[71] Anglo-Saxon, on account of their devotion—supposedly more marked in themselves than in other peoples—to liberty, tolerance, order, and peace, and on account of a generally "idealistic" attitude as native and welcome to them as it is frequently alien and suspect to others. Rationalistic, in their faith in science, intelligence, planning, and in their hatred of institutional authority for anything with which they disagree.[72] Liberal, because in almost everything their appreciation of the new seems too eager, ill considered, well meant, and con-

[68] *ibid.* Note the failure—typical of humanism, because inherent in its outlook —to provide for a spiritual plane distinguishable from those of culture and material comfort.

[69] "Aristocracy," "personal dictatorship."

[70] "Proletarian dictatorship."

[71] Though this is probably true as a sweeping summary, it apparently does not apply, for instance, to Dr. John Dewey. If there is any authority in the review of his *Liberalism and Social Action* in *The Liberal*, November 25, 1935, he "repudiates the theory of class conflict. The real conflict is 'between institutions and habits originating in the prescientific and pre-technological age and new forces generated by science and technology.' In other words, the conflict is not a class conflict but a battle between the scientific method and technological applications on the one hand and older institutions and habits on the other. Another interesting theory of Dr. Dewey's is that technology and not capitalism is responsible for modern conditions." In a letter to *The New Republic* (April 12, 1939, p. 281) Mr. Mark Stone attributes to Dr. Dewey "a dated, middle-class liberalism and the naïve notion that our turbulent society will have successful issue when impregnated with the methods of science and technology."

[72] Instead of rejecting authority, humanists usually transfer it from the cultural to the scientific tradition.

fused to those commonly called conservative, and timid, over-scrupulous, well meant, and confused to those commonly called radical. And American as is shown by their language and by their preoccupation with needs[73] elsewhere in the English-speaking world now apparently better taken into account, as in New Zealand, or in the process of being fairly met, as in Great Britain, or, because of local difficulties, tending to be glossed over at the moment, as in South Africa and India.

Though non-Christian theists often condone or commend laissez-faire, anti-intellectualism, and some sort of aristocratic or dictatorial rule involving tyranny, violence, fanaticism, war, propaganda, and exploitation, for ends that they believe to be religiously, morally, or politically desirable; and though many Christians have in theory—and more in practice—defended, as necessary or admirable under certain conditions, all or some of the principles or actions denounced by humanists: probably most Christians, in their calmer moods, when momentarily freed at least in thought from the seemingly fixed social and economic necessities which cramp as well as define their points of view and effectiveness, would sympathize with the desire of humanists to make life more consonant with our highest capacities than it is now. Such Christians would recognize in humanists an "anonymous" attempt, in the spirit of Christ, to realize the will of God on earth. And countless persons unattached to organized religion likewise believe that civilization advances most through intelligence animated by a love almost indistinguishable from that with which Jesus urged us to act towards one another.[74]

To the mythical man-on-the-street, with whose point of view and that of humanism the reader can make for himself such comparisons as he wants, it seems as though we have two things with us always: an unsatisfactory present situation and an aspiration to improve it. We may look back to a Garden of Eden or a golden

[73] Industrial democracy, economic security, I. 4, I. 6, II. 6, III. 3, III. 7, IV. 1, IV. 3, IV. 4. (The numbers refer to Professor Reiser's list.)

[74] For an interpretation of Christian love, see Chap. II of *The Contribution of Christianity to Ethics,* by C. C. J. Webb.

age or we may look forward to a promised land, a city of God, a perfect republic, a utopia, a classless society, or a communist international. Or, if we are "practical men" of a "one step enough for me" sort, we may make the most of the present situation, unsatisfactory though it is. With imagination, invention, and dogged determination we may acquire control of the limited resources of the earth, which nature gives to those that take and keep, and create new products and new wealth. For a while people bless those that do that, praising them for establishing a material order better than any until then. In some cases this is justified. In others, those that have gained the world see in their mirrors

"A face devoid of love and grace,
A hateful, hard, successful face,"[75]

and around them little change in the fundamental conditions of life. Squalor, poverty, waste, injustice, class conflict, war, and depressions trail us like everlasting shadows. And though, as compared with the past, the situation of any moment is (for optimistic believers in progress) ordinarily an advance, like all advances it has mitigated some evils simply by changing their clothes and in the place of those it has destroyed it supplies new ones. The leaders of the advance, who have raised the standard of living for the many to a point from which they would be loath to recede, are generally blamed the most for its attendant evils by those who have done the least to initiate and guide the new order and who, by "the law of nature," least deserve its rewards.

The result is a state of perpetual friction requiring continuous adjustment, which is ever liable to be misunderstood and exploited by greed and malice. Those who rule may too often do so with "full-blown commercial insolence,"[76] for private gain regardless of public weal. And the ruled may too often "act accordingly." Socialism and communism (in their innumerable forms, each with its own confident "answer") instead of working as beneficent influences then may degenerate into belligerent groups denouncing

[75] Emily Dickinson, *op. cit.*, p. 46.
[76] Irving Babbitt.

competition, seeking public ownership for party benefit, fanning class hatred and calling for cooperation, censuring oligarchy and "the profit motive" and forging autocratic "profit-seeking monopolies" instead of responsible unions. On this amoral level malignly ascribed to nature there is no choice but the sorry one of the gang in which one happened to be born and no emotion higher than shame and pity for us all.

As men, however, we are not merely animals living on an entirely natural plane. We dream of and work for a day when we shall pursue a common end as zestfully as separate ends in common; when "the public" and "the people" will be a fact and not, as socialists themselves admit, an ideal; when each group that moulds an individual will appreciate other groups on a live-and-let-live basis; and when those that are above the average will share their surplus talents with those that are not. Capitalism, we are told in the same breath, has never worked and yet has worked so well that we are all its slaves. Socialism and communism, their more plain-spoken advocates confess, have accomplished nothing except in so far as they have adapted themselves to capitalism and have been assimilated by it. They can accomplish nothing properly, their proponents complain, on a scale smaller than that of the whole earth. Than that of the whole universe, their critics add, presuming that nothing less than minute and absolute control of every factor can insure even the mirage of the security to which a radically collectivistic society would allegedly sacrifice everything else.

The blundering, mythical man-on-the-street, therefore, seeks a compromise allowing the fullest play of forces and interests compatible with survival, peace, justice, and good will. With Christianity and the Church, he puts first, men as complete personalities, rather than as abstractions, like the manual laborer, the professional man, the capitalist, the artist, the unabashed enjoyer of life, and other attenuated descriptions of luxuriant human beings. He is less sure than humanists that we are good, scientific, and civilized, though he hopes they are right in supposing we may become somewhat so. He is not convinced that the world is designed for

179

our pleasure or, considering human nature, that he or anyone else (no matter how fair his momentary state) has in the long run a better than even chance of keeping body and soul together. Under these circumstances, and because he thankfully believes that whatever he has is entrusted to him by gift rather than begrudgingly awarded on account of some fancied right or merit of his own, he finds faith in God not an opiate but a tonic that dispels bitterness and despair and strengthens him with love and courage to carry on.

With these shabby—or, if you must, frank, fearless, wide-eyed—crotchets to determine his response to the intricacies of specific measures, our obliging fellow-in-the-street (put to this mannequin duty as a foil for humanism) is not inclined to suppose that democracy as a principle, aspiration, or ideal, is ever likely to mould the recalcitrant material of life to a noticeable extent without ceaseless effort. He rejoices that, at least in tendency, our American class lines are flexible; our political representation by geographical regions (neatly gerrymandered) attempts to speak for men as complete personalities; our partisan interests are more or less confined to lobbies; our "public opinion" strives to be free and worthy of attention. Instead of the usual "of, by, and for the people," he concludes that the most we can expect of democracy is a political, industrial, and social order run by some of the best, with the consent of a passably informed and conscientious majority, and for the welfare of all. Eager to save the essence of democracy from its cant, he is not inclined to accept at face value everything advertised as "liberal," or to alter the prudent if unintoxicating standards embodied in our constitution and laws, by any means or for any ends less sober and well balanced than those generally recognized as right. Because (outside religious orders and similar associations) in one form or another adequate private property and its inheritance are, like our physical bodies, usually necessary bases for spiritual stability, continuity, and independence, he would restrain their abuse and foster their extension. And because the resources of man and nature are such that it does not seem wise to assume there can be within the foreseeable future sufficient private (or collective) property for all, he feels that everything possible should be done to make the lot of the propertyless not merely the bare minimum that they may wring by force but as adequate as can be for a decent and self-respecting life for all able to live it. Because the man-on-the-street walks through Main Street, Wall Street, Mayfair, the Latin Quarter, Unter den Linden, and Slum Alley, he assumes that emulation, imitation, the love of lucre, the "right to rise," and the impulse "to keep up with the Joneses" form a complex appetite (some psychologists call it a "sentiment") as ineradicable, as exacting of minimum satisfaction, as useful in its place, and as disastrous when inordinate, as any other appetite. Hence in his naïve and simple way he would have it function as inconspicuously and gracefully as possible for the furtherance of higher ends.

A less prosaic foil to set off the brilliancy of humanism is provided by a well known French philosopher. In scanning Professor Reiser's list one is struck by certain similarities and differences between the social program of the "new positivists" and that of their noted predecessor, Auguste Comte. If men are to create for themselves a rational civilization through "the institutions of democratic government," does that imply the exercise of universal suffrage? By apparently limiting suffrage to those voters that can meet "minimal intelligence tests" (likely to increase in difficulty with increasing complexity of public affairs) and by apparently eliminating elected officials incapable of passing "information tests," humanists seem tacitly to endorse Paul Bourget's conviction (shared by those who are "out" when the "wrong" party is "in") that mere numbers neither create nor recognize competence and that universal suffrage means government by a majority of charlatans "elected" by a majority of the ignorant.[77] Though

[77] cf. *L'Étape* (Paris: Plon, 1902), p. 197. That "comradely" radicals join undemonstrative conservatives in holding as modest an opinion of others (in or out of the party) as they hold of themselves is intimated by the following passage from a letter written, February 13, 1851, by Friedrich Engels to Karl Marx: " . . . Haven't we for God knows how many years been pretending that Tom, Dick, and Harry were our party, when we really haven't had any party and when the people who, at least officially, we counted as belonging to our party, *sous réserve de les appeler des bêtes incorrigibles entre nous*, didn't understand even the rudiments of what we were getting at? How can people like us, who

praising democracy, humanists seem in theory driven to restrict the masses almost as much as Comte was. Except in case of revolution, he would not allow the proletariat (whose rule, he believed, meant anarchy) "to take a direct part in government and to have the final decision of political matters."[78] But government, he maintained, must seek the common good, which, on account of their numerical superiority, is chiefly that of the masses. Unlike humanists Comte shares with certain bourgeois social reformers today the soothing notion that the masses are more noble and disinterested than any other group of people. The masses themselves, not to mention doctors, lawyers, sociologists, politicians, teachers, and others in daily contact with them, realize that the odds are against this. In view of those odds, instances of nobility where they could least justly be expected are rightly the most appreciated. The reflected radiance of exceptions and sympathy with the underdog tend to bewitch reason as regards the common run. Their Puritanical background, with its stress on industry, thrift, and independence, and its corresponding impatience with the "improvident," probably leads humanists farther in distrust of the populace than the Catholic tradition of charitable relations with the poor could have led Comte. By developing for every man the inner peace and strength necessary for his station in life, Catholic charity, with an honest recognition of limitations and inequalities, creates a fellowship that transcends without confounding natural differences—a fellowship, or household of Christ, where envy, pride, and vain pretensions bend to understanding love. The pitfall of that kind of charity, like the enemy of any ideal, is acceptance, for selfish reasons, of what is (of present limitations and

avoid official positions like the plague, ever find ourselves at home in a 'party'? We have always spat on popularity and we have always become doubtful of ourselves as soon as we began to be popular, so what should we do with a 'party,' that is, with a collection of asses, who swear by us because they take us for asses like themselves? Truly it is no great loss if we don't figure any more as the 'correct and complete expression' of these half-witted idiots, with whom we've been thrown these last years." (As translated by Mr. Edmund Wilson in *The New Republic*, February 8, 1939, p. 21.)

[78] *A General View of Positivism*, translated by J. H. Bridges, p. 147.

inequalities) without making suitable efforts to bring about what can and ought to be.

On account of his high appreciation of the proletariat, Comte looked to them, to women,[79] and to philosophers (in whose beneficence and power he had a touching faith) to support order and to hasten progress. They were to do this by their moral and spiritual influence, by remaining unspotted from the world. Its business would be the care chiefly of conscientious private capitalism. Their eagerness for capital taxes and political ownership of anything that might be construed as of public utility seems to head humanists towards state capitalism or state socialism with its easy transition to the totalitarianism and the dictatorships that they fear. Their "minimal intelligence tests," "information tests," and similar classroom paraphernalia, suggest a longing, like Plato's, for philosopher-kings (disguised as philosopher-presidents), or, worse, for a pedantocracy. And their "equal rights for women" and "unionization of labor" seem to advocate the use of physical and economic means in physical and economic matters. Women and the masses, made "equal" in materialistic self-interest to the predatory bourgeois males, approach them in wealth, political power, and (like the Church in similar circumstances) spiritual mediocrity. Comte's chivalry, love, and reason thus disintegrate into a "realistic" struggle of selfish groups.

Woman's place is in the home, for Comte, above all in the nursery and the drawing room. He found nothing in nature to support equality of the sexes or to indicate that "equal rights," implying equal duties, would be anything but disadvantageous to women and annoying to men. The positivist education for women, aiming at the development of cultivated wives and wise mothers, would be about the same as that for men, but without technical, scientific, business, or professional emphasis. Considering the family and the household the best school for social feeling, Comte would probably want to know more about humanistic proposals for making divorce and illegitimacy easier, in order to allay his

[79] "The two elements of society in which we find the greatest amount of good sense and right feeling." *ibid.*, p. 99.

suspicions that moves to weaken the family "are regarded in the present day with far too favorable an eye . . . on account of our dislike of all subjection."[80] As incarnate spirits can hardly worship something not mediated through the imagination and the senses, Comte, inspired by Catholic devotion to the Madonna, proposed that men worship women as a means to the worship of humanity and as the best introduction to love and feeling, which, contrary to the "new positivists," he claimed should govern intellect and action. But what women should worship he left to the ingenuity of Mme. Clotilde de Vaux, who unfortunately died before solving the problem.

In their proposals for disarmament, the curbing of nationalism and economic imperialism, and cooperation with the League of Nations and the World Court, humanists follow Comte's desire to subordinate nationalism "to larger feelings of international fraternity."[81] His Republic of Western Europe (France, Britain, "with which may be classed the United States,"[82] Germany, Holland, "the most advanced portion of Germany,"[83] Italy, Spain, and Portugal) envisaged a limited league of nations founded on social, industrial, artistic, and scientific affinities. "Accessory members," like Greece and Poland, would be united to the Western Republic by bonds analogous to family relationships—in many cases resembling most those of distant cousins.

The meaning of their principles, as humanists like Professor Reiser are aware, may be debated. Discussion of time, place, manner, extent, and other points pertinent to the application of them, may unfortunately obscure the needs and the spirit that they express. Assuming that, if it is not already present, no efforts here can evoke agreement with the longing of humanists for a better life in a better world, and that technical details of law, ethnology, biology, medicine, education, industry, diplomacy, and finance suffer more than they gain from amateur handling, we may at least

[80] *ibid.*, pp. 105-6.
[81] *ibid.*, p. 91.
[82] *ibid.*, p. 93.
[83] *ibid.*

consider in a crude general way whether or not the trends of the humanistic social program—sketchy though it avowedly is—indicate a coherent policy.

Of the many actors in the cast, we must confine the spotlight to "democracy" and "education." What do humanists mean by what Mr. Stuart Chase calls "that more or less indefinable swear word 'democracy' "?[84] Dr. L. M. Birkhead refers to democracy as "the widest possible diffusion of a share in the control of common affairs. Democracy believes 'in counting heads instead of breaking them.' "[85] "Ideally," adds Dr. C. W. Reese, "democracy is the faith of those who believe that within the limits of natural possibilities the fortunes of human society are in the hands of the people, to be worked out cooperatively in the light of growing ideals of individual integrity and social well-being and by means of whatever techniques and powers are available."[86] If these definitions are looser than those of a dictionary they are also more realistic; for, in the United States at least (originally a republic in which democracy prevailed more in the legislative than in the executive and the judicial branches), democracy, no longer content to be an element in government, now seeks to embrace all the "common affairs" and "fortunes of human society." It has become roughly synonymous with the influence of the majority on the spirit of the nation. Democracy plain and simple apparently has unquestioning confidence in something called "the people." Humanists, more critical, occasionally proffer "conditions," like those compiled by Dr. C. W. Reese, "for the successful operation of democratic society": "will to democracy; an educated populace; nobility of character; competent leadership."[87] It might be questioned whether Anglo-Saxons (and especially humanists) really desire so much the rule of the majority, right or wrong, as, for every man, freedom and opportunity recognized by him as appropriate to the place in society for which he is fit. In that case they accept the sway of

[84] "Are Radicals Crazy?", leaflet published in 1926 by The League for Industrial Democracy, p. 2.
[85] *The Liberal*, March 27, 1935.
[86] *Humanist Religion*, p. 60.
[87] *ibid.*, pp. 60 ff.

the majority not as intrinsically just but as to date the best available means of assuring minimum rights for the average man against the power of a superior few. In fact Dr. Reese confirms this impression when he writes: "Democracy aims not to level down, nor to level at all, but to equitize. Above certain just and adequate minimum standards of living, and within certain fair limits, there must be ample room for individual initiative and achievement. But no man should be allowed to build his monumental achievement at the cost of underfed, poorly clothed, and inadequately housed men, women, and children."[88]

The general trend of humanism is towards what might be called a scientific natural aristocracy—a state of affairs in which, as far as a sense of decency allows, scientific knowledge and natural ability take precedence over all other considerations. "Equality of opportunity according to capacity" leads to results quite different from those of an artificially imposed egalitarianism, which in revolutions, elections, and moments of crisis, is usually proclaimed somewhat too fervently as the essence of democracy. From what humanists and liberals deem to be urgent measures of reform they must tacitly conclude that after a century and a half of "democratic" régime the greater part of the population of the United States still suffers from outworn institutions, legal and political corruption, crime, sexual and racial injustices, biological degeneration, dangerously little learning, debased standards, heartless exploitation, and, as might be expected, inability to manage domestic and foreign relations well enough to escape disasters. Though the world has suffered from these before—and is long likely so to continue—under various types of government, economy, industry, religion, and ethics, that is the situation humanists now face.

Owing to lack of information about the exact manner of effecting "the social objectives of humanism," one can only suppose that (as in the case of James Mill and most utilitarians) the first step of humanists in meeting this gloomy state of affairs would be the

[88] *ibid.*, p. 75.

education of the "populace" to a sufficient "will to democracy" and "nobility of character" to ensure "competent leadership."[89] Under such leadership laws embodying humanistic social objectives would presumably be passed with sufficient unanimity to make practicable subsequent education for their observance. The fate not merely of Prohibition but of many of the 32,647,389 laws in the United States proves the futility of law alone, if it manifests ignorance or is met by it.

The success of the education indispensable before and after law naturally depends upon the people to be educated, the persons in charge, and the methods used. If the humanistic state is governed by a small group of eugenically bred, intelligent liberals crammed with information, it could hardly be a democracy, for all that humanists say, because no democracy ever has or is ever likely to elect and long to maintain a government so different from most of the people whom it represents. A pure democracy presupposes the education of the masses. Even the maintenance of a humanistic "equitable" democracy (or scientific natural aristocracy, as distinguished from an egalitarian democracy) requires enough popular education to make the majority of the people support a ruling body of scientific moralists. If this support is not voluntary, the humanistic state falls, or prevails by a dictatorship contrary to the principles of humanism. Supposing the impossible, namely, the invention of a thoroughly satisfactory system of education (working not only in schools but in families, churches, clubs, the press, movies, etc.), that education can save the world (for humanists long for salvation as the ancient Hebrews longed for a Messiah) only if the majority of mankind has ability equal at least to that of those now displaying the highest attainments in their several lines. Who is the humanistic paragon, if not the "successful man"—ordinarily the man successful in what for them is the most important sphere, business and community affairs? Humanists complain of Jesus "that he was not an educated man, that he had

[89] "Reasonable and manly attitudes," according to the eleventh affirmation of the Manifesto, "will be fostered by education and supported by custom." p. 53, *supra*.

no business or political experience, that he had never travelled or never mingled with the great minds of the times."[90] His greatness, if not a fiction, was relatively unimportant, they insinuate, because He was not fundamentally conventional, respectable, and "successful."[91] If He whom countless Christians profess to revere was not "successful," is there much likelihood that His followers will become so, except in so far as they abandon Him? Substituting any other standard of excellence for that of the humanists, the question remains: can and will most people so use circumstances as to reach the same level now (and so far always) occupied, if at all, by a few? Supposing the few to have ordered conditions to suit their own best interests (which should include those of others), are the many capable of constructing an equally stable and better society? Most well disposed people probably hope that these questions can be answered in the affirmative. Certainly a Christian's obligation of love towards all would be easier if he could believe that accidents of social structure make men seem more unequal than they are rather than that native human inequality makes civilization seem more unjust than it is. Only if the above questions can be answered in the affirmative will democracy and education be more than superficial. Though their encouraging applause of humanity leaves no doubt that humanists desire an affirmative answer, their actual estimate of human conditions, if true, obliges one to expect that answer, if at all, only as a "dim, far-off, divine event."

The paucity of humanists and their slight official influence might not work to the disadvantage of their presumed method of education, did not the method reflect the limitations of its promoters. Those limitations in turn reveal a flaw in the present functioning of the American system of public instruction. With about two hundred and thirteen sects in the country, public schools, though

---

[90] *Humanism—A Religion for Today,* p. 17.

[91] " 'Had the Apostle Paul any regular job?' No, he had no regular job. 'Had he then a salary?' No, he had no salary. 'Did he earn much money in other ways?' No, he did not make money in any way. 'But at any rate he was married, was he not?' No, he was not married. 'But then Paul was not a serious man!' No, Paul was not a serious man—every tradesman especially will easily understand that." Kierkegaard, quoted by Dr. Walter Lowrie, *op. cit.,* p. 433.

fostering private and civic virtues admired by all denominations, cannot do much more than refer vaguely to a religious background that, while not necessarily forming the primary or immediate basis of morality, nevertheless completes and invigorates it. Though in their most susceptible years high school and university students may freely investigate religion and have often, at home or in church, been previously initiated in its practice, parental information is usually so indifferent and ecclesiastical training so slight that over half the population, on reaching years of discretion, is predisposed more to some sort of secularism than to any kind of religion.[92] Deprived of the stimulus, buoyancy, and freshness of a wholesome faith in God, they are thrown back for their tastes, standards, and interests upon the ordinary level of public commerce around them. "There is," we are told by a psychologist, who has apparently studied American public education from the point of view of "a practical man," "no body of evidence in the whole field of psychology that proves any definite growth of character or personality as the result of higher education in its generally accepted forms."[93] An education that fails to do that is inadequate. To trust in it, as humanists recommend, is to go through life with a hole in one's shoe. As most people are (always have been and probably ever will be) condemned to that anyhow, why should one, humanists might ask, require an education that develops abilities beyond their average use? Though that may be all that can be expected on a wholesale basis, it does not justify exclusion of religious training or confidence that a radical improvement of mankind can be achieved by such faulty means. Americans possess an ability to transcend their cultural heterogeneity in a common pursuit of present practical interests. But their racial and religious heterogeneity is still so marked that educators and legislators avoid meddling with it. From the nature of things it is unlikely that racially and religiously Americans will

[92] cf. "The Other 65 Million," by Bart Andress, *The Standard*, February 1938, p. 131.
[93] Henry C. Link, director of the Psychological Service Center, New York, N.Y., in his *The Return to Religion* (New York: Macmillan, 1936), p. 145.

soon reach the uniformity or neutrality that to a convenient degree they have attained in intellectual and practical matters. If, as has perhaps been evinced, religion—communion with God (at least in the sense of an effective though possibly inarticulate conviction that what we prize most in ourselves points, like a compass arrow, to an ultimate reality evoking, answering, justifying, and perfecting it)—forms a valuable and inextinguishable element of our individual and social constitution, and if religion manifests itself in definite, historical cults, it would seem to be better for us not, like humanists, vainly to repress, ignore, or dilute it, but to foster (difficult though that will be) a publicly encouraged education by the cults in their best contributions to a symphonic, rather than a sectarian or an insipidly nondenominational, practice and appreciation of it.

If there is any truth in this chapter, popular humanism is aware more of the failings than of the merits of religion, especially of Christianity; its optimism towards progress and the annihilation of evil is as uncritical as its faith in personality; and its conception of ethics, though on the whole temperate and humane, is chaotic in itself and incoherently related to human nature. Of the two commonest ways of escape from this situation, the first—that of the grand manner—suggests: "Ours is the responsibility of conserving, transmitting, rectifying and expanding the heritage of values we have received that those who come after us may receive it more solid and secure, more widely accessible and more generously shared than we have received it. Here are all the elements for a religious faith that shall not be confined to sect, class, or race. Such a faith has always been implicitly the common faith of mankind. It remains to make it explicit and militant."[94] Sufficiently abstract and general to meet with universal acceptance, this merely asserts, what everybody knows, that civilization must be improved. Though it may perhaps be called by courtesy a religious faith, it does nothing to discriminate between actual types of religion or to meet detailed difficulties with

[94] John Dewey, *A Common Faith*, p. 87.

which more concrete schools of thought struggle. The other way might be described as cultivating one's own garden. "Be intelligent . . . be tolerant . . . be courageous . . . be honorable . . . follow the truth . . ."—these commands, writes Dr. Birkhead, "summarize my present idea of religion."[95] For most people they summarize the elementary prerequisites of civilized man, qualities he should possess in every sphere of thought and action, but no more exclusively or characteristically religious than they are uniquely artistic, political, or scientific. Not because it is "too negative" or "too destructive," but because it is only a beginning rather than a full flowering of religion, do "religious people" find the "kind of religion" preached by Dr. Birkhead and many other humanists as "unsatisfactory" as he suspects they do.[96]

[95] *The Religion of a Free Man*, Little Blue Book no. 1485, pp. 27, 28, 29.
[96] *ibid.*, p. 27.

CHAPTER VI

SYNOPSIS OF CHAPTER VI

Though most humanists accept as a matter of course contemporary, Anglo-Saxon, liberal morality, their scholars seek reasons for doing so. "Starting from the common humanistic postulate that values reflect our nature and little else," Professor Sellars eventually finds in them indications of the structure of reality also. He leaps the usual humanistic fence between objective facts and subjective values, only to limp along under the impression that facts are ontologically more "intrinsic" than values. Such a belief, as Mr. Lippmann shows, deprives ethics in its higher forms of vital connection with reality. Some humanists, like Dr. Ames and Dr. Curtis Reese, attempt to establish that connection through recognition of cosmic forces making for righteousness, which many of their colleagues treat, however, and even invoke, as personified abstractions. Professor Hartmann's theory of value. His misunderstanding of Christian ideas of immanence and personality as they apply to God and of the relation of God's will to ours.

CHAPTER VI

HUMANISM AND SPECULATIVE ETHICS

ORDINARILY humanists do not go beyond the limits outlined in the preceding chapter. To give a contrary impression might make the movement seem to be more academic than it is. Humanist metaphysicians, however, seek reasons why we do and should cherish our "heritage of values." The popular principles of humanism make this imperative. That feeling and cognition thwart one another, so that scientific reason alone finds facts, while emotion projects illusions; that facts exist in spite of ourselves, and values only as reflections of our moods;[1] that we are "victims in the realm of fact," because reality is "omnipotent matter," which, "blind to good and evil, reckless of destruction, . . . rolls on its relentless way," and "kings in the realm of value" solely because "the lofty thoughts that ennoble" our "little day" are "created" by us:[2] these assumptions, though expressed in the words of Bertrand Russell, are (with little modification) the stock in trade of everyday humanism. Were they true, it would be idle to waste time and spirit in Russellian "disdain" and "proud defiance" of a "wanton tyranny" unconscious of our antics. And if we stared in the face this "slow, sure doom . . . pitiless and dark," we should find it impossible to maintain that cheery confidence in the supremacy of personality, which characterizes the mass of humanists. Aware of this, their philosophers

[1] " . . . when we assert that this or that has 'value,' we are giving expression to our own emotions, not to a fact which would still be true if our personal feelings were different." Bertrand Russell, *Religion and Science* (London: Butterworth, 1935), p. 230.
[2] cf. Bertrand Russell's essay "A Free Man's Religion" in his *Mysticism and Logic and Other Essays* (London: Longmans, Green, 1925; quoted by permission from Allen and Unwin, Ltd.), and *What I Believe*.

195

attempt to save the optimism of the clan by virtually denying its popular assumptions.

Starting with the common humanistic postulate that values reflect our nature and little else, Professor Sellars—this chapter will try to show—"evolves" to the point of finding in them indications of the structure of reality also. His wavering advance and subsequent relapse, his naturalism must answer for. It prevents him from admitting that, despite differences, values and "facts" (like the primary qualities) are equally essential to reality. Without that presupposition, as Mr. Walter Lippmann notes, morality, eviscerated especially in its higher forms, becomes meaningless. Some humanists, like Dr. E. S. Ames and Dr. Curtis Reese, seek a compromise by recognizing cosmic forces making for righteousness. But this strains the imagination of the majority of their colleagues. These, if they recognize powers of goodness at all, address them as personified abstractions masking personal desires or impersonal currents in the universe. Almost the only notable humanistic effort to reach a theory of value beyond positivism and individual or racial subjectivism is Professor Hartmann's. Misapprehensions of Christianity seem to keep him from realizing that the profoundest aspects of his realm of values are latently theistic and that failure to develop their theistic implications decreases their relevance to religious experience without enhancing their worth for ethics, science, and philosophy.

Professor Sellars maintained, in 1928, that "truth, goodness and beauty are expressions of man's aspirations rather than supersensible realities alien to his nature. This means that we must think of the spiritual as rooted in man's nature and not as alien and introduced in some miraculous fashion from above.[3] . . . But when I say that value is never intrinsic to things external to the valuer, I wish to be understood. The value we set on things expresses our connection with them in the way of feelings, pur-

[3] *Religion Coming of Age*, p. 238. Why should the supersensible—e.g. higher mathematics—be "alien" to us? Are not many things "outside" and "above" us— e.g. sunsets—as much "in" us as our hearts and brains? Where do "we" stop?

poses, ideas and desires. In this sense value is egocentric and socio-centric. It is not something which is out there to be discovered by science.[4] It is a halo around things put there by ourselves. It is our value-interpretation of them. Nevertheless, this halo is not artificial; it is in its own way as objective as a thing can well be. Given the living soul with its interests, emotions and outlook upon life, and the value assigned to objects is inevitable.[5] These are the kinds of objects, perhaps, which call out the soul's deepest emotions and mean much to it as a consequence. The value of an object is what it signifies in the economy of our lives."[6] Though Professor Sellars recognizes objects as evoking our emotions, certainly this description of values is anthropocentric, psycho-logical, subjectivistic, and projectionistic in tendency—not quite, though almost, as one-sidedly so as that of popular humanism.

Four years later, however, Professor Sellars tried to strike a bet-ter balance: "I may remark in passing that I have been astonished by the tendency among American philosophers working in this field to reduce value to some generic psychological form such as liking, desire, or interest. . . . It is evident that I must have at least a tendency to desire an object which I find desirable; but it does not seem to me to be quite the same whether I assert that it is a fact that I desire this object or that this object is desirable. In the first, I state a fact about myself; in the second, I am valuing the object.[7] . . . Now I take it that when we say that a thing is agreeable to taste we are characterizing it in terms of a meaning founded on our affective experience and attitude and not project-ing our feelings into it. In other words, value-predicates are not subjective desires and emotions read into the object but meanings of a specific kind in terms of which we now *think* the object. But we are not thinking it cognitively but valuatively. We are appraising

[4] Which alone finds what is not "sociocentric"?
[5] Inevitable, granted; but more or less illusory than scientific values or—should one say—facts? ("Science is only one of the values of life." *Religion Coming of Age,* p. 229.)
[6] *Religion Coming of Age,* p. 228.
[7] *The Philosophy of Physical Realism,* p. 464.

it in the light of our experiences relevant to it.[8] I have long argued that the clue is to distinguish two ways of thinking an object. In strict cognition we are trying to get at the nature of the object as it is apart from ourselves and to decipher structure and behavior. In appraisal we are, instead, estimating how it has or might connect up with our lives. The reference is objective but we have a different intellectual task.[9] . . . The thesis which I have been advancing is that the value-predicate in terms of which we think the object valuatively is founded on the experience we actually have with the object or on the experiences we anticipate that we would have.[10]. . . A good which is not a good *for* someone strikes me as meaningless. It is the possession and enjoyment of things which makes them values for us. There must be implied at least the *possibility* of connection with our lives. In other words, value is not an attribute, like size and composition, which is out there to be known. It is, to use G. E. Moore's term, not a natural property; that is, not the kind of property disclosable by sense-data.[11]. . . Note, then, that value-meanings are not predicates of the cognitional type. They do not pretend to disclose what the object is in itself. It is in this sense that *good* is a non-natural property. It is

[8] cf. "To suppose that, in values, we are immured in ourselves merely experiencing desires and feelings in a subjective, introspective sort of way seems to me a quite unjustifiable position to take. [*ibid.*, p. 463.] . . . It seems to common sense when it is immersed in its commerce with things that they are in some sense perceived as good, harmful, useful, beautiful, etc. The value-meaning is attached to them as directly as any other attributes. And I take this to be the actual case. In other words, valuing is as natural and as automatic as perceiving. Once we have made up our minds about things, the characterization of them follows automatically. [*ibid.*, p. 462.] . . . On the other hand, to look upon values as intrinsic qualities of external things which we have only to discover in an intuitive, cognitional sort of way is to be the victim of an impossible theory of knowledge. Even in perceiving there is interpretative characterization." (*ibid.*, p. 463.)

[9] *ibid.*, p. 465; italics his. cf. "What I have desired to bring out is that judgments of value are perfectly objective in their reference; only they have two references. And this is why judgments of value are at the same time objective and subjective. It follows that values cannot be simply intrinsic in the same way that the properties are which are known; and yet they are objectively assigned." *ibid.*, p. 473.

[10] *ibid.*, p. 466.

[11] *ibid.*, p. 459; italics his. If values are not disclosable by sense-data, they come perilously near to being "supersensible realities."

not like color or shape or structure. It is simply a value-property, that is, what the thing means to our lives in the light of its nature and of its power to affect us, we being what we are. It is an interpretation of the object in the light of factors which are relevant to our appraisal of it in these relations."[12]

Though a conjunction of quotations runs the risk of gaps and false stresses, it would be difficult in any other way to present Professor Sellars's thought as directly as it deserves. Doubtless aware of differences among values and of distinctions that a profounder study of the subject would reveal Professor Sellars chooses —and, to meet him on his own ground, we must accept—a discussion of values in general, on a relatively elementary plane.

"The fundamental dualism" underlying the whole philosophy of humanism, according to Professor W. M. Horton, is "an absolute cleavage between the realm of fact (which is objective and belongs to science) and the realm of value (which is purely subjective and human)."[13] By taking "as objective a view of value as possible";[14] by admitting that values, like "facts," are founded on experience and related to and partially determined by "external" objects not of our creation; by recognizing that the interpretative aspect of valuation corresponds to the interpretation (or apperceptive mass) inseparable from perception; and by acknowledging that such interpretation is not incompatible with objectivity: Professor Sellars would bridge the chasm of popular humanism between objective facts and subjective values. By speaking of them as equally objective (and equally subjective) but as different intellectual tasks (valuative thought and cognitional thought), he would apparently mark their differences without detriment to what they have in common.

In reality, however, he transfers the humanistic cleavage to a deeper if less obvious level. The gulf between the two kinds of thought (cognitional and valuative)—or between the two kinds of values, scientific values (or "facts") and cultural, humane, or

[12] *ibid.*, p. 472. Italics his.
[13] *op. cit.*, p. 83.
[14] *The Philosophy of Physical Realism*, p. 445.

spiritual values—remains as yawning as the original abyss between subjective feelings and objective discoveries. The original difference in objectivity is disguised as a difference in intrinsicality. In both cases the difference rests upon a misunderstanding of science. That values have "two references"—to ourselves and to objects that we distinguish from ourselves—that they are thus connected with our lives, and that they indicate what a "thing means to our lives in the light of its nature and of its power to affect us, we being what we are": is the undisputed realism of common sense. Humanists apparently cannot understand that the same is true of primary qualities.[15] And if it is true, either science is roughly on a par with valuation, as far as degree of intrinsicality or objectivity is concerned, or valuation is roughly on a par with science. In view of the dubious position granted to values by humanists and the high esteem in which science is generally held by occidentals, probably most people would prefer to promote values to the rank of facts—as regards objectivity and intrinsicality—rather than to degrade facts to the questionable status of values.

Inability to recognize what they have in common, in the matter of objectivity, comes from magnifying differences in purpose into ontological differences. Generally we regard both moral values, for instance, and physical characteristics (size, composition, color, etc.), in reference not only to external objects but to our purposes

[15] Perhaps the relative lack of organization and standardization of valuative acts as compared with scientific cognitive acts makes reference to our aesthetic and moral tastes appear to be more incoherent, individualistic, and subjective than reference to our scientific tastes and purposes. A difference in "intellectual task" and in degree of organization does not necessarily imply more than a difference in degree of "intrinsicality"—it does not necessarily imply that scientific qualities are intrinsic and values not intrinsic. Much of the uneasiness felt by some towards a "realm of values" arises from an apparent inability on the part of defenders of the realm to observe a hierarchy of values. Though any proposed order of precedence, like that of Professor Nicolai Hartmann's, may be debatable, there is need to note in values distinctions analogous to those between primary and secondary qualities in physical objects. Presumably, some values are as "real" and indispensable to morality, for instance, as primary qualities are to mechanics. Recognition of a moral order through acceptance of the reality of moral values should no more involve one in an apotheosis of spiritual eccentricities than should recognition of a physical world through acceptance of the reality of physical qualities involve one in a glorification of tone deafness, astigmatism, or any other anomalies of perception.

and needs. The gaiety of this chair's graceful lines, or the solemnity of that table's massive planes, are as objective features as their size and color. In ordinary life one is more aware of the aesthetic, the moral, and the religious quality of a cathedral, or a house, or a landscape, than of their measurements. People brought up in the same cultural tradition will respond to spiritual values with roughly the same uniformity as people brought up in the same scientific tradition will respond to impressions of weight, distance, and solidity. In any situation we find, according to our ability and training, various facts and values distinguishable but conjoined, as original, essential, inescapable data. Subsequently they may be so dissected that we forget the given whole from which we started. In an effort to explain physical motion in the simplest way possible, we can disregard secondary for the sake of primary qualities. We can thereby devise a view of the world that has no place in it for color or for values. On that theory color and values do not belong to the external world (i.e. to the physical pattern we are momentarily concerned with) but are tossed or projected, like quoits or haloes, by our minds on to reality. The inner consistency of the theory, its wide applicability, and the confusion of an attempt "to get at the nature of an object as it is apart from ourselves" with the inconceivable success of such a paradoxical venture apparently lead humanists to believe that that supposedly scientific theory reveals the nature of objects as they are apart from ourselves, intrinsically, absolutely, "in themselves," and "out there." Once they have dreamed this dream, they are unable ever to shake it off fully. "Why talk about a 'world of values'?"[16] asks Professor Sellars a year after taking "as objective a view of values as possible." He is willing to grant that "man's valuations are expressions of his life in relation to his surroundings, expressions of what he admires and hopes to accomplish, etc."[17]—he is, unwittingly and despite his protests to the contrary, thus apparently willing to sink back into an "astonishing" tendency to reduce value to some "generic psychological form such as liking, desire, or

[16] "In Defense of the Manifesto," *op. cit.*, p. 12.
[17] *ibid.*

interest"—but he, and *a fortiori* the majority of humanists, does not yet seem to realize not merely that there are competing scientific pictures of reality, each true to its own point of view and postulates, so that it is absurd for a scientist to talk about "reality" except within a given frame of reference, but also that none of these theories (nor all of them together) attempts to do justice to more than a few data abstracted from an original (and now much neglected) experience.[18]

"What confronts us in actual life," writes Professor A. E. Taylor, "is neither facts without value nor values attached to no facts, but fact revealing value, and dependent, for the wealth of its content, on its character as thus revelatory, and values which are realities and not arbitrary fancies, precisely because they are embedded in fact and give it its meaning.[19] . . . There must be at least as much to learn about the inmost character of the real from the fact that our actual spiritual life is controlled by such-and-such definite conceptions of good and right, such-and-such hopes and fears, as there is to learn from the fact that the laws of motion are what they are, or that the course of biological development in our planet has followed the lines it has followed. It may be that this is a grave understatement."[20]

Turning hopefully to "such-and-such definite conceptions of good and right, such-and-such hopes and fears," we may agree with what Mr. Walter Lippmann writes of "heroes," "sages," "explorers," "inventors and discoverers," "pioneers and patriots," namely, that "though there is nothing in our current morality [he means the morality of humanism] to justify their unworldliness, we continue to admire them greatly."[21] Professor Sellars describes the universe as "something within which to work in a human way, bravely, creatively, gently, wisely. Here is a new attitude, that of an adult

---

[18] At the risk of surrendering the fort to the humanists, one may own that "original experience" at times looks like a mythological monster. It is referred to above in uncritical fashion simply to keep the game going; the analysis of such a fundamental concept would require more attention than humanism itself.

[19] *The Faith of a Moralist* (London: Macmillan, 1930), Vol. I, pp. 61-2.

[20] *ibid.*, p. 65.

[21] *A Preface to Morals*, p. 157.

shifting for himself, set on carving out his own fortunes, aware that life is not a bed of roses, knowing that tragedy may claim him, and yet fighting a good fight for whatsoever things are honorable and of good repute. Here we have man and religion coming of age."[22] Is all this irrelevant to "a world of values"? Is "the universe" merely "not unfriendly,"[23] "not hostile to values in some absolute sense"?[24] Are we to assume this simply because it tolerates our existence as we tolerate the existence of mosquitoes and flies—simply because "it is the natural scene" of our "birth and achievements"?[25] Anybody would admit that courage, creativeness, kindliness, and wisdom are normally pleasures in themselves. Even when carried to an extreme of unworldliness they provide at least some (though for most people not enough) subjective satisfaction, an exaltation of mind, which others can enjoy through sympathy and admire. But the fact that daily virtues ordinarily escape criticism should not silence the scientific humanist. What he wants is truth, reality, not a fool's paradise of sweet spiritual sensations. True, he will take "the supremacy of personality" at its face value—but only at the cost of suspending science's unquestionable right to question. That was an error not to be repeated.

Now, this "unwordly" preservation of a sense of integrity beyond average requirements, manifested in diverse ways by

[22] *Religion Coming of Age*, p. 156. What is "new" about this attitude? Is it not one held for thousands of years by worthy, sometimes unreligious and unphilosophical people? Man has need of all sorts of things not flattering to his vanity—something on which to depend, something to be devoted to, something in which to believe. For his fullest development, these should ever flee before him and lure him on. Charmed by a vision of "social security" he can easily adopt a "rugged individualism" towards God and the cosmos. He feels that he has outgrown the childlike attitude, that he is shifting for himself, that he is "mature," "adult," and independent (in one way or another humanists seem unduly concerned lest we forget they are "of age"), whereas he has merely shifted his dependence to a narrower, smaller, more tangible, less mysterious, and less stimulating object—himself or his fellows. When he transfers his devotion to politics or reform, he feels superior to religious worship. When he can swallow "science" whole, he rightly depreciates the credulity of believers. And in the end, with words of repudiated hymns and scriptures, he affirms—and often "stoutly" —ideals he might have shattered, had he been right.

[23] *ibid.*, p. 156.
[24] R. W. Sellars, "In Defense of the Manifesto," *op. cit.*, p. 12.
[25] *Religion Coming of Age*, p. 156.

"heroes, sages, explorers, inventors, pioneers and patriots," and considered by many people as fundamental to morality, what can be said of it in the light of cold, humanistic, scientific reason? Every day someone has an opportunity to shirk an important obligation without attracting notice, and to save himself and his family from scandal, penury, or death, at the cost of sullying his own sense of honor. Without reproaching him if he took the easier, apparently "sensible," "altruistic" course, and without condoning a choice recognized as none the less base, everyone knows that honorable men are better for themselves and for others than are those who prefer anything else to integrity. But when honor is on one side— to make matters worse, let us suppose that the sense of honor is in this case as near right as could be desired—and everything else on the other, what can humanism do? Up to this point, it can say, "Reality is not absolutely hostile to your valuative act, otherwise it would never have permitted its birth. I don't think you can dismiss your awareness of the right as an individual failing or a purely subjective racial illusion. Remember that even an hallucination has some external object. But what does drive me to despair is that you can possibly suppose that justice or honor is in any way as intrinsic to reality, apart from ourselves, as 'extension, figure, motion, rest, solidity or impenetrability, and number.'[26] Those primary qualities are 'out there.' For a reason that I prefer not to divulge, if values were 'out there,' they would be 'alien' and 'supernatural.' We might be in danger of childishly 'submitting' not merely our intellects but our wills to the ordering of an 'external' reality, instead of relying on that mature 'creativity' which is at once our glory and your pain." If one were persuaded of the truth of that position and if one wanted reality rather than "wish-fulfillment," one would be obliged to prefer primary qualities in some form or other to values. If the voice of conscience is not merely faulty but represents a subordinate and incidental rather than an ultimate aspect of reality, its commands cannot be categorical imperatives. Then one may agree with Mr. Lippmann that humanism

[26] Berkeley (referring to Locke's distinction between primary and secondary qualities), *Principles of Human Knowledge*, Part I, section 9.

makes morality meaningless. "We cannot base a terrestrial optimism on cosmic pessimism."[27]

This is an awkward position for those whose religion is ethics. If Dr. Felix Adler was right in saying that "the ethical movement will prosper and last in proportion as the number who have that sense of sublimity, the holiness feeling about the moral life, increases in our midst,"[28] humanists and their Ethical Culture kin must find a theory of morality that will justify rather than preclude such reverence. Dr. E. S. Ames apparently agrees with Dr. Curtis Reese in seeking this through a recognition that "purposive and powerful cosmic forces" abet morality. "Some call them cosmic processes, others call them God."[29] If the difference is only in name, these humanists seem to be on the road to theism. Certainly their reasoning recalls teleological and moral arguments of theology. They recognize that "in the long run" goodness triumphs, or, to put it less implausibly, ugly, unjust, stupid systems and actions eventually fail a bit more surely.[30]

> "Round the decay,
> Of that colossal wreck, boundless and bare
> The lone and level sands stretch far away."[31]

In spite of the confusing imperfections of our moral and religious systems, the fact (the more profound, if the less apparent, the

[27] Izoulet, quoted by I. L. Holt, in Chap. IV, p. 128, of *Humanism, Another Battle Line,* edited by W. P. King, Nashville, Tenn., Cokesbury Press, 1931.

[28] Felix Adler, "The Quest for the Eternal," *The Standard,* October 1934.

[29] C. W. Reese quoted by J. W. Buckham in Chap. III, p. 84, of *Humanism, Another Battle Line,* edited by W. P. King, Nashville, Tenn., Cokesbury Press, 1931.

[30] "Is the universe friendly to man? . . . Friendly to man in what respect? With respect to ease and comfort, to material success, to egoistic ambitions? Or to his aspiration to inquire and discover, to invent and create, to build a more secure order for human existence [and to obtain ever more satisfactory personal relations with God]? In whatever form the question be put, the answer cannot in all honesty be an unqualified and absolute one. Mr. Breasted's answer, as a historian, is that nature has been friendly to the emergence and development of conscience and character. . . . Growth has not been confined to conscience and character . . . it extends also to discovery, learning and knowledge, to creation in the arts, to furtherance of ties that hold men together in mutual aid and affection." John Dewey, *A Common Faith,* p. 55. Interpolation in square brackets mine.

[31] Shelley, "Ozymandias."

higher one goes) that some sort of mental or physical injury pursues him who wilfully violates the best in his code suggests that moral values belong at least as much as physical qualities, to the structure of ultimate reality. If the working test of reality and objectivity is that which, unless we would be deformed, we must accept, that from which we cannot escape (except by false choice and its consequences—not a real escape at all), moral values, in one form or another, are as ontological as anything can be. If, choosing among countless definitions, one may say that "freedom and the carrying of moral values" are "the two elements of personality," reality, subject to nothing beyond itself and manifesting itself to us through values, is personal in the highest degree.[32] Our personality, humanists concede, grows through cooperation with "cosmic processes" so well adapted to evoke and to sustain the best in us—a "personal" response *par excellence*—that they are better described in the words of Dr. Shailer Mathews as "the personality-producing forces of the universe."[33] Though these are not the only cosmic forces, humanistic logic in defense of humanistic optimism would seem impelled to reach the theistic conclusion that, despite "the problem of evil," they are the supreme forces. Ultimate reality thus becomes worthy of our communion, devotion, joy, and appreciation, which in various ways and degrees it arouses and

[32] Though the definition is suggested by Professor Nicolai Hartmann's *Ethics,* the above point of view—especially in finding a bond of union between the axiological and the ontological and in concluding that reality (God) alone is fully personal (if, as Trinitarian doctrine suggests, His unity admits diversity) —is antithetical to his. His discussion of "The Metaphysics of Personality" (*Ethics,* Vol. I, Chap. XXIV) and of "Metaphysical Personalism" (*ibid.,* Chap. XXV) is almost irrelevant to the Christian idea of God because it ignores its Trinitarian characteristics, which, never originally devised to meet criticism like his, anticipate many of his difficulties concerning the rôle of sociality and subjectivity in personality.

[33] "So when one undertakes to set up personal relations with the personality-producing forces of the universe, one cannot avoid the conclusion that there is in the cosmos that which can make such personal adjustment possible by some sort of personal response. . . . The more one thinks of one's characteristic human personal power, the more one must believe that powers which can produce personality in men and continue as an environment for humanity must, in the nature of the case, be susceptible of making personal response to personal adjustment." Shailer Mathews, *Humanism, Another Battle Line,* p. 144, edited by W. P. King, Nashville, Tenn., Cokesbury Press, 1931.

satisfies. Though response from our nature as a whole is, for us, a fully personal response, owing to our limitations it will take in one the form of an *amor intellectualis,* in another, something more sensuous and concrete—in each according to his nature and training, without the implication, however, that, though each responds as well as he can, every response is equally adequate. But such a reality and such a response, when amorphous generalizations are properly defined by historical cults, are (so far as anything can be said in such matters) God and religion.

Humanists, however, stop short of that with a strange medley of religion, ethics, and science. For a personal God they substitute personified abstractions to which they address petition and worship.[34] "Clear, O Spirit of Truth, our inner vision, that we may see. . . ."[35] "O thou Universal Life, we rejoice in the signs and tokens of thyself. . . ." "For all the holy fellowship of life, we give thanks."[36] To whom? To one another? No, it is a reaching out to ultimate reality—an aspiration presupposing, if it is not vain, that reality is in some sense personal. "For the poetry of spring

[34] More logical humanists refrain from such worship. But their number is few compared with those accustomed to formulas like the ones mentioned above. " . . . the Humanist says that it is . . . useless for us to try to bring ourselves into direct communion with the ultimate center and source of all power and blessing. . . . The all-important thing is that we strive to bring ourselves continually into better relations with that portion of reality with which we come into actual contact." J. H. Dietrich (passage slightly altered in expression but not in meaning), "The Advance of Humanism," p. 37.
"What could be more fatuous than to suppose that there is no God but the God idea and yet try to use the God idea religiously—that is, as a guide in seeking religious adjustment to reality? I well remember hearing a good many years ago a prayer offered in the pulpit of Dr. Ames's church in Chicago, not by Dr. Ames himself, but by the supply of the day, in which the opening apostrophe was, 'O Thou Idealization of our highest desires!' How can the would-be worshipper take up a really religious attitude toward what is confessedly the product of his own imagination? This, however, is what humanism would make of prayer to God: 'O Thou Objectification of our highest ideals!' 'O Thou Projection of our sublimated libido!' 'O Thou Symbol of the highest social values!' 'O Thou Personification, Idealization, and Glorification of the world, including humanity!' 'O Thou Wish-Being!' 'O Thou Substantiated Abstraction!'" D. C. Macintosh, *Humanism, Another Battle Line,* pp. 62-3, edited by W. P. King, Nashville, Tenn., Cokesbury Press, 1931.
[35] Unitarian Services for use in The Fellowship of Liberal Religion—a humanistic group—, Ann Arbor, Mich., Service no. V.
[36] *ibid.,* Service no. VI.

. . . we lift up thankful hearts."[37] They lift them up, of course, to "O thou eternal Goodness," "Life of my life," and even "my Lord."[38] But, as scientific humanists, should they not simply observe that they are glad, or note their temperature, respiration, and pulse? "For all the unknown toilers of mine and field, in factory and office, whose strength has redeemed us from want, whose blood has purchased our welfare, the fruit of whose labor is our rich inheritance; we lift up thankful hearts."[39] If there is no God capable of appreciating and acting on this, if cosmic forces in spite of their "cooperation" are deaf, dumb, and blind, if emotions are misleading, meaningless luxuries, is not this indulgence of them as much "diverted aspiration" as anything censured by humanists in theism? After the religion that made such emotions seem natural, significant, and fruitful has vanished, what is left but sham and sentimentality? Were it convinced of its irrelevance to indifferent "cosmic processes," true thankfulness (like Christian love of neighbor) instead of gloating over itself would seek those unknown people allegedly bleeding for us and would show its gratitude by remedying their lot. Irenic humanists intimate that they and theists are in reality worshipping the same mysterious "Source of power, whose symbol is the thought of God."[40] No doubt there is some truth in the assertion. Nevertheless theists cannot help believing that what is commonly suggested by the words "God" and "religion" is, despite their metaphorical nature and obscurities, more appropriate to the object of humanistic reverence (where it is genuine and not primarily an "esthetic" exercise) and to that reverence itself—and hence less artificial as "symbols"—than are pseudo-scientific abstractions and the inevitably embarrassed fashion in which they are employed.

Probably the best humanistic defense of a moral universe without God is in Professor Nicolai Hartmann's *Ethik*.[41] In almost

[37] *ibid.*, Service no. I.
[38] *ibid.*, Service no. IX.
[39] *ibid.*, Service no. I.
[40] From a hymn in the same book of services.
[41] Translated into English by the leader of The Ethical Church in London, Dr. Stanton Coit.

every respect, except that of refusing to subordinate man to deity, Professor Hartmann differs from the majority of humanists. Instead of aping science and reiterating—as could hardly be expected of a German—recent, popular, Anglo-American ideals, prejudices, and ignorances, he reveals more than a verbal contempt for naturalism and subjectivism, an unapologetic faith in ethics as an autonomous level of human life, and a preoccupation with philosophers, like Plato, Aristotle, Kant, and Nietzsche, noticeably above the usual humanistic "authority." Relying largely upon Kant[42] as the best exponent of the spirit of morality and (with important qualifications) as the best purveyor of its metaphysical machinery,[43] and upon Aristotle (with insights of Nietzsche) for description and appraisement of specific virtues, Professor Hartmann models his final theory of value primarily on Plato's theory of Forms.[44] But the development of Platonic theism in the *Timaeus* and the *Laws,* Aristotle's (and subsequent) criticism of Ideas, and the historical affinity between Platonism and Christianity,[45] in no way shake Professor Hartmann's confidence in his own eclecticism.

Overlooking the fact that Christianity attributes to God not everything that is inexplicable[46] (baffling forms of evil, for exam-

[42] And the Stoics.

[43] Notably Kant's "ethical apriorism."

[44] Professor Hartmann is influenced by the moral, or Socratic, aspect of Plato's theory of Forms, rather than by the mathematical and logical, or Pythagorean, aspect of the theory. Plato's (and Spinoza's) appreciation of the beauty of logical perfection untainted by human concerns hardly appears in the German's *Ethics.*

[45] The affinity is so close that some (like Dr. W. R. Inge and Professor A. E. Taylor) dwelling—with the mystics—on the Form of the Good, and others (like Dr. Paul Elmer More) exemplifying rather what Dr. Friedrich Heiler calls "prophetic religion" and influenced by the "unabashed dualism" of Plato's "natural theology," have found the culmination of Platonism in Christianity.

[46] When driven back to God's "inscrutable wisdom," the religious man, rather than attribute to Him anything unworthy, suspects his difficulties of arising from almost any other source—generally some form of human folly. Archbishop Søderblom's description of the psalmist is relevant here: "He is sure of God despite the contradiction of the senses and the events. Let soul as well as body languish, God is yet his portion and his all. The Saviour on the Cross, the saint in 'the dark night,' Martin Luther with his heaviness of spirit, here is revealed the mystery of religion, its paradox, a certainty of God *quand même,* in spite of the bitter contradictions of life and, what is more, of one's feelings and

ple) but only qualities that, in the light of the Church's experience, seem applicable to Him, Professor Hartmann charges that "the religious man attributes to divinity everything of which he does not know the source; foremost, consequently, he attributes the moral commandments to it."[47] Even in *Exodus* and *Deuteronomy* the real reason why the Ten Commandments, for instance, are ascribed to God is less their unknown source than their felt congruence with His holiness as apprehended by the children of Israel. Values expressed in moral commandments, Professor Hartmann continues, are prized by Christians only as stepping-stones to heaven. Christianity is an "individualistic eudaemonism."[48] "The devaluation of this world is the reverse side of the teleology of the Beyond."[49] Although it could probably be shown that the supernatural, properly understood, perfects rather than nullifies nature;[50] that the values we see through a glass darkly are as precious, indispensable, and permanently incorporated in our growing experience as the values of childhood and adolescence are in the experience of adults; that the social aspects of Christianity are as fundamental as its individualistic ones; and that egoism and eudaemonism, inevitable in any human point of view, need not assume alarming proportions in Christianity or any greater influence there than they actually though not explicitly exert in Professor Hartmann's own

one's own nature." *The Living God* (London: Oxford University Press, 1933), p. 283.

The writers of the Old Testament "were so assured of the existence of God, and *therefore* of his providential rule, that in all times of trial and disaster, to however contrary a conclusion the events, taken by themselves, might seem to point, the assurance remained unshaken. Not being obtained by reflection upon the course of events, it could not be overthrown by them." N. Kemp Smith, "Is Divine Existence Credible?" pamphlet reprint from Vol. XVII of the *Proceedings of the British Academy*, 1931, pp. 13-14.

[47] *Ethics* (London: Allen and Unwin, 1932), Vol. I, pp. 111-12.

[48] *ibid.*, p. 135.

[49] *ibid.*, p. 134.

[50] Professor Hartmann's view of religion—at bottom the bald notion that "as compared with God everything, even man, is nothing" [*Ethics* (London: Allen and Unwin, 1932), Vol. III, p. 264]—overemphasizes its transcendental strain. By neglecting the immanental and the Incarnational aspects of Christianity, he caricatures this kind of theism as a form of deism. Almost everything he says about religion falls under criticism directed by Baron Friedrich von Hügel against "exclusive mysticism" in one guise or another.

theory: although this could probably be shown, it nevertheless remains true that specifically Christian morality exists less as a congeries of "self-sufficing moral principles" than as a way of walking with God.[51] Professor Hartmann, with Plato, Aristotle, the Stoics, and Nietzsche to supply him with other than Christian material and norms, sees this more clearly than most humanists. They seem to think that the morality fostered by Christianity[52] as necessary and appropriate to "children of God" and "joint-heirs with Christ" remains self-evident and vital not only if we do not "suffer with Him"[53] but even if we reject Him and His Father. To the extent that Christian morality embodies features common to many ethical traditions, the humanistic judgment of it as satisfactory in so far as it lacks God resembles the view that dancing is at best a mild kind of gymnastics because, its distinctively social characteristics being overlooked, it is a form of physical exercise.

Although Professor Hartmann apparently believes that morality can englobe science without destroying the latter's autonomy in its own field, he cannot see how ethics, without being cramped and distorted, can possibly fit in religion's wider scheme. Not simply a methodological desire to treat morality apart from religion and metaphysics, nor a humanistic horror of God, but, as Dr. Webb observes, a "profound sense of the dignity of human nature as invested with the freedom and autonomy presupposed by man's moral consciousness"[54] moulds Professor Hartmann's conception of the relation between religion and ethics. "That anything whatsoever in heaven or on earth, even though it is God himself, should take precedence of Man would be ethically perverted; it would not be moral; it would be treason to mankind, which must rely upon itself alone."[55] Professor Hartmann trembles lest people fancy that good is good by divine fiat. Good is good by itself, he maintains,

[51] "Nor is Christian salvation anything else than a veil for the highest good to which yearning aspires—for purity, spiritual health, and union with God." *Ethics* (London: Allen and Unwin, 1932), Vol. I, p. 144.
[52] The morality in which most of them were trained and to which, like Christians, regardless of the sway of the world, they continue to pay lip service.
[53] Rom., viii, 16, 17.
[54] *Religion and Theism* (London: Allen and Unwin, 1934), p. 69.
[55] *Ethics* (London: Allen and Unwin, 1932), Vol. III, p. 264.

half implying that God, if He exists, may be despotic or wrong. To Christians convinced that God is goodness, truth, beauty (as the sun is its rays—and more)—who believe not that they may not err but that there can be no ultimate conflict between the way, the truth, and the life, and God (who is that to them)—to Christians the notion not merely of any discrepancy but of any distinction between His will and absolute goodness—although it has been debated in their theologies—must (like many other debates) be meaningless and repugnant.[56]

If, however, it is "treason to mankind" (rather than a recognition of our place in reality) to accept something other than ourselves as an object of admiration and reliance, Professor Hartmann, in devising, for our devotion, one of the most difficult and distant "realms" ever imagined, falls under his own condemnation. "There is a realm of values," he asserts, "subsisting for itself, a genuine κόσμος νοητός which exists beyond reality just as much as beyond consciousness—an ethical sphere, not manufactured, invented or dreamed, but actually existing and capable of being grasped in the phenomenon of the feeling for values—a sphere which perdures side by side with the ethical real and the ethical actual sphere, just as the logical ideal realm exists side by side with the ontological real and the gnoseological positive realm."[57] Values "are that 'through which' everything which participates in them is exactly as it is—namely valuable. . . . Values emanate neither from the things (or real relationships) nor from the percipient. . . . They are not 'formal' or empty structures, but possess contents; they are 'materials,' structures which constitute a specific quality of things, relations or persons according as they attach to them or are lacking. . . . Not only are they never merely 'invented' . . . but they are not even capable of being directly grasped by thought; rather are they immediately discerned only by an inner 'vision,' like Plato's 'Ideas.' "[58]

An attitude of worship pervades the *Ethics*. "The object worshipped," as Dr. Coit observes, "is the Ideal, Self-existent Realm of

[56] cf. C. C. J. Webb, *God and Personality*, pp. 173 f.
[57] *Ethics* (London: Allen and Unwin, 1932), Vol. I, p. 226; cf. *ibid.*, p. 165.
[58] *ibid.*, p. 185.

Values as a Creative Power impinging upon the world of the senses and of human society and calling for man's cooperation."[59] Probably more than anything else the spirit of worship, cropping out here and there like a vein of gold, tempts humanists and theists to explore the vast and often difficult terrain of Professor Hartmann's thought. Instead of regarding values in the same cool light that he regards the "logical ideal realm," he "constantly uses language which seems to cry out for a belief in God to give it meaning."[60] "Joy," "gratitude," "reverential wonder" are excited in him by "the richness of life," "the unbounded abundance of things that are of worth," and "the presentiment that the values of existence are inexhaustible."[61] And this humanist, inclined to keep morality on a social plane, and to deny "ethical impress"[62] and disinterestedness to love of God, finds the culmination of ethics in "love of the remotest," which "excels . . . every other virtue."[63] "Only a deep and mighty faith, permeating a person's whole being, is equal to it. It is a faith of a unique kind, different from trust between man and man; a faith which reaches out to the whole of things and can do no other than stake all it has. It is faith on the grand scale, faith in a higher order, which determines the cosmic meaning of man. . . . In a pre-eminent sense the expression 'Remove mountains' may apply to it. And this energy is harmonious with a similar feeling—hope, when it is raised to its highest power, the basic feeling of ethical idealism, which bears all things and gladly suffers for an Idea, never despairing: hope, the peculiar assurance which takes hold on one who risks all on a single issue."[64]

Believing, unlike most humanists, in "an inborn aprioristic *ordre du coeur,* or *logique du coeur*"[65]—an "apriorism of emotional acts," which "is just as pure, original, autonomous, and transcen-

[59] *ibid.,* p. 13; cf. *ibid.,* p. 7.

[60] C. C. J. Webb, *Religion and Theism* (London: Allen and Unwin, 1934), p. 72.

[61] *Ethics* (London: Allen and Unwin, 1932), Vol. II, pp. 210, 243.

[62] *ibid.,* p. 278.

[63] *ibid.,* p. 330.

[64] *ibid.,* pp. 330-1.

[65] Pascal quoted by Max Scheler, as quoted in Hartmann's *Ethics* (London: Allen and Unwin, 1932), Vol. I, p. 177.

dental an authority as the logical and categorical apriorism in the domain of theory"[66]—Professor Hartmann accepts our feelings of reverence, gratitude, and love, directed to something beyond and greater than anything we know, as spontaneous, inevitable, and right. But how can anything less than personal be a fully suitable object of these affections?[67] Indeed is not this attitude towards values virtually "such a 'personification' of them in relation to ourselves as is in fact equivalent to the affirmation of personality in God, when this is taken . . . not as an arbitrary transference to the infinite and absolute Reality of predicates essentially finite and relative, but as the inevitable expression of an actual religious experience of that Reality by individual persons"?[68] Professor Hartmann's presentiment of the unbounded abundance of values strikes theists as being almost indistinguishable from faith in the goodness of God. It is difficult to see how his grateful reverence could be warranted without the existence of a Reality "personal" enough to inspire in us a trust analogous to that created "by intercourse with a just and sympathetic personality."[69] And this unique and mighty faith "in a higher order," "which reaches out to the whole of things," which in its utter devotion stakes all it has, this "love of the remotest," which "excels every other virtue" and is the crown and fulfillment of morality, "what is this but precisely the love of God with all our heart and soul and mind and strength, in which Christianity finds the complement, or rather the basis, of the brotherly love, wherein lies the essence of our duty to our neighbor?"[70]

[66] *Ethics* (London: Allen and Unwin, 1932), Vol. I, p. 178, quoted in Webb's *Religion and Theism* (London: Allen and Unwin, 1934), p. 73.

[67] *Religion and Theism* (London: Allen and Unwin, 1934), p. 73.

[68] *ibid.*, pp. 74-5; cf. Dr. Webb's *God and Personality* and *Divine Personality and Human Life.*

[69] *Religion and Theism* (London: Allen and Unwin, 1934), p. 73.

[70] *ibid.*, p. 78. "To me it seems that this insistence on the necessity of finding a place in our morality for the 'love of the remotest' is in fact a recognition at least that morality cannot but in the long run involve . . . not Religion only but Theism. The first great commandment of the Christian law means for me . . . 'that morality rests upon a principle transcending the individual consciousness and belonging to the spiritual principle of unity in all reality, a principle conceived of in Christianity as revealing its nature in the experience of mutual love.' This truth . . . 'cannot be disregarded without imperilling morality' itself. 'In other words, morality cannot dispense with Religion; not in the sense that it re-

214

As an object of the worship reaching out to the whole of things Professor Hartmann prefers a perduring realm of values to God, because his conception of deity is more marred by "anthropomorphism" and "anthropocentric megalomania"—to use his own expressions—than is that of intelligent theists.[71] They think of Him not as a finite person indefinitely magnified, but as a Reality that religious experience finds and presupposes as supporting our love, reverence, and trust, to an extent merely adumbrated in love among finite persons. But finite love and finite personality, though differing from divine love and divine being, are (for Christians, in Christ) the least unworthy analogue, inkling, or manifestation of one, and perhaps for us the most important, aspect of God's nature. A love (like *Fernstenliebe*) greater than that among finite persons, if it is not delusive, must have an object at least as concretely real as a finite person is. Even if Professor Hartmann's values are not (what most humanists would call them) "hypostatized abstractions," they lack the "actual concrete reality" of persons. "In our consciousness of self . . . we have . . . the model and standard of reality, of which even the most sublime ideals fall short, so far as, taken in abstraction from an individual being or individual beings who conform to them, they do not have that same sort of actual existence of which we are aware as belonging to ourselves."[72] According to theism, God possesses a concrete reality greater than ours. As a Being in whom "Essence and Existence are one—a Being who not only *has* but *is* the power, wisdom, goodness which we adore in him"[73]—He meets, better than any lesser object, the religious demand for ultimacy, of which *Fernstenliebe* is a reflection.

And such a God furnishes also what every religion requires, an intimacy excelling that among finite persons. This, Professor Hart-

quires an external sanction, but in the sense that, except as interpreted by Religion, it must appear as an unintelligible fact, incoherent with the rest of experience, and so come easily to be suspected of being no more than an obstinate prejudice which the wise man will endeavor to disregard.' " *ibid.*, p. 79; quotations from *Contribution of Christianity to Ethics*, p. 116.

[71] e.g., A. E. Taylor, W. R. Inge, C. C. J. Webb, F. R. Tennant, W. Temple, V. Monod, D. C. Macintosh, and F. von Hügel.

[72] *Religion and Theism* (London: Allen and Unwin, 1934), p. 139.

[73] *ibid.*, p. 138. Italics his.

mann's ideal perduring values, in so far as they have (despite a "permanence and fulness of significance" surpassing the individual personality of their worshipper)[74] a concrete reality less than that of persons, cannot furnish; for though his values "constitute a specific quality" of persons—as well as of things and relations—they still remain, no matter how much we cherish them, qualities, abstractions, elements, not living wholes, much less real persons with whom we can commune. Intimacy among persons—to repeat —only faintly represents God's immanence. He is apprehended—in worship, for example—as Other, transcendent, over against us, to an extent not even suggested by any person or thing belonging to the plane of "nature" or "creation." And at the same time He is in no way sundered from us. "Closer is He than breathing, and nearer than hands and feet."[75] Finite persons are fundamentally insulated from one another—not mutually transparent. God certainly is dazzling rather than transparent to us, but He permeates our being in a way that the sun's permeation of our bodies and influence on our minds despair to imitate. Only through certain objects (human bodies or the products of human agency) do we become acquainted with one another, but any object, at any time, in any place, may arouse "a consciousness of the numinous" or, at a higher stage, a sense of the Presence of God, "because that of which we are aware in religious experience is immanent in all reality."[76]

His fear lest the providence of an omnipotent and omniscient deity involve a thoroughgoing axiological determination of the real (or transformation of values into ontological categories) gives Professor Hartmann another ground for distrusting theism. We must have, he maintains, a causally determined world in which to act; for moral conduct requires ability to effect events in depend-

[74] *ibid.*
[75] Tennyson, "The Higher Pantheism." cf. *Religion and Theism*, pp. 82-3, 141-2, 154.
[76] *Religion and Theism* (London: Allen and Unwin, 1934), pp. 142-4. It is important, Dr. Webb writes, to "distinguish carefully between social and religious experience, just because the critics of Theism are so apt to assume that Theism is an undiscriminating transference to the latter of categories belonging only to the former." (*ibid.*, p. 142.) On this point see Dr. Webb's "Our Knowledge of One Another," *Proceedings of the British Academy*, 1930.

216

able fashion.[77] But the validity of our sense of responsibility and of our feeling of remorse when we disregard conscience presupposes, according to Professor Hartmann, that our will is free to "insert" its "finalistic determination" into the causally determined world around us.[78] As we are good or bad, we accept or reject the values we discern.[79] If we accept them, we can to a certain extent—in the process of "actualizing" them—mediate the creation of reality by ideality. "Man, a vanishing quantity in the universe, is still in his own way stronger than it: he is the vehicle of a higher principle, he is the creator of a reality which possesses significance and value, he transmits to the real world a higher worth. Nature is bound down to its own laws; man alone carries in himself a higher law, whereby he—or more correctly the law through him—creates in the world, or from Non-Being brings forth into Being, that which was prefigured in its ideality.[80] . . . It is only possible for man to have a task in the world, however restricted it may be, provided there are values which without his cooperation remain unactualized.[81]. . . In a world, determined axiologically throughout, a moral being is an impossibility. A thorough cosmic teleology utterly nullifies ethics. It is a theory of predestination—whether theistic, pantheistic or atheistic—and leaves fatalism as the only standpoint for man."[82]

[77] *Ethics* (London: Allen and Unwin, 1932), Vol. I, p. 277.
[78] *ibid.*
[79] *ibid.*, pp. 236-8.
[80] *ibid.*, p. 243. "The *generatio ex nihilo*, which is otherwise an impossibility in all realms of Being, here is possible." *ibid.*, p. 238.
[81] *ibid.*, p. 242.
[82] *ibid.*, pp. 287-8. Although he would probably dismiss Professor Hartmann's ideal realm of values as a dangerous interpretation and glorification of purely human, social, regulative ideas, Dr. John Dewey voices a similar objection to a universe axiologically determined throughout. "It is argued that the ideal is already the final reality at the heart of things that exist, and that only our senses or the corruption of our natures prevent us from apprehending its prior existential being. Starting, say, from such an idea as that justice is more than a moral ideal because it is embedded in the very make-up of the actually existent world, men have gone on to build up vast intellectual schemes, philosophies, and theologies, to prove that ideals are real not as ideals but as antecedently existing actualities. They have failed to see that in converting moral realities into matters of intellectual assent they have evinced lack of *moral* faith. Faith that something should be in existence as far as lies in our power is changed into the intellectual

217

Though the idea of fate (Μοῖρα, Kismet, and so on) is frequent in religion, the more extreme forms of election, foreordination, and predestination have been only temporary, local vagaries of Christianity, which as a rule has shown slight need or desire to defend them. Accordingly one would not expect Dr. Webb to disagree fundamentally with Professor Hartmann about fatalism. Perhaps for that reason the former's illustration of travelling by train from one place to another[83] does not reach the heart of the latter's objection to "a thorough cosmic teleology." That, under certain conditions, purposive action is possible in a system axiologically determined, travellers prove daily when they utilize trains the routes and the hours of which are prescribed by a railroad company. But in so far as the traveller's purpose is not also determined by the railroad company, the world of Dr. Webb's illustration is not "axiologically determined *throughout*" by one and the same source of determination, which is presumably the condition stipulated by Professor Hartmann. "Divine providence . . . is teleologic, a finalistic determinism. Its ultimate ends are the determinants. And because their determining power is infinite and almighty and moreover permeates every event in the world—even in the little spiritual world of man—, over against it man with his teleology is impotent. . . . What to him appears to be his self-determination is in fact the power of divine providence, working onward through him and above him. . . . All initiative, all setting up and pursuit of ends is transferred to God. . . . In this way finalistic determinism of divine providence abolishes ethical freedom. But if we grant validity to personal freedom, it inevitably abolishes the finalistic determinism of divine providence."[84]

belief that it is already in existence. . . . Moreover, when conditions are adverse to realization of the objects of our desire—and in the case of significant ideals they are extremely adverse—it is an easy way out to assume that after all they are already embodied in the ultimate structure of what is, and that appearances to the contrary are *merely* appearances. Imagination then merely supervenes and is freed from the responsibility for intervening." *A Common Faith*, p. 21. Italics his.

[83] *Religion and Theism,* p. 151.
[84] *Ethics* (London: Allen and Unwin, 1932), Vol. III, p. 267.

Christian theism—eager for the whole of reality, regardless of its apparent paradoxes and contradictions—is as jealous of man's freedom as of God's omnipotent goodness. Our privilege of adopting or rejecting values, which seems to constitute morality for Professor Hartmann, St. Augustine accepts as a characteristic of the imperfect liberty of finite persons. *Posse non peccare, magna est libertas; non posse peccare, maxima est.* Only God, on this basis, would enjoy the true liberty of being goodness itself, a liberty incompatible with "freedom" to be or to do anything evil. Though this "higher morality," to misapply a phrase of Professor Hartmann's, does not and cannot belong to us, sin-sick mortals may understandably long for and strive after a slavery to goodness so complete that its service is perfect freedom.

As far as freedom of the will, evil, and the supremacy of goodness (or the providence of God) are concerned, Christianity and Professor Hartmann struggle along in the same boat. Neither "explains" the age-old "problems," although Christianity has impressed more people as meeting the facts better. Except for its greater intimacy and ultimacy, the attitude of Christians towards God is much the same as Professor Hartmann's worship of values. In his more devout moods he stresses what Christians might call God's prevenient grace. When "beholding" values, the subject, he maintains, "is purely receptive; he surrenders himself to them. He sees himself determined by the object, the self-existent value; but he himself, on his side, determines nothing."[85] Even when asserting man's initiative and the need of his cooperation to actualize the ideal, Professor Hartmann corrects himself, saying that it is values or their "law" or "principle," rather than man, which create the real "through" man. As the good theist is the most amenable to God, so the good Hartmann-humanist is the most susceptible to values. To ascertain the type and the degree of determination exercised over men by God and by ideal values is a task of about the same sort and difficulty in both cases. In each case, man proves his strength less by wrong choice or merely by the fact of choosing than by the fact of being possessed or intoxicated by God or values.

[85] *ibid.,* Vol. I, p. 219.

For better or worse, those most convinced of being vessels of God have in the course of history shown an energy and indomitability unequalled by persons not sure of such backing or inclined to resent infringement of their "moral" right to refuse it. Rather than abolish human freedom, divine will in fact reinforces it. And human freedom, buoyancy of life, and the ripening of our deepest emotions seem to require a faith in the inexhaustibleness of values equivalent to belief in divine providence. The realization of un-bounded values, or of God's immortal love, working in ways we need not and cannot chart, no more absolves an individual from constant effort than does the realization of his small part in building a skyscraper excuse a workman from his work. Though our place in the world depends upon ourselves—which should be enough to keep us morally and practically active—luckily the world itself does not. The providence of God, or the inexhaustibility of values, means not that we need not work but that in so far as we do our best (even if it leads to failure and evil), the resources of Reality are such as to evoke and merit our wonder, reverence, gratitude, faith, hope, and love.

CHAPTER VII

SYNOPSIS OF CHAPTER VII

Approach to Christian theism is blocked for some, like Dr. L. M. Birkhead, by a low opinion of the clergy. Other objections—ecclesiastical dogmatism, disagreement as to the significance of tradition and emotion, and a failure to grasp what Christians mean by "the personality of God"—lead Professor Huxley to an identification of religion with a "sense of the sacred" incompatible with his own metaphysics and ever verging on theism. Professor Auer's definition of religion in terms of psychological function, as the integration of personality through projection and apotheosis of ideals. Dr. Dewey's theory of religion as the function of unifying life by the realization of the ideal in the actual. His picture of the Christian God as "a particular Being" possessed of static, "prior, complete embodiment" outside nature. Humanistic views of prayer.

HUMANISM AND RELIGION

HUMANISTS agree in rejecting theism as much as they disagree on what to accept in its place. Though personal animosities will betray themselves, generally good taste keeps discussion of theory on the plane appropriate to it. But often enough to be noticed, as in the case of Dr. L. M. Birkhead, familiarity with theists breeds contempt of theism. On account of their bewildering variety of substitutes for belief in God, we must limit ourselves to a few humanists of notable constructive ability. We shall consider their proposals in an order of increasing definiteness and objectivity, as they rise from vague religious feeling, through conscious self-integration, to recognition of something more than human and endowed with some of the attributes that believers ascribe to God.

Professor Huxley holds himself exiled from churches he never entered, on account of a misapprehension of the theistic conception of deity, on account of dogmatism and authoritarianism, and on account of the relation of beliefs (like that in an after-life) to primitive sources, conservatism, and desire. His religion he finds in the sense of the sacred, which looks more like an incipient theism than a fit consort to his hermaphrodite of science and philosophy.

Professor Auer would define religion in terms of psychological function. What we worship in God, he asserts, are projected human ideals. Religion is integration of personality through apotheosis of the best in us.

Distrust of the supernatural and of other "historic encumbrances" prompts Dr. Dewey to start also from the seeming

223

certainty of religion as the function of unifying life. Whatever unifies life is "religious in quality." But in the end only something "inclusive" and "deep seated" will do. The uniting of the ideal with the actual—the realization (through our creative imagination) of the former in the latter—marks for him the work of deity. "Use of the words 'God' and 'divine' to convey the union of the actual and the ideal" he allows as long as we do not identify God with "a particular Being outside of nature." His view of the relation of God to nature, men, and existence, provides additional food for reflection.

But practice as well as theory composes religion—practice that transforms spirit as well as outer conduct. For humanists what is the equivalent of prayer? Some, like Dr. C. F. Potter, "call upon their own reserves." Professor Sellars effects this through "music, poetry, and a quiet walk into the country." Professor Leuba, however, distinguishes between relaxation and adoration. The possible effects of Christian prayer, he avers, require a cause like the Christian God. "Possession of an ethical purpose" and of sufficient life- and fire-insurance, alas, is as close as he can get! Both those who have them and those who have them not realize, sadly or happily, that if God does not take the place of insurance and good intentions neither can they take His place. Without Him (and, as most men know, imperfectly with Him),

> "Whatever be our lot,
> In marble palace, or in hut of straw,
> We long for what is not."[1]

But "passons au déluge."[2]

To the principal practitioners of a way of life or to the officers of an institution an inquirer first turns for evidence of the worth of what they represent. Though the attitude of most humanists towards official representatives of the theism they know best—that is, towards the Christian clergy—is not always as unfavorable as Dr. Birkhead's, yet, like him, humanists as a rule probably find

[1] *Japanese Poetry,* by C. H. Page (Boston: Houghton Mifflin, 1923), p. 55.
[2] Racine, *Les Plaideurs,* Act III, scene iii.

less exaggeration than others do in a book by his friend Mr. Sinclair Lewis, called *Elmer Gantry*. Meditating on this novel, for the author of which he was a "technical adviser," Dr. Birkhead compiles a long list of clerical flaws, which (with, of course, some exceptions) may be allotted to two types of clergymen. "Peevish," "sentimental," "affected," "sanctimonious," "petty," "purposeless," "morbid about sex," intellectually weak, "professional sympathizers," "ignorant of life"—the trouble with parsons like these, says Dr. Birkhead not bothering to name the "seminary professor" whom he quotes, "is that they look as though they were descended from a long line of maiden aunts."[3] Others, who go beyond the "hell" and "damn" way of expressing themselves, which Dr. Birkhead associates with the few ministerial "good sports"[4] escaping his censure, he chides for being "crude," "boisterous," "coarse," "vulgar," "thoroughly commercialized," "hypocrites," "hired advocates," "actors," "mountebanks and demagogues," "intolerant and very bad-mannered."[5] Though every profession fosters undesirable as well as good qualities, Dr. Birkhead does not observe that the faults he mentions are as common in similar types of people in other callings and that generally they are to be found among clergymen only in a milieu in which, if one believes its failings to exceed its virtues, one need not move. Dr. Birkhead himself does not divide clerics into the two classes mentioned above. Rather he seems to imply, in any individual divine, a more general blending of the characteristics that he notes than would appear to be likely. The charge (which he brings up elsewhere) that religion is apart from "real living" in home, market place, shop, mine, and mill,[6] might, for example, better apply to "descendants of maiden aunts" than would the charge—more appropriate to "too good sports"—that religion is usually "on the side of persecution, ignorance, and oppression."[7]

[3] *Is "Elmer Gantry" True?* Little Blue Book no. 1265, pp. 29, 30, 32, 34, 35, 36.
[4] *ibid.*, p. 8.
[5] *ibid.*, pp. 13, 19, 20, 22, 27, 28, 32.
[6] *The Religion of a Free Man*, Little Blue Book no. 1485, p. 7.
[7] *ibid.*, p. 16.

Without occasionally attending, like Dr. Birkhead, "revivalistic orgies," or listening to evangelists like "Billy" Sunday, Aimee Semple McPherson,[8] "Father Divine," and a certain Reverend Ora D. Hurley, whose "revival meeting . . . has been in session nightly for several years at the Victoria Tabernacle, in the Armourdale section of Kansas City,"[9] one can hardly imagine the picture of religion they present. If the average "church supper" or religious periodical is enough to turn the fastidious into atheists, exposure to "uplift organizations," like the Anti-Saloon League, the Anti-Cigarette League, the Anti-Evolutionists' League, the Bible Crusaders, the Clean Book League—to choose a few from Dr. Birkhead's list[10]—exposure to such societies for temperance, prohibition, and public morals, might conceivably turn people without theistic propensities to endure all things into misanthropists rather than humanists. That men and women familiar with such ideas of religion and with leagues that, in the eyes of their members, express the humanistic "quest of the ages for a good life in a good world,"[11] should become humanists and should want to call their point of view "religion," proves once more that man is fearfully and wonderfully made.

Humanists have ordinarily been more exposed to such influences than have "reputable theologians." And such influences (which reputable theologians rarely dream of referring to), much more than abstract scientific difficulties, continue to "humanize" people discriminating enough to be repelled by frequent travesties of religion and morality but not well enough trained or richly enough endowed to see far beyond them. This fact, which is again and again evident in popular humanistic writings and which colors the relations between their authors and others of less picturesque background, deserves to be indicated because it is often politely suppressed, with the result of distorting major differences in life into minor differences of thought. There is no more reason, however, for

[8] Little Blue Book no. 1265, pp. 20, 39 *ff*.
[9] Little Blue Book no. 1371, p. 20; cf. *ibid.*, pp. 23, 25.
[10] *ibid.*, p. 8.
[11] A. E. Haydon, *The Quest of the Ages*, p. 167.

humanists like Dr. Birkhead deliberately to seek and feed upon faults more trying to theists than to anyone else[12] (as flaws in the cathedral at Chartres pain the French more than the Tibetans), than for theists to dwell on the shady sides of humanism. None may abide a test sufficiently extreme to mark what is done amiss. No desire to minimize a shameful situation (no matter how provincial and passing it may be) or to rebut with a justifiable *tu quoque*, but common sense, suggests that this game of beam and mote is at best an idle pastime.

Professor Julian S. Huxley, though possibly aware of this prevalent, powerful, and, to that extent, important, bickering, is, needless to say, one of the refreshing humanists totally immune to it. The sideshows of Christianity do not pique his curiosity. He "is not and has never been a member of any organized church."[13] For probably the same reason that caused Dr. Johnson to define "pastern" as the "knee" of a horse,[14] "the whole Christian scheme, theologically considered, remained" for Professor Huxley throughout his youth "wholly incomprehensible."[15] The strength and the purity of his religion make him sensitive to what he supposes are infirmities and subterfuges characteristic of theism. His disinterestedness and magnanimity cannot tolerate base notions of personality, which—in our opinion, erroneously—he associates with the Christian idea of God. Though theists can hardly endorse his interpretation of their position, of science, and of the relation between the two, they can admire the motives that animate his pursuit of a truer and nobler religion than he can find among them. He is, in some respects, they find it flattering to think, too Christian to be what he imagines a Christian is.

[12] No humanist has ever criticized the clergy, the "scandal" of official Christianity, and the "criminal mockery" of public divine worship more tellingly than the Christian believer Kierkegaard. cf. Walter Lowrie, *op. cit.*, pp. 487-582.

[13] *Religion Without Revelation* (London: Benn, 1928), p. 101.

[14] "A lady once asked him how he came to define *Pastern* as the *knee* of a horse: instead of making an elaborate defense, as she expected, he at once answered, 'Ignorance, Madam, pure ignorance.'" Boswell's *Life of Johnson*, edited by G. B. Hill (Oxford: Clarendon Press, 1887), Vol. I, p. 293.

[15] *Religion Without Revelation*, p. 12.

One thing that helped make theology incomprehensible to Professor Huxley, and that flourished more in his youth than it does now, was a dogmatic attitude towards dogmas. "While a new discovery in science, however revolutionary a change it necessitates in accepted systems of thought, is regarded as an advance and a triumph; in religion the abandonment of a traditional outlook is almost always looked on as a defeat—a battle lost; and to this more than any other single cause," writes Professor Huxley approvingly of Dr. A. N. Whitehead, "he traces the loss of influence and prestige which the organized religion of the Christian churches lament today."[16]

Many reasons exist for this contrast. Revolutions in science have generally occurred in its higher reaches. The great mass of people find nothing lacking in Euclid. Lobatchewsky and Riemann are scarcely names to them; Einstein is proverbially said to be understood by not more than twelve specialists. Only when science touches a common human interest—as in Darwin's study of our past—does the populace assert the "democratic right"—relentlessly exercised over religion and morality—of legalizing or outlawing what happens to please the majority.[17] Religion has too many ramifications in daily life to allow great difference if not in thought at least in expression between its experts and their Praetorian Guard. The sanctity appropriate to the object of religious worship often, as Professor Huxley shows, extends to doctrines connected with it. The faith once for all delivered to the saints is put away like an heirloom, a mummy in its pyramid, a relic in its altar, to be cherished more than used.

But where and when that attitude grows strongest, it tends to arouse opposition to a corresponding pitch. As the Roman Catholic Church, for example, neared infallibilism (the goal of its authoritarian tendency), the concept of development, sponsored by Newman, spread as a counterbalancing influence. With the disintegration of Newtonian physics and the elaboration of sciences like geology and biology, the intellectual trend, as indicated by Darwin,

[16] ibid., pp. 93-4.
[17] Tennessee at one time restricted the teaching of "evolution."

Bergson, and Einstein, has been to emphasize consciousness, life, *élan vital,* in contrast to matter and mechanical "forces"; relativity, novelty, creation, as against absolutism and completion; above all (and the triumvirate's chief point in common), time as more fundamental than, or at least as important as, space. What "dates" the present generation of Christians—except "fundamentalists" —is an attitude towards dogma that ranges from the casually critical, through the scientific, to the sceptical. For them the dogmatic attitude towards dogmas—as immutable and absolute truths —is almost inconceivable.

This does not necessarily imply a weakening of conviction. In fact the surer the belief in the reality of God, the less it fears being tested. Though reason affects communion with Him, He is not prized primarily as an inference or a formula. He is apprehended by the religious in a way comparable to the appreciation of beauty, moral fitness, or personal love, in the sense that each of these types of apprehension is (though not equally developed in everybody) normal, *sui generis,* and, though providing reason with material to work on, not entirely a product of discursive thought. Thus it is possible to be as loyal to the object of religious experience, while submitting proposed descriptions of it to every available pertinent means of criticism, as it is to be convinced of the reality of the external world despite the vicissitudes of scientific speculation. But the fact that religion can be studied in all its aspects as scientifically as love, space, skiing, or graptolites, does not justify the inclination to equate religion with merely its scientific aspect, to suppose that one or two types of scientific discipline drawn from other fields are peculiarly appropriate to the scientific examination of religion,[18] or to confound ephemeral crystallizations of science with its living spirit. Lack of appreciation of what religious dogmas stand for, rather than a glorification of them as such, is the style today.

[18] Professor Huxley advocates "the reform of theology on the three-fold basis of agnosticism, of evolutionary natural science, and of psychology." *ibid.,* p. 58.

Another of Professor Huxley's objections to theism concerns personal immortality. Christians and others who hope for life beyond the grave are perhaps more aware of the difficulties involved (which are continually thrown in their faces) than are humanists. Were not the phrase already copyrighted by the latter, Christians might be disposed to boast of their own obstinacy as "tough mindedness." They cannot help noting that humanism itself points towards immortality. "Believing as he does, that human personality is of supreme value, and self-perfectible, the Humanist will not assume any dogmatic position against immortality, if immortality is conceived as a state of improved and perfected personality. . . . For when man has asserted his immortality, he has been simply using the best words and thought-concepts he had to express his confidence in the supreme value of his own personality."[19] What leads Dr. Potter in the end to reject something he deems of sufficient intellectual acceptability to be unworthy of dogmatic denial? Its lack of "emotional efficacy and imaginative reality"?[20] The proverbial heroism of Mohammedan soldiers disposes of that, for simple souls. What disturbs Dr. Potter and most humanists is that "the real heaven-hunters have no interest in improving the conditions here." That, however, as mentioned before, is true only of certain aberrant people.[21] Ordinarily the desire to inherit

[19] C. F. Potter, *Humanism, A New Religion*, p. 108.

[20] Corliss Lamont, *The Illusion of Immortality* (New York: Putnam, 1936).

[21] "Divine Providence is an excuse for the poor whom we have always with us; for the human improvidence which produces whole broods of children without reflection or care as to how they shall live; for not taking action when we are lazy; or, more rarely, for justifying the action we do take when we are energetic." *Religion Without Revelation*, p. 18.

The abuse of an idea reflects less on the idea than on those abusing it. Nobody argues that bad religion or bad science is good. The question is whether at their best they are not favorable to satisfactory life. It is so easy to blame Christianity for our selfishness and apathy that we forget it brings about, against great odds, possibly, more good than has or does any other force in history.

"Humanism has existed from the days of Comte and before, but we have no record of its achievements in building hospitals and orphanages or in rescuing submerged human beings from the filth and immorality of the slums." (W. P. King, *Humanism, Another Battle Line*, p. 271, edited by W. P. King, Nashville, Tenn., Cokesbury Press, 1931.)

"A very large fraction of the altruistic and humanitarian and forward-looking work of the world, in all its forms," Professor R. A. Millikan states, "has today

the kingdom prepared from the foundation of the world[22] is a stimulant rather than a sedative. St. Catharine of Genoa, St. Vincent de Paul, St. Francis of Assisi (not to mention Jesus)—various types of Christians believing in immortality—were—and the world with them—aided rather than hindered by that belief. The "worthwhileness of life on this earth" is, as far as it goes, taken for granted by normal people. Heaven, instead of conflicting with earth, encourages humanity in moments of weakness.[23] For many, life without immortality would be a frivolous or an appalling farce. It is hard to see how humanistic "faith in the supreme value and self-perfectibility of human personality"[24] can be more than an empty phrase if it fails before the first real obstacle of life, death. "The frank acceptance of mortality"[25] is only a pretty way of congratulating ourselves on our resignation, our prompt surrender, our loss of heart. Perhaps the chief embarrassment concerning immortality felt today by people sophisticated enough to hold nothing true unless, like Descartes, they can clearly and distinctly perceive it, is its meaninglessness, its unimaginability.[26] No matter how firmly one may be persuaded that good is more ultimate than evil and that moral effort has what Baron von Hügel called "abiding consequences," the belief that anything in us of permanent worth will survive lacks definite content, because, although we must trust our best judgment, we cannot specify in detail what God wants to preserve. Moreover, a living person, even if he knew what ought to survive, can fancy what life after death

its mainsprings in the Christian Churches. My own judgment is that about 95 per cent of it has come, and is coming directly or indirectly, from the influence of organized religion. . . . My own judgment is that, if the influence of American Churches in the furtherance of socially wholesome and forward-looking movements, in the spread of conscientious and unselfish living of all sorts, were to be eliminated, our democracy would in a few years become so corrupt that it could not endure." (Quoted by W. P. King, *ibid.*, pp. 271-2.)

[22] Matt. xxv, 34. The text makes it obvious that, for Christians, admission to heaven depends largely on "improving the conditions here."

[23] Belief in immortality no more hebetates sensible people than the expectation of going to a university retards children in their work at school.

[24] *Humanism, A New Religion*, p. 109.

[25] R. W. Sellars, *Religion Coming of Age*, p. 197.

[26] Complete extinction is equally hard to conceive.

is no more easily than he can guess what death itself is for one who dies.

> "Nous naissons, nous vivons, bergère,
> Nous mourons sans savoir comment:
> Chacun est parti du néant:
> Où va-t-il? . . . Dieu le sait, ma chère."[27]

Christians, like anybody else, must leave to God what has little significance without Him.[28]

Professor Huxley discards belief in immortality on grounds often accepted by humanists as valid for the general rejection of religious tenets: the belief is of primitive origin; it is held on account of "man's enormous conservatism"; it is "merely the expression of man's deep desire and longing."[29] From the point of view of academic logic one might say that two and two are four regardless of the antiquity of the belief or the conservatism and the affection enveloping it. Ordinary experience, on the contrary, is apt to value highly anything that time has driven deeply in our hearts. Humanists themselves appeal to the tests of antiquity, conservatism or survival-value, and human appreciation, when they rejoice in unbroken descent from Confucius, or maybe the sophists, or at any rate the guiding spirits of the Renaissance. They appeal to the same tests when they argue that early Buddhism's indifference to immortality was so significant that nobody can defend belief in an after-life on the ground that it was long, widely, and warmly held. The objection might have more weight if primitive Buddhism had not been quickly obliged to adapt itself to man's longing for a god or gods and for something more than this life's brief span. Arguments from need and the incompleteness of life, as Professor Huxley remarks, are not in themselves logically compelling. He notes that love does not inevitably ensure its satisfaction. But though individuals sometimes fail to make "the right adjustment," generally speaking the wherewithal exists to meet

[27] Voltaire, "À Madame Lullin."
[28] Baron von Hügel (in his *Eternal Life*) and Professor John Baillie (*And The Life Everlasting*) find the core of immortality in life with God.
[29] *Religion Without Revelation*, p. 31.

232

our dominant needs—knowledge and God, as much as food, shelter, and love. If "desire and longing" cannot be accepted by us today as uncritically as they were by Rousseau, there is still no reason to swing beyond Kant and to maintain, as humanists often seem to, that the more we long for anything the falser it is. Rather the truth seems to be that longing for things incompatible with a good life destroys itself, while desire for things conducive to a good life gains with its own momentum. It would be perverse to mistrust anything of wide fruitfulness simply on the ground that we view it with "deep desire and longing," and it would be incredible that intelligent people could steadfastly view anything with "deep desire and longing" unless it were widely fruitful. The question arises whether normal or standard, as distinguished from careless average, human beings do have a "deep desire and longing" for immortality. But we are here concerned not with immortality itself but with the humanists' attitude towards it in so far as that is typical of their general relation to religion. If immortality—or anything else—is as deeply desired as Professor Huxley asserts, anyone but a humanist (and a humanist for everything but opinions contrary to his own) would conclude that it is not therefore less but more likely to wear "a precious jewel in its head."

Feeling as he does that theism is essentially dogmatic, outworn, and emotional, Professor Huxley seeks a substitute for it in a "scientific humanism."[30] The kernel of his religion is "the sense of sacredness"[31]—surely a sense as dogmatic in its unarguable convictions and as ancient and emotional as anything that he condemns in theism. From his point of view, "the concept of God as a supernatural personal being" is merely a by-product, "a stop-gap explanation,"[32] of the more primitive, original, and empirical sense of the sacred. Deity is—we may suppose—a shape taken now and then by fumes issuing, through volcanic vents of separate religions, from the all-pervasive subterranean flames of the sacred.

[30] *ibid.*, p. 9.
[31] *ibid.*, p. 12.
[32] "Advanced to stop the gaps in pre-scientific thought." *ibid.*

As Baron von Hügel virtually said of the supernatural,[33] "this high sense of sacredness and transcendent value may be vouchsafed in many ways and in many objects."[34] "All philosophy and science, all great art, all history, all lives of men—one and all may inspire to reverence or exaltation, or be made the subject of reflection which, being concerned with great problems in a grave and reverent way, is more truly religious than any pietism."[35] The "religion of the future must have as its basis the consciousness of sanctity in existence—in common things, in events of human life, in the gradually-comprehended interlocking whole revealed to human desire for knowledge, in the benedictions of beauty and love, in the catharsis, the sacred purging, of the moral drama in which character is pitted against fate and even deepest tragedy may uplift the mind."[36] "The consciousness of sanctity in existence" is not, despite Professor Huxley's implication, a novelty for the future. It is, in some form or degree, a characteristic not only of Christianity but of other past and present religions.

Indeed reverence and exaltation are so common and so often go astray that Professor Huxley prefers some types of the sense of the sacred to others. As Dr. Rudolf Otto insisted in the foreword to the English translation of his *Das Heilige*, the *numen ineffabile* should not overshadow the *ratio aeterna*. Mana, numen, *mysterium tremendum*, the sacred—these non-rational elements of religion can be vague, undirected, casual, and destructive, apart from adequate esthetic, intellectual, and moral control. The sense of sacredness, Professor Huxley is aware,[37] does not always attach

[33] For thoughtful Christians today "the supernatural," instead of suggesting, as Professor Huxley seems to think it does, something magic, suggests rather the spiritual (as an omnipresent quality or influence, not as the strange, tenuously material) and "unconditional value" and what they presuppose. cf. J. Oman's *The Natural and the Supernatural* (Cambridge University Press, 1931).—A prominent humanist said that he would like to replace the supernatural by telepathy, clairvoyance, and "extra-sensory perception."

[34] *Religion Without Revelation*, p. 326.

[35] *ibid.*, p. 304. This recalls what von Hügel observed of the "anonymously supernatural": any worthy endeavor or experience when pushed to its end reaches, or at least nears, religion.

[36] *ibid.*, p. 326.

[37] *ibid.*, p. 35.

to supernatural beings. They may not be conceived of at all, or, if they are, they may be deemed unworthy of reverence. In India certain sects have venerated the cow. And others have bowed before inanimate fetishes and impersonal, non-moral powers. "This primitive idea of God as non-moral power tends to survive in the background of more developed religions."[38] In the foreground of many allegedly "scientific" substitutes for religion Professor Huxley might have discerned, in the place of deities, "mere powers, as little ethical as the 'natural man' of primitive societies: morality has at this level not yet become linked with the idea of God."[39] He himself tries to avoid a low sense of the sacred by defining religion as a way of life "relating the objects of its feeling of sanctity to the individual's desire for salvation or righteousness, and to a definite set of beliefs or scheme of thought about the mystery of the universe and man's destiny therein."[40] "What we live by must be organized. . . . This is where organized religious thought makes its contribution to civilization.[41]. . . The experience of the universe as affecting human life and therefore as invested with sanctity is a reality, and is the proper object of religion.[42]. . . A developed religion is one which is so organized that it helps to unify the diverse human faculties, and to give to each of them the fullest play in a common task."[43]

Such a description of religion goes far—but not far enough—towards meeting Dr. Webb's requirements of ultimacy and intimacy. The religious person is concerned with what is ultimate for him—the universe and destiny. And his reverent communion with the ultimate integrates his own nature and puts him in better rapport with society and "all things both great and small." A religion like this is its own reward. It need not envy, fear, or prohibit, less satisfactory kinds. It may, however, suggest, with lordly humility,

[38] *ibid.*, p. 202.
[39] *ibid.*, pp. 201-2.
[40] *ibid.*, p. 327; cf. *ibid.*, p. 34.
[41] *ibid.*, p. 328.
[42] *ibid.*, p. 331. Why "therefore"? We do not revere everything that affects us, e.g. the noise of aeroplanes. Is the "experience" the object of religion except in so far as the object of the experience makes the experience significant?
[43] *ibid.*, p. 342.

"that those who pursue other approaches shall try and see whether their ideas are not narrow, whether they cannot be related to a wider sweep of reality."[44]

Perhaps the chief difficulties in Professor Huxley's theory of religion are that it is incompatible with what he believes to be the scientific picture of reality and that, if it would not be superficial, it presupposes the theism it would oust. As we desire salvation or righteousness, we must, on humanistic grounds, suspect that longing, no matter how hard, apart from its fulfillment, it is to think of the universe as sacred. Though science is yet "infantile" "on the human side,"[45] where art, literature, morality, and religion are more mature, orthodox humanists usually grant it everywhere a sovereignty as unquestioned as the one it wields over "physics, chemistry, and pure biology." Submitting (in fact, if not in words) to this humanistic dogma, Professor Huxley reports that nature is chaos[46] (which does not disturb his faith in its uniformity[47]). Out of this chaos we obtain unity apparently by imposing order upon it, as an artist composes his picture. Professor Huxley discovers "God, under one aspect, as a number of vital but separate facts, some material and some spiritual, but regarded as a unity, as a creation of the human soul (albeit a necessary and fruitful one), compounded of the hard facts of soulless nature and the spiritual and intellectual aspirations of the nature of man, the two organized into a single whole by the organizing power of the human mind.[48]. . . Communion with God . . . is an organizing of our experiences of the [chaotic] universe in relation with the driving forces of our soul or mental being [itself presumably of "Nature's chaos"], so that the two are united and harmonized."[49] If reality were thus and if human beings could create the harmony

[44] *ibid.*, p. 327.
[45] *ibid.*, p. 96. cf. Dr. Webb's *Religion and Theism*, pp. 55-8, for limitations of science in its dealings with human consciousness.
[46] *Religion Without Revelation*, p. 41.
[47] *ibid.*, p. 74.
[48] *ibid.*, p. 40.
[49] *ibid.*, p. 50. Interpolations in square brackets are mine.

necessary for religion, who would not worship them? Who would not be a humanist?

But with the restraint of one that respects the freedom of others Professor Huxley abandons an apologetic that might compel rather than persuade recognition of human ascendency. He turns instead to a totally different picture. "All reality consists of 'events, which are all events in the history of a single substance,' which, 'looked at from outside are matter, experienced from inside are mind.' "[50] At first Professor Huxley found unity only in the mind; and now, "out there" in the single substance. He offers no solution of the problem invented. As it is impossible to revere chaos, so likewise "communion" with the ultimate (which Professor Huxley attributes to religion) is, in any full sense, as impossible as communion with a wall, if the ultimate be a single all-embracing substance in no way reciprocating attention. Dr. Webb, apparently with thought and extension chiefly in view, likens the single substance that Professor Huxley leaves veiled in mystery to the single substance that Spinoza "called indifferently God or Nature."[51] But as Spinoza allowed for a kind of mutual love between God and men,[52] Professor Huxley's substance might also (as far as the impossibility of communing with it is concerned) be compared to Aristotle's Prime Mover, which in no way returned, or was affected by, love directed to it. Though not every man need show ground for the faith in him and though his faith may be true even if it cannot be proved, it is disappointing that Professor Huxley does not offer a theory more likely to strengthen than to sweep away the "facts," as he calls them, of his religion.

"Reverence," "respect, veneration, propitiation, service," "conviction of sin, desire of righteousness, sense of absolution, peace of communion," "the feeling of forgiveness and grace to a soul struggling with the sense of sin, the poignant experience of the value of others' atonement, or of one's own suffering, the sense of

[50] C. C. J. Webb, *Religion and Theism* (London: Allen and Unwin, 1934), p. 45, quoting from *Religion Without Revelation*, p. 76.
[51] *Religion and Theism* (London: Allen and Unwin, 1934), p. 45; cf. *ibid.*, pp. 53-4.
[52] cf. Spinoza's *Ethics*, Part V, proposition xxxvi.

communion with and peace in the realities that are around us"[53]—
these, Professor Huxley asserts, are facts essential to religion.
They are, moreover, phrases, attitudes, and experiences typical of
theistic religion. After due allowance for Professor Huxley's dependence upon the theistic language of his environment and for
his special interpretations and modifications of that language, it
seems to be true, as Dr. Webb argued in his *Religion and Theism*,
that Professor Huxley, like Professor Hartmann, claims as
essential to religion facts and experiences that theism better than
anything else explains and justifies.

What impels Professor Huxley to bolster his religion on two
theories each incompatible with it and with the other, instead of
accepting the theistic explanation for which it calls? Largely a misunderstanding, so it would seem, of the theistic conception of
God. "The next great step which religious thought must take . . .
is the liberation of the idea of God from the shackles of personality which have been riveted on it by man's fear, ignorance,
servility, and self-conceit."[54] A deity "of the same spiritual and
mental nature as a personality but on a higher level,"[55] Professor
Huxley believes, does not exist. It is a "product of evolution"[56]
and a "projection." "The ascription of personal being to religion's
external object is best thought of as in origin a natural and inevitable error of primitive thinking, now surviving in highly
modified form, a mistaken projection of personality into the non-
personal."[57] This "crucial assumption" once established, was
"worked on by man's intellect and by his ethical sense to give such
high conceptions as that of the God of the Jews from after the
Exile, or the God of most Christian churches; but which now must
be abandoned if further religious progress is to be made."[58]

No one conception of God can claim to be "the" theistic conception; for the best idea of Him at a given moment—"the" idea of

[53] *Religion Without Revelation*, pp. 34, 154, 361, 49, 317, 365, 366. cf. Webb's
Religion and Theism, pp. 44, 46, 49, 50, 51, 54, 55.
[54] *Religion Without Revelation*, p. 12.
[55] *ibid.*, p. 29.
[56] *ibid.*, p. 188.
[57] *ibid.*, p. 49.
[58] *ibid.*, pp. 172-3.

Him—inevitably reflects to some extent the peculiar circumstances of those who use it. Doubtless the highly anthropomorphic notion of God which Professor Huxley ascribes to Christians has had sufficient currency among them to come to his attention. Without denying its existence, or its faults (of which Professor Huxley suggests only a few), while at the same time holding that it may be the best thing available for certain people in certain situations (and therefore is not to be exchanged for anything less satisfactory), one may nevertheless agree with Dr. Webb that it does not belong to "the classical theology of Christendom."[59]

Ten years before Professor Huxley's *Religion Without Revelation* was published, with its description of the Christian God as a deity "of the same spiritual and mental nature as a [human] personality but on a higher level" [a "supernatural, personal being"] —ten years before Professor Huxley published this description, Dr. Webb had shown its deficiencies in his Gifford Lectures.[60] "It would probably surprise many critics of traditional language," he wrote, recapitulating some of the results of his Giffords, "to learn . . . that 'the personality of God' is a phrase unknown to Christian theology until well within the last two hundred years; that 'personality' was not reckoned among the divine 'attributes' so-called, and was long ascribed to God only in connexion with the 'three persons' worshipped by the Christian Church as one God; and that even the early Socinian divines were not concerned to insist upon ascribing 'personality' to him, but only to contend that, *if* the term were employed in reference to God (which employment they were inclined to deprecate), he should be spoken of as *One* Person and not as three."[61]

Professor Huxley's description of God as a "supernatural, personal being" might apply to the gods of Homer or of Epicurus or of the Norsemen. If ever gods were "persons," or glorifications of man and projections of his image, their gods were. The only difference, as far as Professor Huxley's description goes, between

[59] *Religion and Theism* (London: Allen and Unwin, 1934), pp. 46-7.
[60] *God and Personality*, especially Chap. III.
[61] *Religion and Theism* (London: Allen and Unwin, 1934), p. 47.

these pantheons and the Christian deity would seem to be that the latter is more "civilized" and lonely. The isolation of one human personality from another (reflected in the relations among the Homeric gods themselves and between them and men, and raised by Epicurus to a condition of mutual indifference between mortals and immortals) characterizes Professor Huxley's idea of the Christian God. Genuine immanence is there impossible. For that reason, among others, Professor Huxley rejects what he calls the Christian God; and for that reason, among others, "the classical theology of Christendom" never adopted such a god.[62]

"The affirmation of personality *in* God [as distinguished from the personality *of* God] has been a characteristic of Christian theological terminology since the third century of our era."[63] Personality in God has been affirmed by Christians as implicit in their doctrines of the Trinity and of Divine Incarnation.[64] Disregarding (as above the level of this discussion) the claims of those doctrines and the ways in which they have enriched the idea of personality, we may restrict ourselves to ascertaining what is generally meant by the now popular phrase "a personal God." Those who (like Trinitarians) affirm personality in God and those who (like theistic Unitarians) affirm the personality of God hold in common "the possibility of personal relations—of worship, trust, love—between oneself and God."[65] "What is meant by calling God 'personal' is ultimately not that we cannot explain the world otherwise for the purposes of natural science than by attributing its origin to a being like one of ourselves; but that our religious experience is experience of a communion, different indeed from the social intercourse which we enjoy with our fellow human beings, yet not merely metaphorically described by terms appropriate to that intercourse, but rather described thus *a fortiori,* that which gives meaning to those terms, the 'warmth and intimacy' . . . of the

[62] cf. Dr. Webb's *God and Personality* (London: Allen and Unwin, 1920), pp. 79-81.
[63] *God and Personality* (London: Allen and Unwin, 1920), p. 65.
[64] *ibid.,* pp. 82-3.
[65] *ibid.,* p. 70.

response, being present here in a greater rather than in a less measure, as compared with the reciprocal relations of finite spirits."[66]

To have any form of religion at all, we seem obliged to accept religious experience, in its varying degrees of adequacy, as "an inalienable and inexpugnable element in our response to our environment."[67] If our attitude towards reality is only disinterested admiration, we have to that extent burst through human pettiness without reaching a typically personal stage of religion. If the colossal indifference of the universe purifies rather than daunts our sense of communion with it, or with a Presence in, through, and beyond it; if we find an ever deeper zest in, and assimilation of, truth, goodness, love, power or being, and beauty, so that they become, as it were, our life; if we cannot help but worship what we find responding so overwhelmingly, so austerely, and, in its own indisputable and exacting way, so appropriately, to our greatest needs and potentialities: we are entering the stage of personal religion. Then we can or must affirm that ultimate reality is "personal" in the sense of accounting for this state of affairs. Clearly neither chaos, nor a single indifferent substance, nor a magnified human personality suffices to maintain these personal relations, which, apart from our defects and sins, are (according to the testimony of the saints) incomparably satisfactory. Historic religions variously define this incipient theism. Christianity—it could probably be urged not as a racial and regional prejudice but as a result of comparative analysis—does so on the whole best of all. Despite its rendering the idea of God more concrete and vivid, "the classical theology of Christendom" insists that, so far

[66] *Religion and Theism* (London: Allen and Unwin, 1934), p. 51.

[67] *ibid.*, p. 55. It is obvious, especially to those with the least of it, that religious experience (with other rich and complex experiences), like a spring, takes on many of the qualities of its environment. That science, too, suffers and gains from being in part a local as well as an international convention has been illustrated by Russian gibes at "bourgeois science," German scorn for "non-Aryan and democratic science," and the conduct of an eminent American scientist in excluding from his laboratory other specialists in his field, whose ways were more alien to him than is Zoroastrianism to Christian Science.

from being adequately envisaged in anthropomorphic fashion,[68] He exceeds all that we can conceive or desire. To hold such views presupposes that religious experience, like moral, aesthetic, or any other fundamental experience, when thoroughly sifted and co-ordinated with the rest of life, is at least as indicative of reality as science is. Because Professor Huxley apparently cannot believe that—because, in the name of science, he continually denies or warps (as it seems to us) the spontaneous (though theistically colored) expression of his religious nature—he concludes not merely that God is not "personal" in an untenable anthropomorphic way but that ultimate reality is such as to render illusory the promptings of the sense of communion with it, which is in large measure the basis of his and of any other advanced religion.

Though humanists and theists may differ on other points, those differences are minor compared with their disagreement about God. Were the reasons of humanists for rejecting Him valid, their constant search for something to take His place would be irrational. On the assumption, however, that humanists are working through errors towards a better conception of God, theists can find in humanistic writings much to cleanse and invigorate their own religion. Though in part it reflects ignorance of the past, nevertheless the desire for present "facts" simple enough to grasp readily, as distinguished from traditional opinions and a difficult-to-attain and often disappointingly sober consensus of experts, is one of the characteristics of youthfully vigorous, personal experience in religion or in anything else. The satisfaction of the desire for the definite and the concrete, usually had by recourse to some sort of empirical immediacy, like the sense of the sacred, is an essential, but not the only essential, of a well rounded philosphy.

Instead of taking the sense of the sacred as the chief fact and foundation of religion, Professor J. A. C. F. Auer, one of the signers of the Manifesto, would proceed from all the observable

[68] Which is valuable analogically, in that God is better thought of more in one way—say, the person of Christ—than in another—say, Professor Huxley's chaos.

effects of religion back to its recondite causes.[69] The conflict between humanism and theism, he says, is the old one between induction and deduction: theism relies, he leads one to suppose, on deduction; humanism, on induction.[70] But if, as seems more likely, both theism and humanism rely on induction and deduction, the question becomes not that of induction versus deduction but of the proper use of both. Letting that pass, however, we may note that in its presumably inductive way (which cloaks a mass of deductive metaphysics) humanism "starts with that which it knows best, man, not with that which it knows least, God."[71] Letting that pass too, "we may accept without question," Professor Auer assures us, "that the effect of religion is the turning of man toward an object of absorbing interest with the whole of his being. Here we have a definition in terms of function to which all Humanists would agree, because it states an effect, the accuracy of which may be verified."[72]

This definition in terms of psychological function, Professor Auer confesses, is general enough to apply to "many things not ordinarily thought religious," like "business, politics, science, or even a consuming hatred of our enemies."[73] There is no more reason to define religion as "life's supreme interest, by the side of which all else becomes secondary,"[74] or as "the force which binds together the loose ends of life until it becomes one,"[75] than to define it Spooneristically as "a reaching forward to the things that are behind." True, a good religion may be life's supreme interest and source of integration. Also one may be honestly religious without religion's taking the supreme place in life or being its principal integrating force. In many people social service or science is more dominant than religion; yet their religion as far as it goes is genuine. It would be absurd to call their science or their social service religion (which, however, may inspire those and other in-

[69] J. A. C. F. Auer, *Humanism States Its Case*, p. 82.
[70] *ibid.*, p. vi.
[71] *ibid.*, p. 103.
[72] *ibid.*, p. 83.
[73] *ibid.*, pp. 83-4.
[74] *ibid.*, p. 84.
[75] *ibid.*, p. 86.

terests) simply on the ground that one's prevailing passion is one's religion. If it may be called so at all, it is by a misleading extension of the word. Even Professor G. M. Stratton's definition of religion—"man's whole bearing towards what seems to him the Best, or Greatest"[76]—is preferable, because it indicates a consciousness by the person involved that the object of his prevailing passion is the best he can conceive—unless, of course, like a drunkard that sincerely acknowledges the superiority of temperance, for one reason or another his "whole bearing" towards "the best" is one of indifference or despair. Professor Auer writes as though the passion itself, regardless of its object, were the only thing that matters. "The important thing to recognize is, that when our attention is wholly focused upon an object of intensest significance to us, a religious process has started." But even in normal life (not to mention pathological cases, like pyromania) focusing of attention upon an object of intensest significance to us is compatible with realizing its insignificance as compared with what generally seems to us to be the best and the greatest. And what seems to us to be the best and the greatest may vary with circumstances and may perhaps, in the light of human experience, be sometimes better described as a personal failing or idiosyncrasy. With due willingness to recognize religion in any degree wherever it may be found, we feel that Professor Stratton's definition of it—and *a fortiori* Professor Auer's—is "far too wide; it takes in too much that is other than religion. . . . The moral consciousness, the aesthetic, the patriotic, or the public-school consciousness could be defined in Stratton's terms. The definition is so broad that it would take up in its sweep the miser, the gourmand, and the libertine."[77]

"It is obvious," Professor Auer remarks of his own view of religion, as presented so far, "that this explanation . . . is incomplete."[78] He shifts us insensibly from religion as almost any "force which binds together the loose ends of life until it becomes

[76] Quoted by A. R. Uren, *Recent Religious Psychology*, p. 155.
[77] A. R. Uren, *Recent Religious Psychology*, p. 162.
[78] *op. cit.*, p. 87.

one" (regardless of the poverty or the richness of that unity), to religion as that which unifies life in the highest and fullest way available. To complete his definition of religion he asks, what unifies life in the best possible way? God, theists answer. Yes, he replies, we may call that God, but let us be wary. Which qualities in God affect us for the best, His exclusively divine ones, like omnipotence and omniscience, or His human-divine ones, like love, mercy, justice? If our conduct is affected by our appreciation of omniscience and omnipotence, then, according to Professor Auer, it is directed by God, who alone possesses those qualities. If, however, we give preeminence to qualities like love, mercy, and justice, we value God "only insofar as he is *like* man."[79] As a matter of fact, Professor Auer writes, "not God's infinitude nor his omniscience draws our admiration, but his justice and his love. Whenever God becomes depleted of purely human qualities, worship becomes psychologically impossible. The qualities which we worship in God are the very ones which we value in man."[80] The real standard is a human standard to which God must conform. As the human qualities in Him alone signify, everything else may be ignored. In a brief historical survey[81] Professor Auer works on the principle—also adopted by Professor Leuba—that wherever a human and concrete quality or factor is present a divine and abstract element is absent or superfluous. Such "reasoning" guarantees an atheistic and "humanistic" conclusion.

But the argument is about as far removed from the facts of religious experience as it could be. The distinction between exclusively divine qualities and others belonging to both God and men apparently springs from verbal negligence and a superficial examination of religion. "Omniscience" and "omnipotence" reveal more clearly than "love, mercy, and justice" the difference between human qualities and their divine analogues. But if one were consistent and used the words all-knowing, all-powerful, all-loving, all-merciful, and all-just, there would be less temptation to suppose

[79] *ibid.*, p. 88. Italics his.
[80] *ibid.*, p. 98. Order of sentences changed without alteration of meaning.
[81] *ibid.*, pp. 88 *ff.*

that some divine qualities are exclusively divine whereas others are human in kind but "divine" only in greater quantity. The truth seems to be that divine qualities are all of them divine (theomorphic) and differ in kind from human (anthropomorphic) qualities.[82] And this difference in kind, this otherness and perfection which refreshingly contrast with and sustain the scattered fragments of our lives, is, as Baron von Hügel eloquently argued, one of the fascinations of religion. A difference in kind apparently does not prevent intimate communion with God. Even in human relationships the word "love" covers a multitude of meanings. Connubial, parental, filial, fraternal, and friendly love differ in kind from one another, from the love we have for God, and from His corresponding response to us. There is no more reason to confound His all-lovingness with "a purely human quality," or to suppose that if it differs from a human quality it is meaningless, than to confound connubial with filial love, or to suppose that all loves are meaningless unless they are of exactly the same pattern. There is no need of this confusion, because, allowing for individual insensibilities, the differences are matter of ordinary religious knowledge.

Though men have beaten their gods and have sometimes thought them dependent for strength on sacrifices from human altars,[83] history furnishes no example of the worship of a God by one who consciously believes his deity to possess nothing in any respect better than "purely human qualities." If we judge the most anthropomorphic religions on record unfairly by how far they fall

[82] "Thus in respect of each and all the ontological attributes the Divine is not known through analogy with the self, or with any other creaturely mode of existence. These divine attributes *presuppose* God's existence, and save in this reference even their bare possibility cannot be established. If, without any antecedent or independent apprehension of the Divine, we have to start from the creaturely, as exhibited in Nature and in man, and by way of inference and of analogy—on the pattern of what is found in the creaturely—through enlargement or other processes of ideal completion, to construct for ourselves concepts of the Divine, then the sceptics have been in the right; the attempt is an impossible one, condemned to failure from the start. We cannot reach the Divine merely by way of inference, not even if the inference be analogical in character. By no idealization of the creaturely can we transcend the creaturely." N. Kemp Smith, *op. cit.*, pp. 13-14.

[83] cf. A. R. Uren, *Recent Religious Psychology*, p. 155.

short of later stages rather than by how far they have advanced beyond earlier stages, we may still excuse them from a charge of mere anthropomorphism; for—using Professor Auer's language— the qualities worshipped in their god or gods,[84] instead of being the very ones prized in men, were something more than men could offer. Without that "more," religion has no reason to exist. To underrate that "more" and "otherness" is to dilute the facts concerned. Mystery, not as an impertinent enigma but as a dimly apprehended situation in which we are concerned and which requires and rewards our best efforts for its fuller apprehension, is the spur of life.[85] If "we love that which we know best and which is most like ourselves,"[86] it is generally with what Voltaire called a "bourgeois love" resting on familiarity, comfort, and habit. Though distance may delusively lend enchantment, and "good fences" may "make good neighbors"[87] in name only, it is also true that humanity has advanced on account of its preoccupation with things other than itself and sufficiently unknown to stir the imagination. The rationalism of humanism is, Professor Auer declares, one of its liabilities.[88]

Strangely enough at a time when science dazzles us with the impressive might of nature, humanists run down divine infinitude, omniscience, and omnipotence. Nobody would claim that those ideas are without obscurity, but neither are the cozier human qualities which humanists think can be more easily projected on the universe. If physicists and mathematicians find reality amenable to their concepts, it might seem that the idea of reality's omnipotence and omniscience (at least in the equivocal sense of—let us say—a prevailing mathematical type of order) might be more plausible than any idea of its being good and mild in a "purely human" way. Yet humanists profess an inability to understand

[84] Religious worship is not worship of "a given quality" as an abstraction, but of a being or beings characterized by certain qualities.
[85] cf. Abbé Nédoncelle's references to Gabriel Marcel, *op. cit.,* pp. 71-2.
[86] Auer, *op. cit.,* p. 102.
[87] Robert Frost, "Mending Wall," *Selected Poems* (New York: Holt, 1923).
[88] *op. cit.,* p. 107.

how people can be interested in God's tremendous attributes. Without arguing for a worship of impersonal and unethical force, one can nevertheless maintain that sheer might—in the sea, in mountain ranges, in earthquakes, in storms, in death, and, on a more puny level, in individual strength and the Napoleonic pomp of arms—is one of the most obvious and imposing aspects of reality. The very notion of reality and of being—the heart of philosophy and of religion—is the notion of that which exists or subsists by its own right and might.[89] Right without might is pathetic, like "an American consul at the scene of a Turkish massacre."[90] If "the required standard of incompetence"[91] is observed, if a finite god, like "a cosmic bell-boy,"[92] "may make mistakes"[93] and trip over his toes, what reason is there to worship him any more than ourselves? Might transfigured by righteousness, truth, and beauty—the holy and awe-inspiring grandeur of God—is the kernel of advanced religion.[94] Adoration is its spontaneous expression. Reverence and homage, "the idea of God" being left "out of the reckoning," but faintly reflect divine worship. Humanism may "wonder whether that type of worship still suits our time and our temper,"[95] because humanism never had Isaiah's vision.[96] A momentary decline in monarchies and increase in democracies has, with due respect to Professor Auer,[97] as little to do with our proper attitude towards God as would a similar tendency in the opposite direction. "King" and "Lord" are applied to Him not primarily according to political

[89] "And God said unto Moses, I AM THAT I AM." Ex. iii. 14.
[90] Wm. Archer, *God and Mr. Wells* (London: Watts, 1917), p. 21.
[91] M. C. Otto, *Things and Ideals,* p. 256.
[92] *ibid.,* p. 263.
[93] *ibid.,* p. 268.
[94] The Psalms furnish countless examples of this. Goethe catches the right note in the songs of the archangels in the *Prolog im Himmel.*
[95] *Humanism States Its Case,* p. 100.
[96] Is. vi. 1 *ff.*
[97] "Democracy is our ideal where earthly relations are concerned; why should this ideal be worthless in religion?" (Auer, *op. cit.,* p. 100.) cf. "'When a nation that has repudiated monarchy in government takes time to reflect,' says Mr. Reeman, 'it will surely not be long before it sees the practical impossibility of retaining in theology what it has felt bound to reject in politics.'. . . We must have a new God, for both theoretical and practical reasons, a God of the people, by the people, and for the people." (M. C. Otto, *Things and Ideals,* p. 261.)

fashions but because we lack better terms to indicate His glory. As far as those words suggest "purely human qualities," one may rightly object to them. As far as they suggest the preeminence of God, they are true to the religious facts that evoked them.

If an "identification of religion with the supernatural" is, as Dr. John Dewey affirms, accepted by theists and atheists—by those that defend the identification and by those that reject it[98]— humanistic discussion of religion apart from the supernatural might resemble discussion of music apart from sound, were not the connection of religion with the supernatural merely an "historic encumbrance."[99] Aside from that encumbrance—that is, in the light of "the best achievements and aspirations of the present"[100] (as we like to term encumbrances not yet historic)—what is religion? Or, because religion in general means nothing to Dr. Dewey and because no specific religion meets with his approval,[101] what, let us ask, is "basically religious in experience" apart from the "inconvenient aspects" of it which appealed to our benighted predecessors.[102]

Dr. Dewey defines religion, like Professor Auer, by its function, by the effect it produces, minimizing the manner and the cause of its production.[103] And, like Professor Auer and many others, he finds that religions effect "a better adjustment in life." "If this function were rescued through emancipation from dependence upon specific types of beliefs and practices, from those elements that constitute a religion, many individuals would find that experiences having the force of bringing about a better, deeper and enduring adjustment in life are not so rare and infrequent as they are commonly supposed to be."[104] As we are each, in any sphere of

---

[98] *A Common Faith*, p. 2. cf. "Religion is a felt practical relationship with what is believed in as a superhuman being or beings." (R. H. Thouless, *op. cit.*, p. 4.) "Social relations with superhuman beings, unless they be devils, is, by common consent, called religion." (J. H. Leuba, *God or Man*, p. 6.)

[99] *A Common Faith*, pp. 6, 9.

[100] *ibid.*, p. 6.

[101] *ibid.*, p. 8.

[102] *ibid.*, pp. 6, 9.

[103] *ibid.*, p. 14.

[104] *ibid.*

thought or action, largely committed to, and confined in, a special type of orthodoxy or heterodoxy, and as almost every way of life has its value, it is a matter of importance to us all to understand how we may enjoy the advantages of another's way of life without subscribing to his absurd beliefs and practices or shouldering his unnecessary responsibilities. In order to rise above the sectarian ties and jealousies which contaminate religions (and anything else of significance), let us "for the moment drop the term 're-ligious,' and ask what are the attitudes that lend deep and enduring support to the process of living."[105] "Deep seated" and "inclusive" enough to unify the self internally and to harmonize it with other selves and the universe,[106] these attitudes "relate not to this or that want in relation to this or that condition of our surroundings, but pertain to our being in its entirety. Because of their scope, this modification of ourselves is enduring. It lasts through any amount of vicissitude of circumstances, internal and external. There is a composing and harmonizing of the various elements of our being such that, in spite of changes in the special conditions that sur-round us, these conditions are also arranged, settled, in relation to us. This attitude includes a note of submission. It is voluntary, not externally imposed; and as voluntary it is something more than a mere Stoical resolution to endure unperturbed throughout the buffetings of fortune. It is more outgoing, more ready and glad, than the latter attitude, and it is more active than the former. And in calling it voluntary, it is not meant that it depends upon a particular resolve or volition. It is a change *of* will conceived as the organic plenitude of our being, rather than any special change *in* will."[107] "And it is pertinent to note that the unification of the self throughout the ceaseless flux of what it does, suffers, and achieves, cannot be attained in terms of itself. The self is always directed toward something beyond itself and so its own unifi-cation depends upon the idea of the integration of the shifting

[105] *ibid.*, p. 15.
[106] *ibid.*, p. 23.
[107] *ibid.*, pp. 15, 17. Italics his.

scenes of the world into that imaginative totality we call the universe."[108]

"It is the claim of religions that they effect this generic and enduring change in attitude. I should like to turn the statement around and say that whenever this change takes place there is a definitely religious attitude. It is not *a* religion that brings it about, but when it occurs, from whatever cause and by whatever means, there is a religious outlook and function."[109] "Whatever introduces genuine perspective is religious, not that religion is something that introduces it."[110]

Theists share Dr. Dewey's desire to make the religious quality of experience—suitable integration of ourselves and adjustment to others and to reality in its most intimate and ultimate aspects— vital, accessible, and free. In his outline of "the attitudes that lend deep and enduring support to the process of living," they admire a description of a genuinely religious frame of mind, entertaining in its insinuation that religions alone are incapable of producing religious results, and charming for its reticent vagueness of expression and its unconsciousness of its vast implications. But they feel obliged to note a limitation of functionalism pure and simple: an "effect" cannot be fully understood apart from its "cause." We need to go on from the religious effect, and find out what does "introduce a genuine perspective." Instead of God as "a particular Being"[111] or "an unseen power controlling our destiny,"[112] Dr. Dewey proposes "the ideal ends that at a given time and place one acknowledges as having authority over his volition and emotion, the values to which one is supremely devoted, as far as these ends, through imagination, take on unity."[113] Imagination provides the

[108] *ibid.*, p. 19. It is hard to see how anything short of theism can provide a suitable intellectual vindication of such wholehearted and happy personal devotion to "something beyond itself," to the universe, to reality in its ultimate form.

[109] *ibid.*, p. 17. Italics his.

[110] *ibid.*, p. 24.

[111] *ibid.*, p. 42.

[112] *ibid.*, p. 23.

[113] *ibid.*, p. 42.

means whereby possibilities, or "things unrealized," "come home to us" and "stir us."[114]

> "To make a prairie it takes a clover and one bee,—
> And revery.
> The revery alone will do
> If bees are few."[115]

Through imagination Morse, for example, acting on possibilities "generated" and "supported" by actual "forces in nature and society," invented the telegraph.[116] "It is this *active* relation between ideal and actual to which I would give the name 'God.'[117] . . . The *function* of such a working union of the ideal and actual seems to me to be identical with the force that has in fact been attached to the conception of God in all the religions that have a spiritual content. . . . This union is active and practical; it is a *uniting,* not something given.[118] . . . A religious attitude . . . needs the sense of a connection of man, in the way of both dependence and support, with the enveloping world that the imagination feels is a universe. Use of the words 'God' and 'divine' to convey the union of actual with ideal may protect man from a sense of isolation and from consequent despair of defiance.[119] . . . A humanistic religion, if it excludes our relation to nature, is pale and thin, as it is presumptuous, when it takes humanity as an object of worship."[120]

Religion having been explained in terms of "ideals," we must ascertain what "ideals" are. Here, unfortunately, Dr. Dewey, largely from assuming that we know what he means by ideals, gives us little and confused help. A pragmatist, he fights against a static, existential, and intellectualistic view of religion. He wants something active, creative, volitional. Theists also recognize those two groups of features characterizing thought and its object. But

[114] *ibid.,* p. 43.
[115] Emily Dickinson, *op. cit.,* p. 116.
[116] *A Common Faith,* pp. 49, 51.
[117] *ibid.,* p. 51. Italics his.
[118] *ibid.,* p. 52. Italics his.
[119] *ibid.,* p. 53.
[120] *ibid.,* p. 54.

whereas they try to find a place for each, he stands out as a partisan primarily of the "dynamic" group. For that reason he lashes out against "a particular Being" or "an unseen power," although each of his ideals has its particular kind of being and unseen "undeniable power."[121] What he criticizes above all "is the *identification* of the ideal with a particular Being, especially when that identification makes necessary the conclusion that this Being is outside of nature."[122] He objects to the notion that the authority and the value of ideals "depend upon some prior complete embodiment—as if the efforts of human beings in behalf of justice, or knowledge or beauty, depended for their effectiveness and validity upon assurance that there already existed in some supernal region a place where criminals are humanely treated, where there is no serfdom or slavery, where all facts and truths are already discovered and possessed, and all beauty is eternally displayed in actualized form."[123] Believers (if there are any) in this "prior complete embodiment" he charges with substituting "adherence to the actual" for "faith in what is possible,"[124] "a system of beliefs about antecedent reality" for "the idealism of action,"[125] the guarantee of "physical force"[126] or of "sheer matter of fact existence"[127] for the intrinsic authority of ideals, and "dependence upon an external power" for "human endeavor."[128]

But his use of "nature," "embodiment," "supernal region," "actual," "prior," "antecedent reality," and "physical force" remains hazy. At one time Dr. Dewey seems to admit as real and existent only objects of sense perception, while at another time he seems to believe that the inherent authority of ideals is as real and existent as objects of natural science, which, presumably, compose "nature." The notions he disparages are so vague and anonymous that it is difficult to attach them as they stand to particular persons

121 *ibid.*, p. 43.
122 *ibid.*, p. 48. Italics his.
123 *ibid.*, p. 49; cf. *ibid.*, p. 43.
124 *ibid.*, p. 23.
125 *ibid.*, pp. 23-4; cf. *ibid.*, p. 43.
126 *ibid.*, p. 45.
127 *ibid.*, p. 44.
128 *ibid.*, p. 46.

or schools of thought. They may, for all one can tell, be unintentional parodies of elements in Platonism, Aristotelianism, and forms of personal and absolute idealism, or they may be products of spontaneous generation. Their attribution to "religions," without indication of the rôle they play in any one, is general enough to be meaningless. That the actual should be contrasted with the possible, belief with action, fact with value, and the influence of other things with our own initiative, in a fashion so exaggerated as to preclude exemplification in ordinary experience or in various types of human beings, is doubtless to be attributed to the philosophical proclivity to transform into irremediable differences and contradictions distinctions and contrasts as closely united as the obverse and the reverse of a coin.

Dr. Dewey's argument is, in pattern, self-refuting. Without relying upon strength other than our own, he urges us to embody ideals. This was in part—if memory serves—the advice of St. Ignatius de Loyola: pray as though everything depends on your prayer; act as though everything depends on your action. But as soon as an ideal becomes "embodied"—certainly when and if it is "embodied" as well as can be imagined, that is, divinely "embodied"—it seems to become, for Dr. Dewey, an evil. We are here concerned not with the antagonism between accomplished good and potential better, but with the suggestion that the best possible embodiment or realization of the best is the worst thing possible. It is the worst thing possible for us only if our relations with God are such that the better He is the more we can afford to be bad. If that is the discovery of any religion, it is by no means Christianity's. If the best possible embodiment of the best is not bad for us, maybe it is bad in itself. But if it is bad in itself (whatever that means), then the whole process of realizing ideals—the gist of Dr. Dewey's religion—leads to ruin. Here too a momentarily fashionable philosophical proclivity is at work: the tendency to glorify becoming or potentiality at the expense of being or actuality, the way at the expense of the end, struggle at the expense of achievement. In a natural reaction to "static," "pre-evolutionary" forms of thought, in a too eager response to recent "dynamic," "creative," "emer-

254

gent," and "relativistic" leadings, Dr. Dewey's enthusiasm apparently "o'erleaps itself and falls on the other—"

Yet, when all is said, theists can sympathize with his main intention. Keenly aware that all is not right with the world, he brushes aside religious experience to deny that God's in His heaven. He would not have mankind leave to God work it should do itself.[129] Besides evil there is, needless to say, good to be explained. Dr. Dewey does not attempt to show how we could recognize evil as evil if the love of goodness and the possibility of its realization were not more strongly engrained in us than the powers of darkness. The possibility of its realization, of its triumph over evil, presupposes, unless we are deluded, that reality is such that, granted our cooperation, goodness, truth, and beauty can (so far as we know, to an indefinitely greater extent than today) prevail in our sphere. Christian theism has maintained this for nearly two thousand years. Probably a misunderstanding of the relation, as Christians see it, between divine grace and human initiative obliges Dr. Dewey to drive God from heaven in order to help men to help themselves. Grace, however, does not take the place of effort; it heightens its quality. God's will acts not like an external power replacing our own but more as a spiritual influence—like that of another person (though far more intimate and profound)— animating by almost any means our thought and conduct. His being is not on the same plane as "matter" or spatially "outside" nature and alien to ourselves, nor is His "perfection" a duplication of this world plus a chocolate coating absent here below. Rather His "antecedent reality" and "embodied existence" may be analogically considered as more like mind informing body without being identical with it. Christians find Him "in" their minds as that towards which their best thoughts and actions tend. His influence is there, and yet always "beyond," in the sense that one must ever seek Him better. Such a way, mere hint that it is, of conceiving His immanence in us and nature, perhaps comes nearer to the require-

---

[129] "Men have never fully used the powers they possess to advance the good in life, because they have waited upon some power external to themselves and to nature to do the work they are responsible for doing. Dependence upon an external power is the counterpart of surrender of human endeavor." *ibid.*, p. 46.

ments of religious experience than do Dr. Dewey's unsympathetic accounts of what he pretends "the churches" and "religions" believe.

"All that an Existence can add," he writes about what might be called the connection of ideals with ultimate reality, "is force to establish, to punish, and to reward."[130] At any rate, that's something! Through pangs or joys of conscience, through the rise or the fall of well or ill founded civilizations, ideals have force "to establish, to punish, and to reward." Though Dr. Dewey, like most humanists, thinks of ideals as goods magnified and "projected" by imagination,[131] he insists that this process, so far from being merely something "in the mind," is rooted in character, personality, and action. It is rooted there not only, if at all, as an aberration of individuals, or as an unsifted accumulation of culture, or as a product of glands, but also as something consonant with our social and physical milieu.[132] And that milieu reflects its environment, the universe (or whatever one calls reality in its fullest scope). If the universe, as Dr. Dewey says, is "friendly" to man in the sense of promoting development of conscience, character, art, knowledge, and better cooperation in all things,[133] we may agree with him that "we are in the presence neither of ideals completely embodied in human experience nor yet of ideals that are mere [cosmically] rootless ideals, fantasies, utopias."[134] In and through man and nature works an influence uniting actual and ideal, by transfiguring present existence or by otherwise bringing about the "emergence" of new creations. This influence, or force, or uniting, plays in fact, though not in the exact terms of Dr. Dewey's philosophy, an important part in the Christian apprehension and idea of God. Though Christianity freely takes truth wherever it sees it, it would probably find Dr. Dewey disappointing as concerns God's perfection (His reality, or what Baron von Hügel called the "isness" necessary to account for the illimitable possibilities of creation) and reward-

[130] *ibid.*, p. 44.
[131] *ibid.*, p. 48.
[132] *ibid.*, pp. 49, 51.
[133] *ibid.*, pp. 55-6.
[134] *ibid.*, pp. 50-1. Interpolation in square brackets mine.

ing in his exploration of hitherto slighted workings of the divine in nature.

We are tempted to dwell on other humanistic specualtions about God. Instead of approaching religion, as commonly understood, in a "superior" and hostile mood, with the intent of cramping it into a naturalistic mould, Dr. E. S. Ames, for example, comes to it with a sympathetic delicacy of perception and a desire to follow its cues as faithfully as "the logic of empiricism" permits. His thought exhibits a growth, a subtlety, and an emotional tone interesting in themselves but less typical of humanism than the reflections of those who have been discussed here at length. Moreover the place he gives in religion to social idealism, God as a name for finite spiritual factors in the universe,[135] and man (in a narrowly "empirical" sense misprizing our apprehensions of the perfect, the infinite, and the eternal) as the measure of all things, resembles that of humanists already referred to.

If humanism is not simply an anthropomorphic and arid theory of reality, if it is "a new religion," in what specifically religious way does it manifest itself? What in it corresponds to prayer and worship in historic religions? From a "strictly logical" point of view, humanism never officially reaches anything like God to worship. Anything less than Him must be felt as unworthy of whole-hearted adoration—as involving, if thus adored, defects of idolatry. From this point of view, Dr. C. F. Potter rightly asserts, "it is very doubtful if we are justified in using the word prayer to describe"[136] its counterpart in humanism. Instead of addressing "a verbal petition"[137] "to an outside deity"—like telephoning to one's senator—a humanist "derives power from himself," "calls upon his own reserves."[138] He turns to "a meditative study of his personality with a view to self-improvement and self-giving in intelligent service to his fellow men."[139] Humanists prefer "as more

[135] "God is the world or life taken in certain of its aspects, in those aspects which are consonant with order, beauty, and expansion." *Religion*, p. 154.
[136] *Humanism, A New Religion*, p. 98.
[137] *ibid.*, p. 103.
[138] *ibid.*, pp. 17-18.
[139] *ibid.*, p. 98; cf. *ibid.*, p. 103. "One's" in the original text has here been changed to "his."

honest" to describe this exercise "in other terms than prayer."[140] "To formulate our needs, to direct our powers to the attainment of our desires [whatever they are?] and to attempt to relate ourselves [in scientific fashion?] to the universe,—none of these needs a personal God, and all of them together are certainly not what has commonly been meant by prayer."[141] Resembling business in its high estimate of "personality," "service," and "efficiency," religion thus understood becomes this-worldly, utilitarian, the Cinderella of sociology and economics. "Relations between parents and children, the economic status of women, the causes of criminality, the lack of financial responsibility among many rich people, international honor"[142]—such matters come to be considered peculiarly religious. Humanistic sermons tend to parallel the following random selection of addresses delivered in Ethical Culture societies: "What Is Back of All These Strikes?" "Russia Enters the League of Nations," "What Next in Germany?"[143] "Are Modern Parents Helpless?" "H. G. Wells's Autobiography," "Plato's 'Brain Trust' and Mr. Roosevelt's," "The Future of Marriage."[144] "It would seem," Professor Sellars remarks, "that man is turning from supplication to manipulation. . . ."[145]

Other humanists—and sometimes those referred to above, when sated with "current events" during the week well enough to do without a rehash of them on Sunday—prefer to think of prayer in a more self-forgetful, passive, contemplative, and—they might be inclined to say—"esthetic" manner. "Many have suggested self-communion, meditation, reflection. I myself," writes Professor Sellars, "find music, poetry, and a quiet walk into the country effective for that gathering together of oneself that is good for one at times."[146] Camomile tea or a nap might also be prescribed. This fits in nicely with Karl Marx's depreciation of religion as the opiate of the people; yet sleep and mild forms of recreation are

[140] *ibid.*
[141] *ibid.*, p. 99. Interpolations in square brackets mine.
[142] R. W. Sellars, *Religion Coming of Age*, p. 281.
[143] *The Standard*, October 1934.
[144] *ibid.*, March 1935.
[145] *Religion Coming of Age*, p. 282.
[146] *ibid.*, p. 280.

"good for one at times." "During mental quietude, the many small things which had assumed an undue and false importance in a too eager struggle for life, fall back into their proper places, while deeper and larger purposes assert their potency. Vision becomes truer; ideas, obscured or impaired in egoistic affirmations of the self, are restored, and the mind is re-centered about the larger and better ends of life. . . . It is," Professor Leuba announces with professional pride, "a psychological effect, quite independent of any specific divine action."[147]

"The more important aspect of the prayer-attitude is, however, not the saving of energy and the refreshment resulting from the relaxation of bodily and mental tensions, but a consequence of that attitude, namely increased plasticity or receptivity. . . . The full measure of the blessings" of prayer (i.e. "strength, peace, and joy") "is not secured by passivity and receptivity alone. An equivalent to that for which God stands in Christianity, must be present in the mind in order to make the state of quiescent receptivity as effective as Christian prayer may be."[148]

Everything hinges upon whether or not a satisfactory equivalent for God can be found. Like Professor Auer and Dr. Dewey, Dr. John H. Dietrich fails to bring this out at once because he defines worship by certain psychological peculiarities—by its form and function—regardless of its content and object. Spinoza venerated Nature or God; T. H. Huxley, truth; R. G. Ingersoll, "the finer sentiments of human character"; and "our own beloved Mr. Firkins, Humanist to the core . . . the highest and best."[149] Though the objects vary, worship always remains, Dr. Dietrich insists, an attitude of veneration. Despite their variations, the objects of veneration have this in common: each for its worshipper is his best access to what in Reality is most significant for him. "Only in so far as religion concentrates its worship upon reality—things as they

[147] *God or Man*, p. 312.
[148] *ibid.*, pp. 311-13.
[149] "Do Humanists Worship?", pp. 1-3, an address delivered by J. H. Dietrich, May 15, 1932, published, as no. 1, series XVI, of *The Humanist Pulpit* pamphlets, by the First Unitarian Society, 1526 Harmon Pl., Minneapolis, Minn.

are—has it any real value for human life."[150] Dr. Dietrich, as might be expected, holds that "a purely naturalistic conception of the universe and of human life are the only fit objects of intelligent worship,"[151] because he believes that such a conception reveals "things as they are." Like Professor Auer, he supposes that "the qualities which people worship in God are the very qualities which they value in man"[152]—meaning less that we revere in men qualities suggesting those in God than that we project upon an imaginary unity qualities that we value in men. (Why we should be irresistibly driven to "project" these qualities, were there not a divine magnet ever drawing us to itself, is not explained.) We need not refer to our previous criticism of these ideas, because Dr. Dietrich shows that in at least one way of "relating ourselves to the universe," to use Dr. Potter's words, we prize, quite as much as human qualities, other-than-human qualities—in this case those of inanimate nature, which, like a Japanese *hokku,* points beyond itself. "Take the man who is touched and lifted by natural beauty, the sense of natural power; the man who loves the woods, who turns and stands to see the glory of a sunset, who is lifted by tides of emotion as he hears the surf beat on the shore, who feels bowed in the presence of the wide night sky of stars, who is uplifted in the presence of mighty hills, who is touched by all natural scenes of beauty and peace and glory. Is not such a man a worshipper?"[153] If we say yes, as Dr. Dietrich probably wants us to, we have gone beyond "a quiet walk" and "meditation, aspiration, self-inventory, and high resolves"[154]—without disparaging their value or denying them a place in worship. We are "so uplifted and moved to admiration of the highest and finest things in life, that we are not satisfied until we have made them a part of ourselves."[155] "Prayer is far more than any form of words or conscious thoughts, although it

[150] *ibid.,* p. 2.
[151] *ibid.*
[152] *ibid.,* p. 7.
[153] *ibid.,* p. 10.
[154] C. F. Potter, *Humanism, A New Religion,* p. 102.
[155] J. H. Dietrich, "Do Humanists Worship?", pp. 14-15.

may employ these.[156] It is an attitude, a habit, a disposition in which is sought the fullest possible participation in that larger reality into which all significant thought and action radiate."[157]

[156] As Baron von Hügel said, a certain minimum of verbal prayer is a necessary skeleton of a well rounded, steady life of worship.

[157] E. S. Ames, *Religion*, p. 219.

Public worship—meaning "fine music, common concentration on a high ideal, the hearing of tried and true words of scripture and of an inspiring address, and association with similarly minded people" in "a humanist meeting" (C. F. Potter, *Humanism, A New Religion,* p. 102)—is generally recognized by humanists as helpful for "those who are more dependent upon the reinforcement which social groups give to the individual" (R. W. Sellars, *Religion Coming of Age,* p. 260). As humanistic theory shows a gradual disintegration of Protestant theology, so its public services reveal a similar trend away from the historic, the institutional, the social, the sacramental, and the splendid, towards the ordinary, the individualistic, the symbolically void, and the current mediocre. The "tone" of humanistic meetings is that of a middle-class gathering bent on "uplift." The program of a typical Sunday Morning Meeting, like that held at All Souls Unitarian Church, Kansas City, Mo., at eleven o'clock, October 2, 1932, runs as follows:

> Organ Prelude.
> Opening Words—Selected.
> Song—"The World is Young." Tune, "Beecher."
> > "Who will say the world is dying?
> > > Who will say our prime is past?
> > Sparks of good, within us, lying,
> > > Flash, and will flash to the last.
> > Still the race of hero spirits
> > > Pass the lamp from hand to hand,
> > And the growing light of knowledge
> > > Casts its rays o'er every land.
> > Still the youthful spirit gathers
> > > Fiery joy from wold and wood;
> > He will dare as dared his fathers,
> > > Give him only cause as good.
> > Still the race of hero spirits
> > > Pass the lamp from hand to hand
> > And the men who work for justice
> > > Are an e'er increasing band."
> Readings and Greetings.
> Organ Interlude.
> Address—"Utopia For All" (Including Republicans and Socialists, Democrats and Communists.) Mr. Birkhead.
> Offertory.
> Closing Words.
> Organ Postlude.

O. W. Firkins, then professor of comparative literature at the University of Minnesota, describes in *The New Humanist* (March-April 1931, p. 4) a regular

261

The truth seems to be, as Dr. Ames asserts, "that prayer is a natural expression of the human spirit. It is not [wholly] destroyed by atheistic views of the world."[158] It withers or blossoms in humanism in proportion to the intensity or the half-heartedness with which humanists cling to naturalism as an adequate guide of life. Worship (to which prayer, adoration, communion with God, or profound and high personal relations with ultimate reality, are central) is recognized by humanists as a measure of man's greatness and as a means of growth.[159] If he worships the best he can conceive, what he worships indicates something of the present capacity of his mind. And in trying to be more at one with the best he can conceive he is able to become better than he has been.

Dr. Leuba, like most humanists, suggests that possession of an ethical purpose or ideal is the equivalent of the Christian God. Apparently on the assumption that

> "Faith is a fine invention
> For gentlemen who see;
> But microscopes are prudent
> In an emergency!"[160]

he also suggests that "financial provision, in the form of insurances against unemployment, sickness, and old age, is, after all, a safer ground of mental peace and contentment than the confidence in God with which one rises, empty-handed, from one's knees."[161]

morning service of the Minneapolis humanists under Dr. Dietrich's régime: "The meetings are held in the Shubert Theatre, and the auditor's wandering eye is solaced by a notice of *All God's Chilluns Got Wings* or *East of Suez* at the oncoming and, so to speak, impatient matinée. The service, with the inevitable deletions, clings to accepted models. There are hymns in which doggerel and poetry are sung with undiscriminating gusto, excellent violin solos, a reading (from the Bible, as 'meat offered unto idols,' is rigorously barred), a 'meditation,' the wraith of prayer, haunting prayer's former domicile, and a benediction defecated of piety to its very name 'Closing Words.' The right epithet for the service is *decent*. Nothing can be less like the traditional Unitarian congregation than the good-natured and intelligent, but unsifted, uncemented, unceremonious audience, so hard to assemble and so easy to disperse that the latest arrivals sometimes meet the earliest fugitives in the aisle."

[158] *Religion*, p. 217. Interpolation in square brackets mine.
[159] J. H. Dietrich, "Do Humanists Worship?", p. 9.
[160] Emily Dickinson, *op. cit.*, p. 28.
[161] *God or Man*, p. 317.

We have already seen the inadequacy of the humanistic concept of ideals as "projections," their thinness as compared with the perfection of a "personal" God, and the absurdity of supposing that for theism supernature dispenses with nature any more than in reality nature dispenses with supernature. In spite of excellent features, humanism fails to appreciate fully facts and experiences leading to the idea of God and to communion with Him. For that reason alone—even were it otherwise satisfactory—humanism cannot carry out its promise to fill the place of God and theistic religion.

CONCLUSION

CONCLUSION

ALMOST everything condemned in religion by humanists is, we agree, hypocritical, retrograde, spiritually encumbering. Differences of terminology taken into account, few theists cherish exactly what humanists reject. Nor is humanism alone in its discovery that science has nurtured not new facts only but new standards and motives, which every sphere of life must note. One need not be a humanist to oppose injustice, sham, folly, and brutality; or a malicious reactionary to see in the ends and the means of the humanistic social program the stamp of the amateur—love lost in innocence, haste, and confusion. The quest for a good life in a good world—nine-tenths of humanism—so far from being the peculiar property of that movement, is a quest as old and as varied as the race. Humanism's distinctive feature—a tenth of its whole—its "new naturalism," is (unless this book has gone astray) not merely "inadequate" but, in general, a benevolent collection of barren, second-hand sophistries, an impoverishment rather than an enrichment of life. That most people already possess the positive values of humanism and that few covet its deficiencies, perhaps explains the slight effect of its aging pretensions.

"The memory of the glorious dreams I dreamed
    In youth, through many a sleepless night,
Make tears start now, whene'er the moon is bright."[1]

Of a founder of humanism it is eulogistically written, "He clarifies and simplifies complicated subjects."[2] Of another, "They will assail [him] for his brevity. But it is precisely by such clean-cut concise definition that the humanist philosophy has found its

[1] C. H. Page, *op. cit.*, p. 58.
[2] "Humanism—A Religion For Today."

267

hearing."[3] Facile simplification, oversimplification, taints the blood of humanism. Impatience with imperfection, not met patiently, fells the tree it prunes—and not trees only, but law, science, business, politics, as well as the Church. Preference for "You may have only what I clearly and distinctly perceive," to "Let us take all we can and hope some day to assimilate it," stands out sharply in the humanistic transformation of the limits of the sciences, as they usually misunderstand and more often misapply them, into the limits of the human spirit.

Their widely prevailing will not merely to renounce for themselves but to deprive others of belief in God marks the peak of the humanists' path of negation. Here humanism parts company with ordinary secularism. Those not only in but essentially of "the world" usually have no interest in denying or in affirming theism. If concerned with religion at all, they are so in a way not primarily religious. But they generally know what most people around them mean by religion and its claims. Knowledge of those august claims prompts them to avoid them as, whether true or false, unquestionably disconcerting. And it makes them aware of the vulgarity and the absurdities of substitutes for God. Controversy between humanism and theism strikes them as being on its lower levels a *tour de force*, a babel of braying words, and at its climax a sacrilege, the profanation of (if not for them, at least for many) a glorious and fearful Name.

Hamlet and Madame Bovary exist in their own right and but incidentally as deputies for Shakespeare and Flaubert. A lyric is rarely mistaken for more than a momentary flash of spirit. But anything long, prosy, pedantic, and plotless, especially on philosophy or religion, though as much a product of convention and art as is a novel, a poem, or a play, has better than even chances of being identified with "the man himself." It seems well to note this danger lest (despite our precaution to refer to persons simply in order to provide ideas with an address where they may be found when wanted) anyone suppose that by reading this book he has become acquainted with humanists and theists named in it rather

[3] E. H. Wilson, *The New Humanist*, March-April 1931, p. 27.

than with a highly restricted and individual sketch of humanism and of some corresponding features of theism. As in law and politics, so here issues are contrasted sharply to accentuate the truth. But differences in ideology should never outweigh common humanity. An artificially stimulated conflict of ideas provides no ground for supposing that their exponents are themselves at odds with one another. They are merely actors filling rôles assigned to them by fate, or advocates sincerely pleading their case. But after the play or when the court adjourns, they will lunch together and laugh at their foolishness and at all they might have done had they only thought of it in time.

Though this digression bids farewell to humanists as actual people, it would be against the rules of the game to ward off from them as sponsors of humanistic ideas (like owners of mischievous dogs) the figurative *coup de grace* with which a study like this is expected to end. In the preceding chapters, accordingly, we found no humanistic objection to theism damagingly valid and no alleged support of humanism so strong as humanists require. On historical, social, scientific, philosophical, moral, and religious grounds, theism appeared better rooted and more fruitful than humanism. The latter's function is chiefly critical: to put what it dislikes through the test of fire. Theism, we believe, emerges from that test purified. We doubt whether humanism in its peculiar one-tenth could survive it at all. Their good, humanists have taken from others but made it no better. Their bad they have borrowed also and by misuse made it worse. It is not an inexcusable exaggeration, we conclude about that last tenth of humanism, to say of the "new naturalists" what Lord Balfour so conveniently said of naturalists a generation before them: "Their spiritual life is parasitic: it is sheltered by convictions which belong, not to them, but to the society of which they form a part; it is nourished by processes in which they take no share. And when these convictions decay, and those processes come to an end, the alien life which they have maintained can scarce be expected to outlast them."[4]

[4] *Foundations of Belief* (London: Longmans, Green, 1901), p. 88.

INDEX

INDEX

Abel, Theodore Curtis, 8 n., 10 n.
Absolute, 33, 88, 98, 99, 114 n., 138, 142, 158, 159, 160, 161, 214, 229
Abstraction, 43, 44, 108, 110, 114, 121, 125, 126, 142, 144, 147 n., 155, 161, 179, 196, 200-2, 207-8, 215-16
Adler, Alfred, 139, 144
Adler, Felix, 163, 205
Adoration, 4, 224, 248, 262
Aeschines, 25
Agnosticism, xi, 20-1, 22, 23, 24, 25, 45, 148 n., 229 n.
Alexander, S., 42, 64, 117 n., 119 n.
Alexander VI, 29
American Freeman, The, 7-8
American life, 12-14, 168, 169 n., 176-7, 180, 185-7, 188-9, 197
Ames, E. S., 17, 20, 70 n., 78, 80, 86, 125 n., 126, 194, 196, 205, 207 n., 257, 261 n., 262
Analogy, 62, 117, 140, 215, 242 n., 246 n.
Anaxagoras, 23
Anaximander, 23
Anaximenes, 23
Andress, Bart, 189 n.
Anglo-Saxon, 163, 176, 185; cf. xi, 177, 209
Anthropology, 52, 78 n., 91, 102, 105
Anthropomorphism, 14, 63, 116, 131, 166, 197, 215, 239, 242, 245-7, 249, 257, 260
Antipater, 25
Archer, William, 248 n.
Aristotle, 18, 25, 64 n., 209, 211, 237, 254
Arnold, Matthew, 158 n.
Aronson, M. J., 10 n.
Art, 11, 18, 27, 53, 62-3, 66, 67, 71, 73, 79, 94, 95, 96, 101, 102, 103, 109, 159, 160, 162, 168, 179, 184, 191, 200 n., 201, 205 n., 234, 236, 242, 244, 256, 268; cf. 34

Atheism, xi, 7 n., 9 n., 22, 23, 29, 39, 86-7, 135, 164, 171, 217, 226, 262
Atonement, 154, 237
Auer, J. A. C. Fagginger, 20, 55 n., 154 n., 159 n., 160 n., 166 n., 222, 223, 242-9, 259, 260
Augustine, St., 35, 91 n., 219
Authority, religious, 33, 36, 37, 58, 67, 70, 92, 96, 97, 103 n., 104, 154, 155, 160, 214, 223, 228, 253; cf. 166; scientific, 57, 66, 101, 102, 108, 124, 125, 176 n.

Babbitt, Irving, 18-19, 178 n.
Backus, E. Burdette, 7 n., 55 n.
Baillie, John, 232 n.
Balfour, A. J., 269
Barnes, Harry Elmer, 10 n., 55 n.
Barry, F. R., 146
Baynes, H. G., 137 n.
Bazin, René, 170 n.
Beach, J. W., 86 n.
Beard, Charles, 169 n.
Beauty, 9 n., 27, 28, 58, 76, 80, 88, 96, 99, 113, 149, 155, 161, 168 n., 196, 198 n., 212, 229, 234, 241, 248, 260
Being, 44, 67 n., 123, 215, 217, 241, 248, 250, 253, 254, 255
Bergson, 39, 43, 111 n., 138 n., 229
Berkeley, 204 n.
Bianchi, Martha Dickinson, 40 n.
Bible, 32, 33, 35, 36-7, 39, 40, 44-5, 61, 134, 148, 162, 226, 262 n.
Biology, 24, 42, 56, 61, 76, 85, 91, 118, 137, 184, 186, 202, 228, 236
Birkhead, L. M., 7 n., 10 n., 55 n., 111 n., 161 n., 167 n., 169 n., 173 n., 185, 191, 222, 223, 224-7, 261 n.
Bithynia, 25
Boehme, 71 n.
Boileau-Despréaux, 4 n.
Boni, Albert, 10 n.

Bosanquet, Bernard, 43
Boswell, 227 n.
Bouquet, A. C., 75
Bourget, Paul, 6 n., 155, 181
Braden, C. S., 6 n., 7 n., 9 n.
Bradley, F. H., 38, 43
Bragg, Raymond B., 7 n., 8 n., 10, 51, 55 n.
Brain, 80, 119-23, 124, 196 n.
Breasted, 205 n.
Bridges, H. J., 9 n.
Bridges, J. H., 56 n., 182 n.
Brown, W. A., 21 n.
Buckham, J. W., 205 n.
Buddha, 2, 20, 21-2, 35, 132 n.; cf. 232
Burke, Kenneth, 103 n.
Burt, 138 n.
Burtt, Edwin Arthur, 10 n., 55 n., 76 n.
Buschman, Harold, 7 n.
Business and industry, 11, 13, 27, 30, 34, 40, 55, 81, 94, 168, 174, 180, 183, 184, 186, 187-8, 243, 258, 268

Caldecott, Ernest, 7 n., 55 n.
Calvin, 31-2, 35, 39
Cantwell, Robert, 13, 14 n.
Capitalism, 30, 176, 179, 183
Cappon, Alexander P., 7 n.
Caracalla, 25
Carlson, A. J., 55 n.
Categorical imperative, 47, 157, 171 n., 204
Catharine, St., of Genoa, 231
Catholicism, mediaeval, 29, 30, 31, 34, 40, 56; Roman, 9 n., 29, 32-3, 35, 37, 41-2, 46, 59, 69, 71, 76, 97-8, 148 n., 159, 160, 166, 182, 184, 228
Cause and effect, 45, 60 n., 62, 75, 77, . 91-2, 110, 113-18, 121, 124, 147-8, 150, 216-17, 243, 249, 251
Cellini, Benvenuto, 162 n.
Channing, 45
Chaos, 57 n., 107, 111-13, 158, 236, 237, 241, 242 n.
Chase, Stuart, 185
Christian, Christianity, etc., assimilative, 3, 4, 155, 160; beliefs of, 44, 62, 65, 68, 69, 71-3, 75, 95, 107, 145, 153, 155, 159, 167, 169, 170, 177 n., 206 n., 212, 214, 215, 219, 229, 230, 232, 234 n., 239-42; and business, 30, 188; clergy, 33, 34, 46, 71, 154 n., 224-7; ethics of, 5, 163 n., 177, 210-12, 214 n.; failings of, xi, 3-4, 57-8, 70, 71, 97-8, 158 n., 160, 170, 171, 177, 190, 218, 227, 238-9; general influence of, 162, 163, 179; good points of, 66, 72, 105-6, 145, 169, 170, 224, 231 n., 234, 259, 262; and humanism, xi, xii, 4-5, 11, 21, 34-5, 41-2, 57-8, 59, 60, 62, 68, 72, 73, 76, 77, 92, 106 n., 107, 120, 136, 153, 154-5, 156, 158 n., 160, 162, 163, 166-7, 172-3, 177, 254-5, 256; and literary humanism, 18, 19-20; misapprehensions of, 58, 72 n., 154-5, 159, 160, 196, 227-8, 239-40, 255; philanthropic, 4, 9 n., 71, 167, 208, 231 n.; and Platonism, 67 n., 209; and Reformation, 30, 31-2, 41; and Renaissance, 26-7, 28, 29; and science, 41, 59 n., 95, 96, 105; and sophists, 26
Christian Register, The, 8
Christian Science, 241 n.
Church, beliefs of, 74; and Christ, 33, 167 n.; corrupts, 154, 159, cf. 183; developing, 155 n.; divine, 31, 33; as a guide, 210; indifference towards, 5; and the masses, 11, 170 n., 179, 189; in the Middle Ages, 30; monopolistic, 57-8, 154; and mysticism, 71; and personality, 179; as a prison, 32, 70; in the Reformation, 31, 32, 34, 36; and scholasticism, 40; and science, 28; and state, 170, 183
Class conflict, 174, 176, 178, 179
Clement VII, 29
Codrington, 78 n.
Coit, Stanton, 208 n., 212
Colet, 29
Columbus, 28
Communism, 76 n., 178, 179
Comte, Auguste, 8 n., 15, 45, 50, 55-6, 152, 156, 181-4, 230 n.
Confucius, 2, 21-2, 26, 232
Conscience, 17, 46, 47, 83, 155, 165, 166, 170, 204, 205 n., 217, 256
Conservatism, 3, 12, 155, 177, 181 n., 223, 232
Cooperatives, 12, 175; cf. 54, 179
Copernicus, 28, 111 n.
Counter-Reformation, 32
Cowper, 35

Creation, 60, 61-2, 64, 96, 217, 219, 229, 236, 254
Creeds, 32, 37, 41, 51, 57, 70, 107, 121, 166
Crime, 12, 174, 186, 258
Cromwell, Oliver, 35
Cult, xi, 52, 70, 97, 190, 207

Dante, 29
Darrow, Clarence, 167 n.
Darwin, 41, 104, 228
Decker, Clarence R., 7 n.
Deism, 45, 53, 210 n.
Democracy, 7 n., 8 n., 10 n., 26, 27, 30, 32, 56, 153-4, 156, 174, 175, 176, 177 n., 180-2, 185-6, 187-8, 231 n., 248
Descartes, 45, 64 n., 231
de Vaux, Clotilde, 184
Dewey, John, 8 n., 10 n., 17, 20-1, 31, 55 n., 67, 69-71, 73 n., 74 n., 75, 86, 93-5, 99, 100, 103 n., 106, 130 n., 154 n., 176 n., 190 n., 205 n., 217 n., 222, 223-4, 249-57, 259
DeWitt, Dale, 7 n.
Dickinson, Emily, 40 n., 65 n., 114 n., 129 n., 150 n., 168 n., 178 n., 252 n., 262 n.
Dieffenbach, Albert C., 7 n., 8 n., 55 n.
Dietrich, John H., 5 n., 7, 8 n., 10 n., 42 n., 55 n., 167 n., 207 n., 259-60, 262 n.
Disinterestedness, 13, 15, 17, 68, 74, 81-2, 92, 103, 105 n., 148, 166, 213, 227; cf. 105
Dogmatism, religious, 26, 35, 37, 57, 59 n., 87, 92-4, 96-8, 135, 155, 223, 228-30, 233; scientific, 93-4, 95-6, 98, 104; social, 87
Dostoevski, 160
Durant, Will, 10 n.

Eddington, Sir Arthur, 42, 92, 143 n.
Education, 10 n., 11, 12, 23, 25, 45, 53, 84, 156, 174-5, 183, 184, 185, 187-8; religious, 87, 189-90
Einstein, 42, 104, 228, 229
Eliot, Frederick M., 7 n., 10 n.
Eliot, T. S., 18 n., 19 n., 155 n., 168 n., 171 n., 172 n.
Elliott, G. R., 20 n.
Ellis, Havelock, 138 n., 167 n.

Emerson, 132 n.
Emotion, feeling, etc., in American life, 13, 168-9; and humanism, 16, 79, 80, 147, 168; and morality, 156, 164-5; and nature, 63, 260; and reason, 45, 62, 195; and religion, 15, 53, 71, 102-3, 129, 130-1, 134, 138, 139, 148 n., 150, 156, 162, 184, 208, 213, 220, 223, 230, 232-3, 235-6, 242; and science, 16, 79, 85, 104, 105, 108-9, 135, 146; and values, 135 n., 196-9, 251
Empedocles, 23
Empiricism, 45, 78, 79, 93, 95, 113, 169 n., 233, 242, 257
Energy, 77-8, 92, 137-8
Engels, Friedrich, 181 n.
England, 7 n., 9 n., 17, 31 n., 177, 184
Enlightenment, 27
Epicurus, 239-40
Episcopacy, 32-3
Erasmus, 29
Eternal, 84, 92, 99, 257
Ethical Culture, 9 n., 37, 46, 55 n., 57 n., 58 n., 163, 166 n., 205, 208 n., 258
Eucharist, 31-2
Euclid, 228
Eunapius, 26
Europe, 29, 31, 83, 184
Evans, D. L., 7 n.
Evil, 63, 72, 83, 154, 156-8, 173, 178, 190, 195, 206, 209, 219, 220, 231, 254, 255
Evolution, 27, 42, 45, 46, 52, 55-6, 64, 75, 79, 91-2, 96, 116-17, 118, 119, 120, 132 n., 144, 157, 158 n., 170 n., 226, 228 n., 229 n., 238, 254

Fact, 40, 95 n., 101, 104, 105-6, 107, 109-10, 111, 126, 153, 161, 195-6, 197 n., 199-202, 237, 242, 245, 254
Faith, xiii, 17, 19-20, 34, 35, 37-9, 45, 58, 63, 69, 70 n., 81, 86, 93-6, 104, 132 n., 156, 158, 167, 170 n., 172, 173, 185, 189, 190, 213, 214, 217 n., 220, 228, 237, 262
Family, 34, 156, 175, 183-4, 258
Fantus, Bernard, 55 n.
Fate, 72, 218
Faust, 158
Feudalism, 29, 169 n.
Fielding, Henry, 145 n.
Firkins, O. W., 259, 261 n.

275

Fite, Warner, 164
Flaubert, 268
Floyd, William, 10 n., 55 n.
Ford, 27
Forms, or Ideas, 17, 46, 47, 159, 209, 212, 213
France, 8 n., 18 n., 55, 160, 181, 184
Francis, St., of Assisi, 231
François, St., de Sales, 35
Free thought, 5, 8 n., 23, 24, 37, 57, 93-4, 96-8, 104, 155, 174
Freud, S., 85, 128, 133-7, 138 n., 139, 142, 144-5, 164-5
Frohman, Daniel, 10 n.
Frost, Robert, 247 n.
Fundamentalism, 41, 58, 98, 132 n., 229

Galileo, 28, 41, 104
Gama, da, Vasco, 28
Geta, 25
God, apprehension of and communion with, 14, 35, 36, 45, 65, 66, 73, 74, 79, 80, 88, 95, 96, 97, 104, 107, 110, 131, 142-3, 145, 149, 155, 158, 159, 160, 161, 163, 166, 190, 206, 207 n., 211 n., 216, 235-8, 240-2, 246, 257, 262, 263; attributes of, 35, 78-9, 116, 130, 136, 138-9, 158, 210, 212, 214, 215, 239-40, 245-9, 255, 260; and creation, 61-3, 96; as a "father-complex," 133-4, 139-40, 148; as finite, 20, 158, 215, 248, 257; and human freedom and responsibility, 15, 17, 21, 35, 44, 54, 66, 67-8, 73, 77, 154, 157, 211-12, 216-20, 250, 255; idea of, 4, 20-1, 31, 45-6, 56, 59, 63, 66, 71, 78-9, 80, 91, 131, 138-40, 159-60, 162, 207 n., 215, 223-4, 233, 234-5, 236-7, 241-2, 245, 252, 256, 263; as an illusion, 4-5, 15, 47, 74, 78-9, 84, 102, 134-5, 142, 148-50, 207 n., 242; immanence and transcendence, 17, 45, 107, 132 n., 138, 142, 154, 158 n., 160-1, 210 n., 216-17, 240, 255; inscrutability of, 136, 209 n., 216, 242; and libido, 138-40, 142-4, 148, 207 n.; as objective, 4, 142, 150; personal, 20, 107, 116, 130-1, 139, 148-9, 206-7, 207-8, 214-16, 227, 233, 238-42, 258, 263; primitive origin of idea, 130, 232, 238; as a projection, 130-1, 132-45, 148, 161 n., 207 n., 223, 238, 239, 360; proof of, 62, 80, 139 n., 148, 160 n., 205, 209 n.; ultimacy and intimacy, 14, 22, 88, 107, 132 n., 142, 143, 163, 166, 215-16, 219, 235, 237, 240-1, 251, 255; value of belief in, 28, 33, 66, 69, 72 n., 73, 97, 107, 131, 134, 138, 140-2, 149, 150 n., 156, 163, 170, 180, 189, 210 n., 224, 231 n., 235, 259
Goethe, 248 n.
Goldman, Edwin Franko, 10 n.
Goodness, 3, 9 n., 17, 20, 26, 57, 58, 63, 76, 80, 87, 96, 111, 149, 154, 157 n., 159, 161, 163, 167, 179, 195, 196, 198, 202-3, 205, 208, 209 n., 211-12, 214, 215, 219, 241, 255
Gorgias, 25
Gould, Lawrence, 10 n.
Gray, Thomas, 171 n.
Greece, 23-5, 27, 28, 69, 184
Green, T. H., 43
Grou, 35

Hamlet, 268
Hampson, Alfred Leete, 40 n.
Hankins, F. H., 55 n.
Hartmann, Nicolai, 16, 17, 47, 163, 194, 196, 200 n., 206 n., 208-19, 238
Hartshorne, Charles, 7 n.
Haydon, A. Eustace, 7 n., 8 n., 17, 50, 55 n., 57 n., 61 n., 74, 82-3, 85, 87, 90, 100-4, 154 n., 156 n., 226 n.
Heaven, 31, 45, 59 n., 66, 93, 133-4, 150 n., 154, 210, 230
Hebrew, Jew, etc., 3, 9 n., 46, 55 n., 58, 169, 187, 210, 238
Hegel, 24
Heiler, Friedrich, 42, 75, 209 n.
Heim, Karl, 42
Hell, 31, 59 n.
Hellenism, 162 n.
Heraclitus, 23
Herbert, George, 72 n.
Herodes Atticus, 25
Hill, G. B., 227 n.
Hinkle, B. M., 137 n.
History, 23, 24, 30, 31, 45, 52, 57, 70, 73, 83, 93, 100, 102 n., 104, 129, 140, 145, 157, 164, 167, 170, 205 n., 220, 223, 234, 241, 246, 249
Hobbes, 157

Hocking, W. E., 64 n.
Hoffman, Irwin D., 10 n.
Holland, B., 118 n.
Holmes, John Haynes, 8 n.
Holt, I. L., 205 n.
Homer, 239
Horton, W. M., 81, 82 n., 86 n., 199
Hügel, Baron Friedrich von, 39, 42, 59 n., 66, 69, 76, 115, 118 n., 145, 160, 165 n., 210 n., 215 n., 231, 232 n., 234, 246, 256, 261 n.
Humanism, atheistic, xi, 4-5, 7 n., 9 n., 10, 15, 17, 20-3, 29, 31, 46-7, 53, 78, 80-1, 84, 86-7, 162, 207 n., 211, 242, 245, 262, 268; beginning of, 8 n., 24, 46, 226; in colleges, 6 n., 11 n.; criticism of theism, 242, 267, 269; a "cultural lag," 6 n.; definition of, xi, 4-6, 59; distribution of, geographical, 8-9; distribution of, social and economic, 10-12, 262 n.; ignorant of Christianity, 6 n., 42, 75-6, 145, 196, 223, 226-7, 238, 242, 245; as an institution, xi, 4, 5-6, 8-10; journalistic, 6 n.; lacks religious sense, 36, 53; mediating school of, 17, 19 n., 20-1, 42, 47, 62, 81, 84, 92, 108, 113; a mood, xii, 6, 17, 130; optimistic school of, 16-17, 81; and oriental religions, 21-2; pessimistic school of, 16-17, 20, 42, 62, 81, 84, 92, 144, 158, 165; present policy of, 5-7; publications, 6-8; and the Reformation, 23, 26 ff.; religious services of, 7, 8 n., 10 n., 12, 141 n., 168 n., 207-8, 258, 261 n.; and sophism, 23-6; style of the day, xi, 6, 51-2; tone of, xi, 6, 11, 12, 46, 56-7, 58-9, 98, 257; vacillation of, 21, 38, 47-8, 63, 66, 79-80, 92, 115, 124-5, 126, 196, 201; vicissitudes of, 6 n., 7 n.
Humanism, literary or academic, 15, 18-20, 27, 47, 84
Humanism, Renaissance, 23, 26-30, 31, 232
Humanist Bulletin, The, 8, 10 n., 155 n.
Humanist Press Association, 6, 8, 9 n.
Humanist Pulpit, The, 5 n., 7, 8 n., 259 n.
Humanitarianism, 19 n., 26-7, 163
Hume, 38, 45
Hurley, Ora D., 226
Huvelin, 165 n.

Huxley, Julian S., 8 n., 17, 90, 100, 103-8, 126, 222, 227-9
Huxley, T. H., 259
Hyde, Lawrence, 20 n.

Idealism, 24, 43, 64, 66, 116, 120, 124, 160, 167 n., 176, 213, 254
Ideals, 3, 9 n., 18, 21, 34, 36, 47, 56, 67, 69, 70, 71, 76-7, 80, 81, 82, 86, 87-8, 92, 96, 99, 109, 113, 124, 130-1, 167, 172, 179, 180, 182, 207 n., 209, 215, 217-18, 223-4, 251-4, 256-7, 262-3
Ignatius, St., de Loyola, 254
Imagination, 28, 149, 184, 207 n., 218 n., 224, 230, 247, 251-2, 256
Immortality, 47, 65-6, 91, 139 n., 153, 170, 223, 230-3
Incarnation, 32, 154, 210 n., 240
India, 8 n., 87, 177, 235
Individualism, 6, 7 n., 9 n., 10, 16, 23, 26, 32, 37, 44, 51, 99, 161, 164, 170, 200 n., 203 n., 210, 261 n.
Induction and deduction, 92, 104, 125, 243
Infinite, 77, 130, 158, 161, 166, 214, 218, 257
Inge, W. R., 75, 81, 145, 209 n., 215 n.
Ingersoll, R. G., 259
Innocent VIII, 29
Institutions, 3, 32-3, 34, 41, 45, 47, 54, 57, 58, 68, 70, 93, 129, 134, 155 n., 174, 176, 186, 190, 207, 224, 261 n.
Instrumentalism, 24, 27, 43
Intelligence tests, 175, 181, 183
International relations, 175, 184, 186
Intuition, insight, etc., 37-8, 66, 69, 80, 87, 93, 103, 113, 158, 165 n., 172, 198 n.
Isaacs, A. S., 141 n.
Isaiah, 248
Izoulet, 205 n.

Jacquerie, 29
James, William, 16, 20
Jesuits, 106 n.
Jesus, Christ, 19 n., 23, 25-6, 31, 33, 34, 35, 37, 38, 40, 58, 59 n., 69, 71, 72, 96, 126 n., 160, 167, 170, 177, 182, 187-8, 209 n., 211, 215, 231, 242 n.
John, St., 159
John of the Cross, St., 71
Johnson, 227

Johnston, Sir Reginald F., 22 n.
Jones, Llewellyn, 8 n., 55 n.
Jowett, 67 n.
Julia Domna, 25
Julian the Apostate, 25, 26
Jung, C. G., 128, 133, 137-45, 148

Kant, 17, 24, 45, 46-7, 114 n., 162, 171 n., 209, 233
Karma, 22
Keller, Adolf, 158 n.
Keller, Helen, 10 n.
Kepler, 41
Kessler, Julius, 10 n.
Kidd, Benjamin, 170 n.
Kierkegaard, Søren, 34, 38-9, 41, 42, 139 n., 188 n., 227 n.
King, W. P., 21 n., 170 n., 205 n., 206 n., 207 n., 230 n.
Knowledge, and God, 142, 216, 243; and metaphor, 121; and nature, 14, 62, 76, 205 n., 233, 256; of ourselves, 120, 243; and psychology, 15, 64, 146-7; and reason, 165 n.; and religion, 41, 51, 234, 246; and science, 42, 70 n., 95, 103, 105, 108-9, 113-14, 115, 125, 135-6, 161 n., 195; and values, 197-200, 214, 253
Knox, 35
Krutch, Joseph Wood, 16, 50, 74, 82 n., 84-6, 165

Labor and the masses, 6 n., 8 n., 11, 164, 170 n., 175, 176, 178-83, 185-6, 187, 189, 208, 228
Lamb, Gilbert D., 10 n.
Lamont, Corliss, 7 n., 230 n.
Lâo-tse, 2, 21-2
Laplace, 41
Lavoisier, 41
Law, order, etc., of nature, 178, 217; scientific, 40, 91, 92, 109-12, 117 n., 132 n., 202; of society, 33, 159, 165, 174, 180, 184-7, 228, 268, 269; spiritual, 118 n., 154, 219
Leach, Henry Goddard, 10 n.
League of Nations, 158 n., 175, 184, 258
Leibnitz, 144
Leighton, J. H., 146
Le Roy, Édouard, 42, 112 n., 121 n.
Leuba, James H., 10 n., 17, 44, 73, 74,
76-7, 79, 161 n., 170 n., 224, 245, 249, 259, 262
Leucippus, 23
Lewis, Sinclair, 13, 14 n., 225
Libanius, 26
Liberalism, 5, 12, 153, 163, 166, 168 n., 169, 170, 176, 180, 186, 187
Libido, 137-9, 140, 142-4, 148-9, 207 n.
Life, 54, 56, 67 n., 75, 76, 103, 115, 119, 120, 126, 131, 133, 138 n., 139, 144, 155, 160, 166, 171, 207-8, 212, 224, 228-9, 241
Link, Henry C., 189 n.
Lippmann, Walter, 17, 50, 74, 81-2, 111 n., 129, 130 n., 148, 194, 196, 204
Literature, 11, 18, 25, 71, 97, 112, 175, 236
Lobatchewsky, 228
Locke, 45, 204 n.
Logic, xii, 23, 24, 35, 40-1, 43, 45, 62, 75, 80, 84, 98, 105 n., 113, 116-17, 125, 136, 159, 206, 209 n., 212-14, 232
Lollianus, 25
Love, and Comte, 56, 183-4; God's, 96, 136, 220, 237, 245-6; of God, 14, 34, 35, 73, 161, 167, 170, 207, 213, 214-15, 237, 240, 245, 246; and libido, 138; of others, 65, 72, 81-2, 97, 130-1, 166-7, 170, 177, 178, 180, 182, 188, 205 n., 208, 232-3, 234, 246; and religion, 9 n., 40 n., 53, 133, 138, 148, 149-50, 155, 182, 214-15, 229, 241, 247; and science, 109
Lovett, Robert Morss, 10 n., 55 n.
Low, Clarence H., 10 n.
Lowrie, Walter, 34 n., 39 n., 41 n., 139 n., 188 n., 227 n.
Luther, Martin, 31, 33, 34, 36, 37, 38, 39, 46, 209 n.

Macdonald, Ramsay, 167 n.
Macintosh, D. C., 87 n., 125 n., 148 n., 170 n., 207 n., 215 n.
Man, as measure, 16, 23-4
Mana, 78 n., 234
Manifesto, humanist, xiii, 26, 51-5, 61 n., 65 n., 72, 73, 80 n., 123, 165 n., 169, 187 n., 203 n., 242; signers of, 55 n.; tone of, 56-7, 59-60
Manitou, 78 n.
Marburg Articles, 31
Marcel, Gabriel, 247 n.

Maritain, Jacques, 76
Marley, Harold P., 10 n., 55 n.
Martineau, James, 45, 105
Marvin, F. S., 7 n.
Marx, Karl, 181 n., 258
Materialism, 22 n., 33, 42, 64, 75, 93, 114,
 121, 146, 183
Mathematics, 56, 61, 75, 80, 84, 95 n.,
 98-9, 102, 106 n., 136, 196 n., 209 n.,
 247
Mathews, Shailer, 206
Mayer, Robert, 137
McCabe, Joseph, 167 n.
McDougall, 171 n.
McPherson, Aimee Semple, 226
Melancthon, 29, 39
Melanesia, 78 n.
Mephistopheles, 158
Mercier, L. J. A., 18
Meyerson, É., 42
Middle Ages, 26, 28, 29-30, 33-4, 44, 46,
 56
Middle class, 12, 13, 176, 261 n.
Middle West, 9, 13, 168
Mill, James, 186
Mill, John Stuart, 20, 41-2
Millikan, R. A., 230 n.
Mind, thought, consciousness, etc., 43,
 52, 56, 61-2, 63-4, 67 n., 74, 75, 77, 80,
 98, 103 n., 107, 110, 114, 115-16, 117,
 119-24, 132 n., 138, 140, 143, 146-7,
 156, 158, 160, 164, 212, 214 n., 229,
 236 n., 237, 244
Miracle, 46, 74, 91, 117 n., 131
Modernism, 9 n., 46, 53, 98
Modernity, 7 n., 8, 21, 42, 51-2, 54, 56,
 84, 92, 102 n., 120, 163
Mohammed, 35
Monasticism, 32, 33, 71
Mondale, R. Lester, 5 n., 7 n., 55 n.,
 131 n., 148 n.
Monneron, Joseph, 6 n.
Monod, V., 215 n.
Moore, G. E., 198
Morality, ethics, etc., 15, 25, 27, 43, 83,
 117 n., 186, 209, 213, 236, 244; and
 humanism, xiii, 16, 18, 38, 39, 47, 63,
 66, 76, 81, 103, 153, 157, 158-60, 168,
 172, 190, 202, 204-5, 208; and naturalism, 79, 81, 196; ontological status
 of, 62-3, 85, 113, 168, 204-6; and
 philosophy, 98; and religion, 17,

19-20, 22, 24, 28, 30, 36, 37, 46-7, 63,
 70, 73, 88, 94, 130, 141 n., 154, 156,
 159-66, 170 n., 189, 210-11, 214 n., 234,
 242; and science, 24, 36, 63, 66-7, 99,
 126, 156, 200 n., 201, 204, 211; and
 theism, 44, 73, 88, 154, 210, 215, 219,
 235
More, Paul Elmer, 16, 18, 19-20, 38,
 47, 209 n.
More, St. Thomas, 29
Morgan, Lloyd, 117 n.
Morse, 252
Murphy, A. E., 106 n.
Music, 71, 103, 224, 249, 261 n.
Muzzey, David S., 57
Mysticism, 33, 56, 71, 78, 79, 99, 117,
 209 n., 210 n.
Mythology, 61, 79, 101 n., 121, 202 n.

Nationalism, 175, 184
Naturalism, 8, 16, 18, 19, 23, 36, 41, 60,
 64, 66, 74-5, 76 n., 77, 79-81, 86, 101,
 102, 116, 120, 121, 146, 196, 209, 257,
 260, 262, 269; "new," 4, 5, 9 n., 17,
 20-2, 27, 29, 36, 41-2, 47, 57, 63, 64,
 66, 78-81, 86, 118, 184, 196, 267, 269
Nature, external, 14, 15, 26, 53, 64, 67,
 79, 81, 82, 85, 96, 107, 109-10, 113-16,
 118-20, 126, 130, 133, 139, 162 n., 172,
 178, 179, 217, 224; human, 14, 183;
 and religion, 68-9, 71-2; the this-
 worldly, 26, 44, 63, 70, 74, 75, 80, 118,
 132, 148, 216
Nédoncelle, Maurice, 59 n., 247 n.
Neo-realism, 17, 75
Neumann, H., 166 n.
New Humanist, The, 7, 51, 55 n., 65 n.,
 101 n., 106 n., 113, 123 n., 165 n., 172 n.,
 173 n., 174 n., 261 n., 268 n.
New Testament, 33, 36, 38, 148, 162
Newman, 228
News Letter, 8, 9 n.
Newton, 41, 228
Nicholas V, 29
Nicholas of Cusa, 28
Nietzsche, 209, 211
Nirvana, 22
Norsemen, 239

O'Dell, George E., 10 n.
Œcolampadius, 29
Ohrenstein, Edward W., 7 n.

Old Testament, 32, 72, 97, 159, 162 n., 210
Oman, J., 75, 234 n.
Order, 28, 56, 111 n., 112-13, 115-16, 118, 158, 176, 183, 200 n., 213-14, 236, 247, 257 n.
Orenda, 78 n.
Orr, H. R., 172 n.
Otherness, 68, 88, 99, 142, 154, 216, 246-7, 249, 250, 260; cf. 166, 212, 214
Other-worldliness, 22, 26, 46, 70 n., 71, 161, 202-3
Otto, M. C., 8 n., 17, 57 n., 71 n., 125, 130 n., 154 n., 248 n.
Otto, Rudolf, 42, 234
Oudah, 78 n.
Oursler, Fulton, 10 n.

Paganism, 26, 27, 34
Page, C. H., 224 n., 267 n.
Pantheism, 43
Papacy and popes, 29, 31, 32, 71, 96
Paracelsus, 28
Parker, 45
Parmenides, 23, 111
Party, 181 n.
Pascal, 38, 213 n.
Past, the, xi, 27-8, 31 n., 51-2, 57-8, 59 n., 66, 71, 104, 155 n., 178
Pauck, W., 172 n.
Paul, St., 36, 71, 159, 188 n.
Personality, 17, 43, 74, 80, 115, 157 n., 215, 240, 256; development of human, 53, 65, 149, 156, 166-7, 189, 257, 262; humanistic conception of, 73, 77, 86, 116-17, 166-9, 187-8, 190; importance of, xi, 63, 114 n., 126, 153, 156, 166-7, 169-73, 195, 203, 230, 231; religious conceptions of, 21-2, 65, 116, 167, 173, 206; functioning as a whole, 39, 45, 162, 179-80, 207
Phenomenology, 43
Philanthropy, 4, 9 n., 19 n., 21, 25, 71, 86
Philosophy, 14, 20, 46, 51, 53, 82, 91, 103, 111, 122, 160, 181, 268; and Comte, 183; and humanism, 66, 77, 101 n., 113, 116, 124, 125, 168, 169, 195-7, 199, 209, 223, 254, 269; and Jesus, 38; and morality, 98, 126, 217 n.; and psychology, 96, 142; recent, 24, 27, 43, 45, 116, 197; and

religion, 62, 69, 106, 126, 160 n., 211, 234, 248; and scholasticism, 40; and science, 109, 126; and sophism, 23-5
Philostratus, 26 n.
Physics, 16, 24, 42-3, 56, 92, 98, 102, 111, 129, 137, 143, 155 n., 228, 236
Planck, Max, 121 n.
Plato, 18, 20, 23, 25, 64, 67 n., 82, 91 n., 99, 116 n., 120, 123, 183, 209, 211, 212, 258
Plymouth Brethren, 106 n.
Poetry, 12, 68-9, 106 n., 207, 224, 258, 262 n., 268
Poincaré, Henri, 42
Pokunt, 78 n.
Politics, 11, 12, 22, 23, 27, 31, 81, 96, 101-2, 153, 156, 180, 182, 183, 186, 191, 203 n., 268, 269
Polytheism, 22, 69
Positivism, 4, 21, 24, 41, 55-6, 95, 181, 183-4, 196
Positivist Society, 8 n.
Potter, Charles Francis, xi, 8 n., 9 n., 17, 21, 44, 50, 55 n., 73, 74, 75, 77, 78 n., 84, 86 n., 110 n., 167, 169 n., 173 n., 224, 230, 257, 260
Pragmatism, 16, 24, 43, 144, 252
Pratt, J. B., 6 n., 7 n., 146, 171 n.
Prayer and worship, and humanism, 21, 31, 53, 93, 168 n., 184, 203 n., 207-8, 212-13, 215, 219, 245, 246-8, 252, 257-62; and psychology, 143, 145; and relaxation, 224; and theism, 14, 74-5, 145, 150, 216, 227 n., 228, 240-1, 254; value of, 35, 72, 150 n.
Priestley, Joseph, 41, 45
Pringle-Pattison, 111
Profit motive, 54, 179
Progress, 18, 20, 26, 28, 41, 45, 55, 68, 91, 130-1, 132, 158, 178, 183, 190
Prohaeresius, 25, 26
Protagoras, 23, 25
Protestantism, 9 n., 29, 30, 32-3, 35, 37, 39, 40, 41, 44-5, 46, 56, 70-1, 75, 97, 145 n., 155, 159, 163, 167, 182, 261 n.
Providence, 58, 72, 210 n., 216, 218-19, 220, 230 n.
Psalms, 35, 65, 69, 110, 209 n., 248 n.
Psychoanalysis, 92, 137, 138 n., 145, 165
Psychology, 12, 18, 24, 64, 96, 107, 138 n., 181, 189; Freud's psychology of religion, 133-7; and humanism,

xiii, 15, 16, 65 n., 66, 67, 77, 81, 129-30, 142, 146-9; Jung's psychology of religion, 137-44; and religion, 32, 81, 92, 104, 105-6, 130, 134, 142, 146, 148, 150, 171 n., 223, 229 n., 243, 259; and values, 85-6, 197, 201

Purification by science and thing, 125, 241

Purpose, teleology, etc., 24, 61, 68, 91, 114 n., 115, 117, 118-20, 196-7, 200, 205, 210, 217-18

Pythagoras, 99

Qualities, primary and secondary, 196, 200-1, 204

Quietism, 65, 73

Race, 169, 171, 174, 186, 189, 190

Racine, 4 n., 224 n.

Racovian Catechism, 37

Radicalism, 9 n., 12, 54, 56, 84, 153, 177, 179, 181 n.

Randall, John Herman, 10 n., 55 n.

Rapp, William Jourdan, 10 n.

Rappleyea, George W., 10 n.

Rationalism, 8 n., 36-8, 45, 47, 62, 141, 167 n., 176, 247

Realism, 14, 43, 129, 146, 183, 200

Reason, 7 n., 12, 18, 28, 36-9, 44-5, 47, 62-3, 99-100, 115-16, 133, 135, 141, 144, 155, 164-5, 170-1, 173, 183, 195, 204, 229

Reeman, 248 n.

Reese, Curtis W., 7 n., 8 n., 21 n., 55 n., 153, 154, 167 n., 168 n., 172 n., 173 n., 185, 186, 194, 196, 205

Reformation, the, 3, 23, 26-8, 30-42, 44, 170

Regiomontanus, 28

Reiser, Oliver L., 7 n., 10 n., 55 n., 123 n., 165 n., 173 n., 174-5, 177 n., 181, 184

Relativity, 123 n., 142, 144, 158, 161, 229, 255

Religion, 15, 21, 27, 30, 33-4, 37, 43, 69, 101, 186, 201; religious attitudes, 35, 53, 63, 68-71, 93-4, 107, 116, 143, 161, 163, 167, 205, 206-7, 213-15, 220, 234, 237-8, 240-1, 248, 250-1, 259; Auer's description of, 242-9; Christian, 3, 169-70; and convention, 70; definitions of, 22, 52, 86-7, 145, 190-1,

223-4, 226, 235, 243-4, 249-50, 251, 259, 268; Dewey's description of, 70, 249-56; and education, 87, 189; religious experience, 20, 37, 79, 88, 95, 139, 140-2, 196, 214-16, 229, 241-2, 245-6, 255-6; and humanism, xiii, 4-5, 16, 25-6, 36, 41-2, 47, 52, 55-6, 60, 63, 66, 72 n., 74, 76, 77, 79, 118, 126, 149, 166, 168, 172, 207, 210 n., 247-8, 258-9; Huxley's description of, 106-7, 227-42; as integration of personality, 20-1, 223-4, 235, 243-5, 249-52; and literary humanism, 18, 19-20; and morality, 28, 46-7, 76-7, 93-4, 130, 141-2, 159-66, 189, 205, 211, 214 n.; outside and inside, 94-5, 97-8, 143; and pathology, 149-50; as a prevailing passion, 243-4; primitive, 78 n., 102, 130-1, 139, 141, 163, 232, 235; as a projection, 113, 130, 133, 149-50; and reason, 38; revivalistic, 226; and science, 6 n., 51, 53, 62, 63, 67, 76-7, 91, 92-100, 102, 103 n., 105-7, 115, 144, 155-6, 229, 236; and sophism, 25-6

Renaissance, the, 26-8, 30, 31, 232

Republic, 178, 184, 185

Republic of Western Europe, 184

Resurrection, 59 n.

Reuchlin, 29

Revelation, 39, 45, 46, 58, 94, 165 n.

Revolution, 26, 55, 153, 174, 182, 186, 228

Rey, Abel, 42

Riemann, 228

Riviere, J., 133 n.

Robson-Scott, W. D., 133 n.

Romanticism, 163

Rombotis, G., 100, 101 n., 102

Roosevelt, F. D., 258

Rousseau, 233

Rural influence, 11, 15, 26, 224, 258, 260

Russell, Bertrand, 8 n., 16, 50, 60 n., 74, 83, 90, 91, 92 n., 98-100, 103, 105 n., 106 n., 108-13, 118 n., 125, 126, 159, 167 n., 195

Sachs, B., 10 n.

Sacrament, 32-3, 34, 58, 261 n.

Sacred, and secular, 33-4, 46, 53, 69, 72; sense of the, 106-7, 223, 233-5, 242

Sahler, Helen G., xii

Salvation, 34, 40, 82, 154 n., 187, 211 n.

Santayana, George, 76 n., 169 n.

Scepticism, 24, 26, 29, 38, 45, 66, 99, 172

Scheler, Max, 213 n.

Schiller, F. C. S., 16

Scholasticism, 39-41

Schopenhauer, 137

Science, 38, 39, 60, 153, 159, 223; acclaimed by humanism, xi, xiii, 5, 8 n., 15, 21, 28, 36, 55-6, 57, 83-4, 110; ancient, 23; cant of, 103; Dewey's description of method of, 93-4; Haydon's description of method of, 101-3; "humanization" of, 15, 56, 126, 168; Huxley's description of method of, 103-8; limitations of, 14, 43, 61, 63, 67, 73, 76, 77, 79, 95, 103, 107-8, 109, 112 n., 119, 123, 124, 125-6, 136, 147, 162 n., 200-2, 229, 241 n., 268; and literary humanism, 18; and reality, 5, 16, 24, 47, 53, 77, 84, 85, 95 n., 98, 101, 103 n., 107-8, 125-6, 135-6, 161 n., 172-3, 195, 200; its popularity, 27; and religion, 6 n., 45, 51, 53, 59 n., 62-3, 66-7, 73-4, 78, 87, 92-100, 102, 144, 155, 160 n., 172-3, 191, 196, 208, 227, 234, 242; Renaissance and subsequent, 28, 41; Russell's description of scientific method, 108-13; Sellars's description of scientific method, 113-18; scientific view of reality, according to Sellars, 118-24; and theism, 14, 16, 51, 91, 93, 116-17, 136, 160 n., 172; its view of the world, 42-3, 202, 236, 267

Scopelian, 26

Scott, Clinton Lee, 55 n.

Secularism, xi, 5, 6 n., 19, 23, 26, 33-4, 46, 189, 268

Seillière, Baron Ernest, 18 n.

Sellars, Roy Wood, 10 n., 17, 55 n., 65 n., 73, 79, 80, 86, 90, 91, 100, 113-25, 126, 130 n., 194, 196-203, 224, 231 n., 258, 261 n.

Sense, sense-perception, etc., 16, 18 n., 28, 62, 79, 85-6, 113, 114 n., 123, 136, 146-7, 155, 184, 198-9, 209 n., 213, 217 n., 234 n., 253

Septimius Severus, 25

Sex, 137, 138 n., 167 n., 183, 186, 225

Shakespeare, 268

Shelley, 205 n.

Shipley, Maynard, 55 n.

Simplification, 43-4, 46, 71, 102, 156, 160, 161, 267-8

Sin, 34, 35, 107, 237

Smith, Logan Pearsall, 84 n., 111 n.

Smith, Norman Kemp, 210 n., 246 n.

Snell, Lord, 9 n.

Social and economic improvement, 9 n., 18, 23, 24, 25, 26, 29, 30, 41, 45, 51, 55, 70 n., 76, 83, 86, 131, 132-3; Christian, 4, 71-2; Comte's program of, 181-4; humanistic program of, 12, 53-4, 73 n., 153-4, 156, 157 n., 166-7, 168, 173-7, 230; man-on-the-street's view of, 177-81

Socialism, 54, 176, 178-9, 183, 261 n.

Socinus, Faustus, 37, 38

Socrates, 38-9, 69, 172, 209 n.

Söderblom, Nathan, 42, 76, 209 n.

Sophists, 23-6, 29, 144, 232

Space, 56, 60 n., 79-80, 91, 92, 98, 100, 113-14, 116, 119, 121, 123 n., 130, 229

Spencer, 45, 55, 81 n.

Spinoza, 162, 209 n., 237, 259

Spiritual pluralism, 43

Standards, 41, 189

Stevenson, R. L., 25 n., 106 n.

Stifler, William W., Jr., xii

Stoics, 162, 209 n., 211, 250

Stone, Mark, 176 n.

Stratton, G. M., 244

Subjectivism, 14, 23, 32, 133, 134, 142, 144-5, 157, 196, 197, 198 n., 200 n., 209

Substance, 237, 241

Success, 25, 178, 187-8, 205 n.

Sunday, "Billy," 226

Supernatural, 22, 70, 204, 223, 234, 235; "anonymously," 21 n., 69, 234 n.; and humanism, 5, 6 n., 21, 53, 57, 66-7, 73-8, 79, 80, 81, 86, 110, 148, 176, 233, 234 n., 239; and literary humanism, 18; and magic, 33, 44, 234 n.; and the natural, 18, 44, 46, 64, 71-2, 73-5, 77, 80, 118, 132-3, 148,

210, 249, 263; in religion, 22, 70-1, 78 n., 130, 249

Swift, Frank W., 55 n.

Swope, Herbert Bayard, 10 n.

Symbol, in religion, 70 n., 139-41, 148, 207 n., 208, 261 n.

Tawney, R. H., 30 n.

Taylor, A. E., 42, 75, 115, 202, 209 n., 215 n.

Temple, William, 75, 88 n., 160 n., 215 n.

Tennant, F. R., 215 n.

Tennyson, 216 n.

Thales, 23

Thayer, V. T., 55 n.

Theism, adaptable, 6 n., 41; culminates in Christianity, 145, 241; defined loosely, xii; faults of, xi, 5, 59, 63, 64, 91-2, 177, 224-5, 227; humanism an arrested development of, 16, 21 n., 36, 77, 87, 107, 116, 132 n., 141 n., 149, 196, 205, 206, 207-8, 214, 223, 236, 237-8, 242, 251 n.; humanism rejects, xi, xiii, 5, 16-17, 20, 31, 34, 53, 130, 132 n., 208, 216, 223, 233, 242, 268; and literary humanism 16, 20, 47; misunderstandings of, 76, 79-80, 106-7, 124, 142, 210 n., 215, 216 n., 223, 238; and morality, 154, 159, 163, 166, 170 n., 208-9, 217; and Platonism, 67 n., 209; and psychology, 130, 144, 148; and religion, 20, 145; and science, 16, 41, 92, 93-4, 105, 129; teachings of, 14, 35, 61-2, 63, 65-6, 68, 69, 74-5, 87, 88, 115, 116, 120, 124, 132 n., 148-9, 155-8, 159-60, 161, 163, 215, 239, 249, 263, 267

Theology, xiii, 9 n., 24, 32, 40, 44, 52, 56, 60 n., 61, 69, 71, 76 n., 77, 92, 102, 105, 115, 142, 153, 155, 159, 169 n., 205, 209 n., 212, 217 n., 226, 228, 229 n., 239-40, 241, 248 n.

Thomas à Kempis, 35

Thomas Aquinas, St., 35, 43, 44, 61, 69, 159

Thouless, R. H., 140 n., 146, 148, 149, 249 n.

Tilney, Frederick, 10 n.

Time, 56, 59, 60 n., 62, 65, 79-80, 91-2, 100, 114, 116, 119, 121, 123 n., 229

Totalitarianism, xi, 174, 183

Tradition, 3, 4, 17, 33, 40, 51, 52, 57, 58, 59, 62, 64, 91, 92, 132 n., 155, 159, 239, 242

Trinity, doctrine of the, 32, 37, 44, 206 n., 239, 240

Troeltsch, Ernst, 42

Truth, 4, 9 n., 16, 17, 23, 24, 25, 35, 37, 45, 57, 58, 59, 60, 80, 84, 88, 94, 95, 96, 97, 98, 99, 103, 105, 106, 109, 111, 113, 115, 134, 141, 146, 149, 153, 155, 160, 161, 165 n., 167 n., 172, 191, 196, 203, 207, 212, 241, 248, 256, 269

Uniat Oriental Churches, 32

Unitarian, 5 n., 6, 7 n., 8 n., 9, 10, 37, 45, 46, 55 n., 131 n., 148 n., 153, 157 n., 167 n., 168 n., 207 n., 240, 259 n., 262 n.

Unity, 8

Universalist, 55 n.

Universe, or chaos, 111, 159; and evolution, 91, 117 n., 120; and humanism, 16, 60, 69, 76-7, 78, 84 n., 86, 111, 113, 130, 132 n., 158, 161, 169, 196, 202, 203, 205 n., 260; and mind, 122 n., 123 n.; and morality, 63, 67, 68, 82, 85, 179, 203, 208, 217, 256; and religion, 14, 52, 66, 130, 132 n., 206, 235, 241, 250, 251, 252, 258; and science, 42, 53, 76, 85, 92, 109; self-existence of, 45, 52, 60-1, 62, 113, 116

Uren, A. R., 78 n., 88 n., 137 n., 147 n., 148 n., 171 n., 244 n., 246 n.

Utilitarian, 41, 55, 157, 165, 186, 258

Utopia, 19, 29, 154, 178, 256, 261 n.

Values, creation of, 131 n., 195, 204, 217, 223, 251-2, 255; judgment of, 24, 135 n., 165, 196-202, 210, 212; "objectivity" of, 16, 17, 47, 68, 82, 87-8, 99, 111, 161, 196, 197, 198 n., 199-202, 206, 212-13, 215, 217 n., 256; personification of, 20, 196-7, 207-8, 214, 215; and religion, 14, 51-2, 59, 69, 70, 86, 87, 88, 96, 115, 130, 133, 139, 154, 162 n., 190, 210, 219, 241, 251-2; and science, 53, 67, 78, 81 n., 105 n., 115, 125-6, 197, 199-202, 203-4; "subjectivity" of, 15, 16, 23, 42, 47, 53, 63, 67, 78, 81, 82, 83, 85,

87-8, 99, 111, 161, 196, 197, 198 n., 195-7, 199, 200, 204, 253-4
Vanderlaan, Eldred C., 55 n.
Vernon, Marjorie, 59 n.
Vespucius, 28
Villard, Oswald Garrison, 10 n.
Vincent de Paul, St., 231
Virgin Birth, doctrine of, 59 n.
Voltaire, 232 n., 247

Wakan, 78 n.
Wakefield, 84 n.
Walker, Joseph, 55 n.
War, 174, 177, 178
Ward, M., 97 n.
Ward, Wilfrid, 97
Webb, Clement C. J., 6 n., 17 n., 75, 79, 88 n., 106, 107 n., 136 n., 142 n., 146, 163 n., 164 n., 165, 177 n., 211, 212 n., 213 n., 214 n., 215 n., 216 n., 218, 235, 237 n., 238, 239, 240 n.
Weierstrass, 100

Weinstein, Jacob J., 55 n.
Wells, H. G., 20
Wieman, H. N., 103 n., 125 n.
Whitehead, A. N., 42, 103 n., 156 n., 162 n., 165 n., 228
Wicks, Frank S. C., 55 n.
Wiggam, Albert Edward, 10 n.
Wilde, S., 146
Wile, Ira S., 10 n.
Williams, David Rhys, 55 n.
Wilson, Edmund, 182 n.
Wilson, Edwin H., 7 n., 8 n., 55 n., 154 n., 268 n.
Women, 174, 183, 184, 258
Wordsworth, 71 n.
World Court, 175, 184
World War, 18, 83, 175
Wright, W. C., 26 n.

Zeno, 23
Zoroastrianism, 241 n.
Zwingli, 31, 32, 36